JAMES C. BIRDSONG, JR.

THE BEST IS YET TO COME

A Testimony of One Young Man's Redemption

Foreword by Dr. Christopher Bowen, D.Min.

Copyright © 2017
James C. Birdsong, Jr.

All rights reserved.
No part of this book may be reproduced, stored in a retrieval system, or transmitted by any means, electronic, mechanical, photocopying, and recording – without the prior written permission of the author.

Scriptural quotations, unless otherwise noted, are from the King James Version of the Bible.

Library of Congress Cataloging-in Publication Data

Birdsong, James Jr., C.
The best is yet to come: a testimony of one young man's redemption/James C. Birdsong, Jr.

ISBN: 978-0-9994121-7-6

Dedicated in the memory of my loving great-grandparents, the late Ed and Ida Birdsong of Greenwood, Louisiana. They made vast contributions in the family legacy. Ed and Ida were the Abraham and Sarah of our family. I know they are smiling, and we will reunite in heaven.

CONTENTS

FOREWORD ix

INTRODUCTION 11

CHAPTER ONE
Just the Beginning 13

CHAPTER TWO
Love Grows 25

CHAPTER THREE
Move on Up a Little Higher 37

CHAPTER FOUR
Miracle at Three Years Old 49

CHAPTER FIVE
The Community Knows You 61

CHAPTER SIX
Daddy's Roots in Louisiana 73

CHAPTER SEVEN
Strength of a Praying Mother 87

CHAPTER EIGHT
Mid-Late Eighties 99

CHAPTER NINE
Cindy, Edwin & Otis Birdsong 113

CHAPTER TEN
1989 125

CHAPTER ELEVEN
Welcome to the Nineties 139

CHAPTER TWELVE
Things Begin to Change 153

CHAPTER THIRTEEN
Innocent Child in the Middle 165

CHAPTER FOURTEEN
School in the Inner-City 177

CHAPTER FIFTEEN
When God Has His Hands on You 191

CHAPTER SIXTEEN
Into the Separation 203

CHAPTER SEVENTEEN
We're No Longer Together as a Family 215

CHAPTER EIGHTEEN
Leaving Richmond for Fairfield 227

CHAPTER NINETEEN
The Pastor of Fairfield High School 241

CHAPTER TWENTY
Losing Daddy 255

CHAPTER TWENTY-ONE
A New Century and Millennium 269

CHAPTER TWENTY-TWO
9/11 283

CHAPTER TWENTY-THREE
Journey in the Gospel Music Industry 297

CHAPTER TWENTY-FOUR
James Talks to the Youth 311

CHAPTER TWENTY-FIVE
The Best is Yet to Come 325

ACKNOWLEDGEMENTS 337

AWARDS AND RECONGITION 345

ENDNOTES 353

FOREWORD

The Best is Yet To Come: A Testimony of One Young Man's Redemption is exemplary of how one's destiny is not defined by his disability alone. This book will add meaning to your life! James C. Birdsong, Jr. uses his developmental disability and life tragedies to show you how you can take what was meant to keep you in bondage, and turn it into the supernatural.

Coming from a family of various artists, James' motivation and determination enabled him to transform his delays and fast forward into becoming a national gospel-recording artist.

James' redemption came when he realized that, "The favor of God is upon my life. It is Jesus Christ that made all this possible." With him being called into the ministry at the tender age of three, and not yet knowing the full extent of his disability, James gives countless examples of how praying parents, teachers, and famous relatives instilled in him the value of life and kept him on the path of success.

Dr. Christopher Bowen, D.Min.
Certified Life Coach
Dream Releaser Coaching

JAMES C. BIRDSONG, JR.

INTRODUCTION

When I authored my first book, titled, *One Marriage, Many Tales, And a Separation: A Message of Hope* at 14-years-old, it became a bible based inspirational autobiography that the Lord placed on my heart. This was during a time when my parent's marriage encountered a major crisis that eventually resulted in their divorce.

Additionally, I wanted to share the message to fathers concerning their responsibility to their children. The focus of *One Marriage, Many Tales, And a Separation: A Message of Hope* became my mission of reaching out to our children and passing on the message of hope to people of all ages and nationalities. Seventeen years after the first publication of One Marriage, Many Tales, And a Separation: A Message of Hope, the story continues with *The Best is Yet to Come: A Testimony of One Young Man's Redemption*.

Published in 2000 by Author House, in Bloomington, Indiana, it opened doors for editorial reviews in many regions of the United States. I have shared my story on television, radio, and print media. The editors of Marquis Who's Who in America nominated me for inclusion in the publication of their 2003 57th Edition.

There is more to the story of my journey. Are you ready to come along with me as I proclaim a message of hope? If so, then welcome aboard.

JAMES C. BIRDSONG, JR.

CHAPTER ONE

Just the Beginning

This story begins with the 1970s as a decade forever remembered by many. Recorded as a "pivot of change" by historians, I will share some highlights of this decade that made global headlines in the media as this chapter becomes the interlude of the redemption. We'll go ahead on this journey of triumphs and storms along the way.

Richard Nixon, thirty-seventh President of the United States, resigned from office on August 9, 1974, after the result of the Watergate Scandal. Vice President Gerald Ford assumed the presidency, which made him the only person in the history of the presidency to assume the role as Commander-in-Chief, without having been elected as President.

The Vietnam War concluded on April 30, 1975, after a 19-year battle between North and South Vietnam. The Fall of Saigon was the capture of Saigon by the People's Army of Vietnam and the National Liberation Front of South Vietnam. The last of the soldiers in the United States Marine Corps evacuated the American Embassy on this same day. It is estimated that there were one million casualties during the Vietnam War.

President Ford pleaded his case to the American people during the 1976 Presidential Election. As the incumbent candidate, he conceded the campaign to his opponent, Governor Jimmy Carter. His inauguration was held on January 20, 1977, at Capitol Hill, in Washington, D.C. The death of Elvis Presley on August 16, 1977, stunned millions of fans and the music world, at large. Known as the undisputed "King of Rock and

Roll," he was only 42-years-old and still in the highlight of his career as one of the most famous entertainers of all time. His record sales continue today with the current figure of 134.5 million sales.

African-Americans also had success in this decade, which included the popularity of the 1977 television mini-series, *Roots*, with an all-star cast, including John Amos from the sitcom Good Times. The film is based on the novel written by the late Alex Haley. Roots received 37 Emmy nominations, with nine wins. Almost forty years later, Roots is still popular today. The novel explains Mr. Haley's family history, starting with his fourth great-grandfather Kunta Kinte. These are some of the many highlights of the 1970s that are now forever recorded in the history books.

In September 1979, a young woman named Belinda Barb, met a gentleman, James Charles Birdsong. A mutual friend of Ms. Barb introduced her to Mr. Birdsong, as a blind date. Both were residents of Richmond, California. Ms. Barb was a single mother of two sons, Demetrius and Alonzo, who were approaching their adolescence years. They resided in a two-bedroom apartment on Pennsylvania Avenue. Mr. Birdsong lived on Maine Avenue, at the corner of Harbour Way South.

Mr. Birdsong lived in a large two-story, five room Victorian house. His 65-year-old mother, Charlene Walton-Birdsong, also resided in the house. The house was built in 1914 and was once owned by the Breuners, owners of the popular Breuner's Furniture Store in the San Francisco Bay Area.

Ms. Barb eventually met Mr. Birdsong's mother, brother, Roosevelt Daniel, Jr., and other members of his family. Mr. Daniel and his late wife, Annette, resided in the house with their children, prior to Mr. Birdsong and their mother. Mr. Daniel had relocated to live with his children in the area. All were natives of Greenwood, Louisiana. Ms. Barb had the opportunity to meet the neighbors in the community, which led to her becoming acquainted with Mr. Birdsong. As the months passed, they eventually dated and developed a strong relationship. Mr. Birdsong came from a large, closely knit family who loved him. He was in his early forties and had already developed a name for himself in Richmond. He earned his high school diploma through the adult school program at Richmond High School in 1970.

Mr. Birdsong continued his education at Contra Costa College in San Pablo, California and obtained an Associate of Science degree, in Social Studies, in 1974. Ms. Barb was previously married several years earlier to Demetrius and Alonzo's father.

The marriage was a challenge for her and ended in divorce. As the courtship of Mr. Birdsong and Ms. Barb continued to flourish, his family already knew she would be a good wife to him. Early in the courtship, Mother Birdsong was not pleased with how her son was treating his girlfriend. One day as Mr. Birdsong and his mother were home on Maine Avenue, she had a serious talk with him.

Mother Birdsong was from the "old school" generation that believed in discipline. She was a person that would remind you of the older women from the television sitcoms, such as, Aunt Esther of Sanford and Son, and Mama Payne from Martin.

The older women in her generation would sometimes communicate in profanity for their position to be heard. You could not approach Mother Birdsong in any way. She did not believe in foolishness and would inform you immediately. As an African-American woman, who was raised in the south, Mother Birdsong held on to her traditions of the family structure. She knew her son had a good woman in his life who loved him unconditionally.

There is a lesson to be learned in this process. Parents want the best for their children as they become productive adults. Parents desire a good person for their children to have as their wedded spouse. Mother Birdsong wanted her son to be married and have a family. She already had grandchildren and great-grandchildren from her eldest son and his late wife. Mother Birdsong was approaching her seventies in five years. The continuation of her family was essential for the future. Mr. Birdsong's treatment of Ms. Barb was not fair in the eyes of Mother Birdsong. I am reminded of the character, Mabel "Madea" Simmons, of the Tyler Perry motion pictures and plays. Mother Birdsong was the "Madea" of her family and needed to give her son a reality check.

"James Charles, this girl goes out of her way to help you," Mother Birdsong said. "She comes over here and takes you places, cooks and prepares your meals, and does things you asked her to do. You have all those credit cards and money in the bank and your pocket. Now you get your ass in gear and take her shopping."

The words of his mother had made a dramatic impact on building this relationship. He realized she was telling the truth and he did not want to have any regrets. When a man has a good woman in his life, he will actively pursue her for marriage. Mr. Birdsong had reflected on his mother's words and made a telephone call to Ms. Barb. He asked her to meet with him at his home. She immediately came over and they went to a popular shopping center.

Ms. Barb drove Mr. Birdsong and his mother to Hilltop Mall. This mall was built during the early seventies and opened to the public in 1975 and is in Richmond, near the suburb of El Sobrante, California on Hilltop Mall Drive. The mall was one of the premier shopping centers in the Bay Area. Upon arriving, they walked inside of Emporium-Capwell. This was a popular department retail store with corporate headquarters in San Francisco, California.

Emporium-Capwell existed in the retail industry until 1995, and later had a merger with another popular department retail store called Macy's. Mr. Birdsong purchased a black dress, shoes, and a purse for Ms. Barb. She had a smile on her face, and this made Mother Birdsong pleased to the fact that her son came to the realization of what a man should do for his woman. Mr. Birdsong and his mother attended church services regularly on Sunday mornings.

They were members of Elisabeth Missionary Baptist Church located on Bissell Avenue. The pastor of Elisabeth was Reverend J.L. Johnson. He was one of the most respected pastors in the City of Richmond and had established himself as a legend and icon in ministry. He and his wife, Mother Ida Mae Johnson, were longtime friends of Mr. Birdsong and his mother.

The friendship between the Birdsongs and the Johnsons extended back to Greenwood, Louisiana. Prior to Elisabeth, Reverend Johnson served as the pastor of St. John Missionary Baptist Church in Vallejo, California. He died in 2012, at 94-years-old.

Mr. Birdsong and his mother were members. Ms. Barb began to attend services at Elisabeth with Mr. Birdsong. She knew his family was devoted to the church, with the lineage of preachers, musicians, and singers who eventually became recognized nationally. As the relationship of Mr. Birdsong and Ms. Barb continued to flourish, one day she visited her mother, Mildred Germany, at her home in Richmond. Mrs. Germany was another respected figure in the community. A member of North Richmond Missionary Baptist Church, the late Reverend

C.W. Newsome was her pastor. He was a respected pastor in Richmond that became a legend and an icon.

The two pastors I have mentioned were friends and colleagues in ministry. North Richmond Missionary Baptist Church is located on Filbert Street. Mrs. Germany was an active member of the National Council of Negro Women and served as the President of the Richmond chapter. She was actively involved in the community through volunteer efforts for the Richmond Rescue Mission.

Mrs. Germany also attended conferences in the Baptist church during the 1960s. Mrs. Germany had the opportunity to meet Mary McLeod Bethune and Dorothy Height. Mary McLeod Bethune was an African-American educator and Civil Rights leader. She was the founder of Bethune-Cookman University, a historically black college in Daytona Beach, Florida. Mrs. Bethune also founded the National Council of Negro Women and served as an advisor on the Black Cabinet for President Franklin Roosevelt during his administration.

Mrs. Germany happened to be surprised about the gentleman her daughter was courting. She said, "I am very familiar with the Birdsong family. They are very famous, and he is related to Cindy, Edwin and Otis Birdsong."

Her daughter mentioned that Mr. Birdsong was the nephew of the late Sidney Birdsong, Sr., of Los Angeles, California. Mrs. Germany immediately grabbed a program from a conference she attended in Los Angeles many years ago.

"Belinda, I remember Reverend Sidney Birdsong and the church he served as the pastor," she said. "When I attended the conferences, he would be there. He was very well known and respected." Reverend Birdsong was the pastor of Solid Rock Baptist Church in Los Angeles. He was Mother Birdsong's brother-in-law. Reverend Birdsong would always visit his nephew and sister-in-law when he had a preaching engagement in the Bay Area.

He died in 1976, at 58-years-old, and his funeral was well attended. There was one famous person who did a musical tribute at Reverend Birdsong's funeral in Los Angeles. That would be none other than Stevie Wonder, who is a close friend of the Birdsong family. I will share more of the story as this book continues to be written. Ms. Barb knew she made a milestone. Allow me to explain my position. When a woman is committed in a relationship or marriage to a man with the status of Mr. Birdsong, she has accomplished a goal in her life.

Most women desire a man who, first and foremost, has the Lord in his life, in addition to values, principles of solid family structure and foundational application. The union will then become their positive development for their future goals. The context of Biblical passages found in Scripture is our guide, as it becomes the voice for marriage and family. There are roles and responsibilities for both men and women, as husband and wife. I am going to speak on the man's role concerning this subject in her life and it was still registering. Scripture becomes an emphasis on the collective voice for marriage.

The passage speaks, "Whoso findeth a wife findeth a good thing, and obtaineth favour of the LORD" (Proverbs 18:22).

Marriage is ordained by God as a union between a husband and wife, in one body. As a man finds the woman he desires to become his wife, it establishes a partnership in the covenant. The definition of covenant is an agreement between two parties. A covenant is also a reminder of a contract being signed. When a person signs a contract, it becomes a legal binding agreement between the two parties. The signature of the contract moves forward in terms and obligations.

A contract can also be breached if one or both parties are

not in agreement. A marriage is more than a license as stated by the marital laws. The husband and wife must be able to have effective communication and growth development in the marriage. As we reflect on the wife's role in marriage, the Bible declares, "And the Lord God said, It is not good that the man should be alone; I will make him an help meet for him" (Genesis 2:18).

Mr. Birdsong and Ms. Barb continued their courtship for the remainder of 1979. One of his cousins, Albert Birdsong, and his wife, Barbara, came to visit him. Albert served as a deacon at Friendship Missionary Baptist Church in Vallejo, California, where Reverend Carol Broadfoot was the pastor at this particular time. He retired as the pastor and now serves as the pastor emeritus. The pastor today is Reverend Dante Quick.

Albert was a man devoted to his family, the church, and his community. He was employed by Sunset Books, a popular book publishing company, in the Bay Area. Mr. Birdsong made a name for himself in Richmond, while Albert was well known in Vallejo. The two of them grew up together as children in Greenwood, Louisiana. Albert was also the father of two sons, Albert Jr. and Orland. They also met Ms. Barb and knew she was a good person. Mr. Birdsong was having a conversation with his cousin about Ms. Barb. I already mentioned he was blind since Thanksgiving Day 1956. Albert observed Mr. Birdsong's facial expressions as they were talking.

Ms. Barb had a difficult moment. She already knew Mr. Birdsong wanted to marry her. There were numerous occasions of discussions of marriage and family. He was a single man in his forties and never experienced a true relationship.

"I don't want to be married," Ms. Barb told her boyfriend.

Those words had affected him and he wanted answers. As the conversation continued, Albert suddenly figured out the problem. He said, "James Charles, she does want to marry you. Belinda loves you and does not mean what she is expressing to you." He then broke the ice of the situation by saying, "She is pregnant." Mr. Birdsong was shocked and stunned.

As Chapter Two is being prepared, I need to talk with the men who are reading this book. For the record, I am not a licensed, certified relationship expert or a psychologist. Relationships can have challenges for both parties. I already mentioned the importance of effective communication. When a woman knows she has a good man in her life there are going to be doubted. This occurs when the marital factor becomes a presentation. In other words, she is going to be afraid. This becomes natural in a relationship.

Ms. Barb was truly in love with Mr. Birdsong. He never had a problem with Demetrius and Alonzo. They knew he was a good man in spite of his disability. Mr. Birdsong was finally going to be a father for the first time in his life. He always desired a son, and the family legacy was essential to him. I am going to impart something that is the truth. When a man wants to have a child, he desires a son to carry on his name. If something happens to the father, then his son would take care of the mother and family. This is the tradition of families for widespread practice. Mr. Birdsong believed in the principles of the family structure from his childhood. God has ordained the family for a purpose on this earth. I am reminded of this one scripture as a statement of multiplication in the land.

It says, "And God blessed them, and God said unto them, Be fruitful, and multiply, and replenish the earth, and subdue it; and have dominion over the fish of the sea, and over the fowl of the air, and over every living thing that moveth upon the earth" (Genesis 1:28).

Mr. Birdsong knew something had to be done. This is where

the decision factor of reality in a relationship is tested on the grounds. He can either continue the courtship with Ms. Barb or move forward to his future as her husband, in marriage. John Gray shares practical insights in Mars and Venus on a Date, as couples are in courtship for marriage preparation. He is known for his best-selling book, *Men are from Mars, Women are from Venus*. The marital preparation includes stages. Gray's position becomes an effective voice on the stage of engagement. He brings this agenda to the table. We recognize our partner to be our soul mate. Not only are we in love; we love this person so much that we want to spend the rest of our life with him or her (Gray, 1997). Mr. Birdsong applied practical advice by family and friends.

They had to remind him of the blessing God had placed in his path. A new decade was on the horizon. The next chapter of this book will proceed to 1980 as Mr. Birdsong and Ms. Barb were planning their future. Mother Birdsong was excited about the expansion of her family. The marriage had been in the discussions among Mr. Birdsong's family for a long time. When a man is educated, financially stable, obtains status among the elite and, most of all, active in the church, he has struck gold. It reminds me of the lottery. A ticket is purchased as winning numbers are broadcast on television. The winner claims their prize worth millions of dollars. Mr. Birdsong played the relationship lottery and became rich. His popularity continued to increase among the residents and dignitaries in Richmond. I can only imagine his expression as the Birdsong family rendered their verdict on Ms. Barb. Before they met, there were women that had their interest in him as a possible husband. Mr. Birdsong believed in class and did not settle for anything less than his caliber. He had his preference of women. Most men desire for a woman to be attractive in looks and personality.

Merriam-Webster defines caliber as a degree of excellence or importance. He strives for a relationship with a woman that shares the same desires and interests. A man of integrity, his vision for a wife and children became the tone for a legacy establishment. Mother Birdsong knew she was getting older in her age. Society classifies a person sixty-five and older a senior citizen.

"I want to be here when James Charles and Belinda are married," she thought one day. Mother Birdsong dedicated her life to her family for fifty plus years. That's inspiration in support of foundational philosophies. The Lord made provisions for Mr. Birdsong and Ms. Barb's journey in the marital stage. God gives us the heart to rejoice in blessings. Although the couple continued to date and engage in conversations for the future, Demetrius and Alonzo entered the stages of adolescence. The two brothers also made the verdict about their future stepfather. They rejoiced for their mother. Admiration of Mr. Birdsong and Ms. Barb's relationship, amid family and friends, sanctioned them to stay on one accord. The couple remained united in the same agenda, discussion of marriage were on their minds.

The Bible addresses this important question, "Can two walk together, except they be agreed?" (Amos 3:3). This scripture speaks more than the nature of relationships and marriages. God desires for His Children to come into agreement with each other. Mr. Birdsong's family believed in this Biblical teaching from their heritage in Greenwood, Louisiana. A tragedy occurred that no one expected. This is where our strengths and weaknesses are tested on families. I have learned there are questions and answers to be addressed. Beginnings of a foundation become the building of dreams. Where do we go from here on the beginner's stage? Only time will tell in the flight path as love grows.

Great grandfather, the late Ed Birdsong, Sr.

Great grandmother, the late Ida Birdsong

Great uncle, the late George Birdsong, S

Great uncle, the late Reverend Sidney Birdsong, Sr. and his wife Josephine

Last surviving great aunt, Glady Birdsong-Murray

Great aunt, the late Myria Birdsong-King

Grandfather, the late Jim Birdson

CHAPTER TWO

Love Grows

In Chapter One of this book, I mentioned a tragedy occurred. Before I share the specifics, there are historical milestones that happened in the 1980s. The populist conservative movement known as the New Right enjoyed unprecedented growth in the late 1970s and early 1980s (History.com, 2015). The early 1980s is the focus of this chapter.

President Jimmy Carter did his re-election campaign in the 1980 Presidential Election. President Carter pleaded his case to the American people for a second term. Since he was the incumbent candidate, his opponent was former Governor Ronald Reagan, a Republican, who served two terms as the thirty-third Governor of California from 1967 to 1975.

Prior to his career in politics, Governor Reagan was also a Hollywood icon in radio and television. After months of speeches, television and radio ads, national conventions of both political parties, and debates between the two candidates, Governor Reagan was declared the winner in the 1980 Presidential Election. President Carter conceded to his opponent. Governor Reagan was elected as the fortieth President of the United States. His inauguration was held on January 20th, 1981, in Washington, D.C.

The 1980 Summer Olympics were held from July 19th to August 3rd in Moscow, Russia that year. This is the leading international sporting event of summer and winter sports competitions of athletes. The date of inception remains a point of conjecture among historians, but it is generally accepted that the Olympic Games found their genesis in Olympia, Greece, in 776 BCE and survived in attenuated form until 393 BCE (Encyclopedia.com, 2016). There was a boycott of the 1980 Summer Olympics. President Carter was in his re-election campaign for a second term in the United States presidency. President Carter had encountered testing of his policies.

In 1980, the United States led a boycott of the Summer Olympics in Moscow to protest the late 1979 Soviet invasion of Afghanistan (2001-2009.state.gov, 2009). Conflicts of this situation created political agendas in the presidential campaigns, as President Carter and Governor Reagan pleaded their cases before the American people. In organizing the boycott and rallying support behind it, the Carter Administration had wanted to express the extent of international displeasure with the invasion of Afghanistan and to pressure the Soviets to pull their armies out of the conflict (2001-2009.state.gov, 2009).

John Lennon was murdered on the evening of December 8th, 1980, in New York, as he and his wife, Yoko Ono, returned to their apartment. An English singer and songwriter, John Lennon rose to worldwide fame.

He was a co-founder of the Beatles, the most commercially successful band in the history of popular music. Songs like Real Love (with the Beatles), Jealous Guy, and Imagine, to name a few, were a testament to his musical genius (Biography.com, 2016). Mr. Lennon's murderer, Mark David Chapman, was a deranged fan, who met him earlier in the day and just hours prior to his murder. John Lennon was 40-years-old and had a young son at the time. The murder of John Lennon made media headlines around the world. His record sales with the Beatles continues to generate revenue today.

There are more current events of the 1980s to be discussed as this book continues to be written. I am now going to resume the conversation about a tragedy that occurred during Mr. Birdsong's and Ms. Barb's relationship. This happened on New Year's Day of January 1st, 1980. Before the New Year arrived, Mother Birdsong realized she was approaching her seventies. She wanted her son to have a family of his own. She accepted the fact there was going to be another addition to the family. There were many thoughts on her mind, and she wanted the best for her son.

One morning Mother Birdsong walked to the neighborhood store, M&A Market, across the street from the house. As she approached the entrance, one of their neighbors, Clim, who was also one of Mr. Birdsong's best friends, greeted her as he was departing.

He smiled and said, "Good morning, Ms. Birdsong. How are you doing today?"

Mother Birdsong replied, "I am doing alright."

Clim knew something was wrong. He said, "Ms. Birdsong, what is going on with you? Are you alright?"

Mother Birdsong was troubled and needed to speak with someone. She and Clim were talking on the sidewalk where M&A Market was located on Harbour Way South. Mother Birdsong knew she could not hold it any longer.

"Please listen to me very good Clim. I need a favor from you about something that is very important to me," she said.

"Sure, Ms. Birdsong, I am listening to you," he answers. Mother Birdsong was a very strong willed woman and made many sacrifices for her sons.

"You have been a good friend to James Charles since our relocation here in this neighborhood," Mother Birdsong said. "I am getting older and I am very happy my son has found a good woman like Belinda. If anything happens to me, please watch out for him."

He applied her words to heart and replied, "Don't worry, Ms. Birdsong. I am going to keep my promise to you." Mother Birdsong then walked in the store and afterward returned to the house. He and his children were close to Mr. Birdsong, his mother, and brother during a period of eleven years before they met Ms. Barb. Clim worked in housekeeping at Brookside Hospital, in San Pablo, California, up until his retirement in 1993. Mother Birdsong did not share the details of her conversation with Clim to her son. She knew he had fallen in love with Ms. Barb.

Joan and Richard Hunt explains goals of choosing your relationship in their book, *Preparing for Christian Marriage*, as the path of flight prepares for takeoff in stages. Marriage implies a community of persons, who cooperate and support each other, in times of joy and in times of trouble (Hunt, 1982). Allow me to explain my position of the flight path. Mother Birdsong was grateful to the Lord for her prayers being answered. Every parent desires a good person as a potential spouse for their children in marriage. Mother Birdsong had confidence in Ms. Barb that she would be a great wife for her son.

Her desire for Mr. Birdsong and Ms. Barb, as husband and wife, became their investment in the love account. This included deposits of support in the good times and the tough times. The flight path of Mr. Birdsong's and Ms. Barb's relationship was about to embark on their journey of marital destination. There were other individuals in Mr. Birdsong's inner circle who accepted the fact he had found true love. Our most basic emotional need is not to fall in love but to be genuinely loved by one another, to know a love that grows out of reason and choice, not instinct (Chapman, 1992). The relationship building continues to include "add-ons" every day in love growth.

The account of love produces our level of maturity in

relationship building. The love language of Mr. Birdsong and Ms. Barb produced their investment in the love account.

Ms. Barb had a dream and had to immediately inform Mr. Birdsong. On New Year's Eve, December 31, 1979, she was at home with her sons on Pennsylvania Avenue. She called Mr. Birdsong and said, "James, I need to share something with you."

Mr. Birdsong stopped what he was doing to listen to his girlfriend. He replied, "What is going on Belinda?"

She continued with their conversation. "I had a dream of two men. They were climbing a mountain trying to reach a woman who was little." She told him the two men did their best to reach the woman but were unsuccessful. Mr. Birdsong could not understand what Ms. Barb had mentioned to him.

The following day on January 1, 1980, Mr. Birdsong was at home with his mother. His brother came over to visit them. In Chapter One of this book, they resided in a Victorian house. Their home had two bedrooms downstairs and three on the second story. Both stories of the house had a bathroom. Mother Birdsong's room was upstairs facing the south on Harbour Way South as it crossed on Cutting Boulevard. From Mother Birdsong's room, there was a view of the Port of Richmond. I will explain more specific details about the City of Richmond as this book continues to be written. While Mr. Birdsong was in his room, Mr. Daniel was downstairs in the living room.

Mother Birdsong sat down in her chair and leaned back. She closed her eyes and never awakened. Charlene Walton-Birdsong died on this day, in her room, at sixty-five years-old. Mr. Daniel went upstairs to check on their mother. When he walked in the room, he called her name and said, "Mother, mother wake up."

There was no response and he yelled, "James Charles, Mother is not breathing."

Mr. Birdsong gets out of his bed and went to the room with his brother, as Mother Birdsong sat lifeless in her chair. The paramedics were called and responded. The emergency medical response personnel took Mother Birdsong to Kaiser Permanente Hospital on Marina Way, in Richmond. She was pronounced dead upon their arrival. Mr. Birdsong and his brother were in mourning over the sudden death of their mother. They now had a major challenge on their hands, with funeral arrangements and telephone calls to various family members. The death of Mother Birdsong was a major shock to the family and the community. Mr. Birdsong called Ms. Barb and said, "Belinda, the dream that you had was about mother. She died today and you saw her death." He had a child on the way and knew his mother was waiting for the birth of another grandchild.

This chapter is titled "Love Grows." We are going to experience tests and trials as love does build growth. There are three things Mr. Birdsong had to deal with. First, he was blind and lost his vision at 18-years-old, in Greenwood, Louisiana. His disability became the determination and acceptance of being different.

Secondly, Mr. Birdsong had a woman who loved him, despite his disability, and wanted a future as one family. Finally, his mother was now deceased and no longer around to watch his child grow up. Mr. Birdsong's father, Jim Birdsong, was still alive when Mother Birdsong died. He resided in Shreveport, Louisiana. Mr. Birdsong's parents were married and divorced in the late 1960s, before the relocation to California. There will be a chapter in this book that will explain more of Mr. Birdsong's childhood and the relationship with his parents. His father later married a woman named Pearl who lived to be 100 years old when she died in 2011.

Rose Manor Funeral Services handled the funeral

arrangements of Mother Birdsong. They are the most respected African-American owned mortuary in Richmond. The founder and owner of Rose Manor Funeral Services, John Stewart, was a friend of Mr. Birdsong and his family. Mr. Stewart died in 1997. The mortuary is located on MacDonald Avenue and continues to serve the citizens of Richmond and surrounding areas, with their funeral and burial services.

Following the funeral, the procession proceeded to Rolling Hills Memorial Park near Hilltop Mall for Mother Birdsong's interment. Mr. Birdsong and Mr. Daniel were joined by attendees for a dinner reception following their mother's burial. The two brothers were still in mourning over their mother's death, and this allowed them to grow closer as brothers. Ms. Barb realized Mr. Birdsong was still mourning. She also realized what his mother wanted.

I am going to reflect on the conversation between Mother Birdsong and Clim. She told him if anything happened to her then he would watch out for her son. I truly believe she already knew the Lord was preparing her to make the transition into eternity. Clim and his family also attended the funeral of Charlene Walton-Birdsong and held on to his promise. Mother Birdsong was proud of her son for his decision about marriage and family.

He wanted to cherish her memory. The process of a relationship becomes our essential voice again as a connection to traits Mr. Birdsong and Ms. Barb had while preparing for marriage in the relationship. There are three stages in the love growth. Mr. Birdsong and Ms. Barb had roles while preparing for marriage in the relationship.

There are three stages in the love growth. The first is friendship level as dating proceeds. As a man and woman meet for the first time, the investigation and analyzation begin in dating. This allows them to learn their interests, likes and dislikes, and future goals. The second is the relationship level as love determines in the development of growth. Once the two factors have been tested on grounds of both parties, the third and final stage is marriage and family level.

Regardless of our philosophy, we cannot make our entrance into the level of marriage and family without completion of the previous tests. It reminds me of children in their education. If they are going to reach the twelfth grade in high school, the steps must first begin in elementary school as a first grader and recognize the family tradition. There is an order in the process of diverse grounds. "Let all things be done decently and in order" (I Corinthians 14:40). God will give us the desires of our heart as dreams are pursued in life and even relationships. Psalm 37:23 also becomes a declaration in the presentation, as it reads, "The steps of a good man are ordered by the LORD: and he delighteth in his way." If we abide in the Will and Purpose of God in the love growth, then our steps of marriage become purpose directed, purpose driven, and purpose focused.

The purpose direction of Mr. Birdsong allowed him to be driven to Ms. Barb in their love growth. He was ready to pursue happiness in marriage with her and wanted to prove himself as a man. Engagement sets the tone of love growth as a man proposes to his woman for her hand in marriage. We will do an examination of the engagement process. There are certain traditions and cultural practices in consideration of the marriage and family stage are brought forth. If a man proposes to a woman for marriage in some cultures, he requests the permission of her father. Respect values integrity in family foundation.

There are also some cases where the man proceeds with the proposal, without the consent of his woman's family. Mr.

Birdsong already met Ms. Barb's family members. There will be a chapter in this book about her story as we continue to proceed. Ms. Barb did not have a close bond among her siblings. If the woman's father is deceased or never involved in his daughter's life, then the man will request the permission of her mother. Situations where both parents are deceased and the man progresses in his proposal becomes a factor in the love growth. Opinions create our Broadway production in relationship transition.

I already shared the definition of love growth. One of the nation's most acclaimed clinical psychologists, William F. Harley, Jr., presents his case on this topic. He is best known for his best-selling book, *His Needs Her Needs Building an Affair-Proof Marriage*, sold more than 1,000,000 copies since 1986. Harley shares practical insights of the love bank. Each person either makes deposits or withdrawals whenever we interact with him or her (Harley, 1986).

Mr. Birdsong invested at the love bank and opened an account. He already knew the love account was going to be joint and not separate. An entrepreneur is going to have risks and takes in their business as their revenue increases. The stock market produces shares of a company for brokers around initial financial investments. A person must be skilled and experience to engage in this position. If you read the daily reports of the stock market, they have highs and lows. Now, the scenario for love accounts is described.

Seeing that a customer makes their deposits and withdraws in the love bank, stewardship must occur always. If the account is overdrawn, immediate action should proceed for the status. Our record follows us through life. This begins at birth as a mother conceives a child, and produces status quotas for various stages. There are gives and takes in love growth. Mr. Birdsong made the acceptance as a man to pursue his desire to be married.

For Ms. Barb's part, she had to open a love account. As a young woman in her thirties, and as a divorced mother of two children, she longed to be a wife and have a real man to be a good father figure for Demetrius and Alonzo. Society has their conceptions of women that are single mothers. The single mothers of that time were either divorced or widowed. They have been married to a husband.

In the 21st century, the concepts have dramatically changed in this perception. We have children today raised in single parent homes, without a father in the home. The mothers are challenged daily in sacrifices as Mama and Daddy. This is a trend in the African-American community. I am very optimistic about striving for a positive future for every man, woman, and child. I applaud the single mothers that are doing their tireless efforts to raise their children to be productive citizens as adults. Throughout the years, I have met and known single mothers that can relate to this position. These single mothers are hardworking citizens. Regardless of what has occurred, I admire the fact they did not allow the ways of society to hinder them from transforming into their destiny ordained by the Lord Himself. It saddens and grieves me on how society passes judgment towards people when all of us have fallen short of the Glory of God.

Matthew writes this passage as it reads, "Judge not, that ye be not judged. For with what judgment ye judge, ye shall be judged: and with what measure ye mete, it shall be measured to you again" (Matthew 7:1-2). I encourage the single mothers that read this book that you are loved, appreciated, and respected.

There is a love account for a single mother that desires a husband. The Word of God clearly points this out thoroughly, "But seek ye first the kingdom of God, and his righteousness;

and all these things shall be added unto you" (Matthew 6:33). If this came to pass for single mothers that have prayed, trusted and believed in God for a husband and a father figure to their children, it can also happen for you. Once He steps in and develops the marital union in this perspective, the love account increases.

The older saints of the church used to say, "I've got a feeling that everything will be alright." Yes, God is going to make this alright and bring your status as a single mother, with the heart's desire to be a wife, to the husband, into fruition as love growth is amended.

The next chapter will explain how Mr. Birdsong made his step as a man to pursue marriage and family. He was blind and had no vision. Did he prepare for a marital proposal? Would his popularity increase in Richmond among the dignitaries and citizens? What would be the reaction of Ms. Barb and especially her sons? Only time will tell in this story. The love train is now departing for the next station.

The late Reverend Sam Price of the Greenwood No. 1 Baptist Church (left).

The original Greenwood No. 1 Baptist Church (below)

CHAPTER THREE

Move On Up A Little Higher

The late Mahalia Jackson recorded a song, *Move on up A Little Higher*, which became a major hit. This song was composed by the late William Herbert Brewster in 1947. Mahalia made history during the 20th century throughout the United States and abroad. She was the most famous gospel singer in the world. Her music continues to inspire millions today.

As I reflect on this song, the relationship of Mr. Birdsong and Ms. Barb comes to mind. The last chapter of this book explained their love growth. We are now about to approach this phase of Mr. Birdsong and Ms. Barb's relationship. They have already had discussions and plans for marriage. Their relationship elevated a little higher in love growth.

Karl Pillemer explains the process of following your heart in *30 Lessons of Loving: Advice from the Wisest Americans on Love, Relationships and Marriage*. Falling in love means that intuition tells you this is the right thing to do, without knowing for sure (Pillemer, 2015). We will experience fear along the way in this process. Criticism of family and friends also becomes a conflict in the element. Our hearts provide clarity and determination in our love growth, regardless of opinions by individuals closest and dearest to us.

Mr. Birdsong asked the important question. He said, "Belinda, will you marry me?" She smiled and said yes, to him. They were now officially engaged to be married. For the record, they did not have a traditional wedding. Mr. Birdsong and Ms. Barb were expecting a child and he was still grieving over the death of his mother. He said, "I am finally going to be married and a father. Mother is no longer here to witness this in our family." I want to share this with you. Mr. Birdsong was a very strong man when it came to these situations.

He was not alone. The Birdsong family was and still is a strong minded and positive thinking people, in both the good and tough times. Since they were famous and respected around the world, their purpose gave them motivation to teach, guide, and prepare future generations to carry lifetime application principles.

Bishop T.D. Jakes shares his counsel with his national best-selling book, *Destiny: Step into Your Purpose*. Once you set your order, you will awaken each day determined to engage those principles to pursue your purpose (Jakes, 2015). I agree with Bishop Jakes in this lesson of purpose Mr. Birdsong and Ms. Barb had already set the order with their love growth, of the marital stage, in their relationship. They made the decision to invest in a road trip to Reno, Nevada. Mr. Birdsong and Ms. Barb could not travel there alone. He requested three of his longtime friends to accompany them as witnesses for the wedding, which occurred on March 7, 1980.

Paul Logan was a longtime friend of Mr. Birdsong. A dedicated husband and father, Mr. Logan practiced as a nurse in the medical field. He lived in Richmond with his wife, Barbara, and their children. The remaining two individuals were Barbara's sister, Diana, and "Pops", their father. The five of them traveled 203 miles in three hours, from Richmond to Reno, in Mr. Birdsong's car. I am going to explain my perspective of the artistic view. While they were riding alongside Interstate 80 East on the road to Reno, the concept of outdoors had beautiful scenery. The snow-covered trees were imparted with heavenly beauty. It reminds me of the angels in heaven singing *Joy to the*

World as a mass choir. This artistic view also brings my attention to the late Leonard da Vinci, for his famous historical Mona Lisa portrait. Mr. Birdsong and Ms. Barb, along with their guests, arrived in Reno after a three-hour journey on the road. Ms. Barb was seven months pregnant at the time. Her sons were already in their pre-adolescence stages. They did not go with their mother and her fiancé to Reno for their wedding. They proceeded to the Washoe County Courthouse to obtain the license for marriage. Once the marriage license was purchased, they headed to Chapel of the Bells, a small wedding chapel. A gentleman named Murrica, a licensed ordained minister, performed the marital ceremony of Mr. Birdsong and Ms. Barb. Once Murrica rendered the declaration of marriage in the ceremony, I am pleased to announce they were now pronounced as husband and wife on midnight of March 8, 1980. Ms. Barb was now known as Belinda Birdsong.

Mr. and Mrs. Birdsong were smiling as they now entered into the new chapter of their lives as a married couple. For excitement and recreation, the Birdsongs and their guests departed Chapel of the Bells and went to the Golden Nugget Hotel, a popular hotel in Reno. For those of you that are familiar with Reno, it is the third major city in Nevada where Las Vegas ranks as the largest. Both cities are well-known internationally for their gambling casinos.

There were more than 300 people at the Golden Nugget Hotel and security was active that evening. The newlyweds and their guests enjoyed the activities of playing casino games. About 6:00 AM in the morning, the Birdsongs and their guests departed the hotel for the three-hour drive back to Richmond. Artistic view once again becomes amended on this agenda. The outdoor scenery arranges the tone of a life production. It reminds me of the angels in heaven singing *Love Lifted Me*, in this description.

Once they returned to Richmond, the Birdsongs began their lives as a married couple. Mr. Birdsong became the stepfather of Demetrius and Alonzo. Mrs. Birdsong and her sons relocated to the house on Maine Avenue, where Mr. Birdsong resided since 1968. The household now consisted of him and his wife, along with Demetrius and Alonzo. During this time, Mr. Birdsong continued to establish himself as a distinguished figure in Richmond. I already mentioned in Chapter One of his role in the community. He was now a husband for the first time. My mind reflects on Charlene Walton-Birdsong, as she wanted her son to be married and have a family.

Mr. Birdsong came to one conclusion. He said, "If only mother was still alive today." Once a man and a woman are married, the real challenge begins. Life is filled with episodes of challenges. Despite what obstacles we endured in our journey, a testimony is built on the tests of our circumstances.

Paul writes about affliction, "We are troubled on every side, yet not distressed; we are perplexed, but not in despair; Persecuted, but not forsaken; cast down, but not destroyed; Always bearing about in the body the dying of the Lord Jesus, that the life also of Jesus might be made manifest in our body" (II Corinthians 4:8-10). God will give us His Divine direction to handle our afflictions in our challenges. "(A Psalm of David.) The LORD [is] my shepherd; I shall not want. He maketh me to lie down in green pastures: he leadeth me beside the still waters. He restoreth my soul: he leadeth me in the paths of righteousness for his name's sake" (Psalm 23:1-3). The strength comes from Jesus Christ in our challenges of situations.

Bishop Jakes mentions another important lesson in the order of fulfilling purpose. When your life is ordered, setbacks and disappointments are regarded as commas and not periods that punctuate your story (Jakes, 2015). Afflictions of challenges allows us to have our teaching moments in these situations. The Birdsongs were newlyweds and were already making plans for their future.Mrs. Birdsong was in her eighth month of pregnancy.

Her husband, along with his friends, decided to organize a baby shower. As a woman is approaching the birth of a child, in her pregnancy, she will receive gifts pertaining to the baby, such as, clothing, diapers, furniture and other accessories. This became a joyous occasion in her life as she was about to be a mother again for the third time. I can imagine the reaction of Mr. Birdsong. He had always desired a family of his own. The baby shower was held at their home on Maine Avenue.

The Birdsongs were preparing for their new addition. There was a 13-year gap in her pregnancy. Her last child, Alonzo, was born on August 22, 1969. During the time of their mother's baby shower, he was 10-years-old while Demetrius was two years older. The brothers knew they were going to have another sibling. They were aware Mr. Birdsong loved their mother and wanted to have a family. Mr. Birdsong's family continued to visit him and his wife at their home. Mr. Daniel relocated to San Pablo where his children and grandchildren were residing. Everyone in Mr. Birdsong's circle, from family members to high profile individuals in Richmond, was excited about the upcoming birth of his child.

Two months later, Mrs. Birdsong was admitted at Richmond Hospital on May 15, 1980. She had approached her ninth and final month of pregnancy. John Gray talks about parenting skills in *Children are from Heaven: Positive Parenting Skills for Raising Cooperative, Confident and Compassionate Children*. All children are born innocent and good. In this sense, our children are from heaven. Each child is already unique and special (Gray,

1999). Heaven was rejoicing and the active doors were opened. The child of James and Belinda Birdsong was born on May 16, 1980, at 10:10 AM. This beautiful baby weighed nine pounds and was twenty-one inches long.

Did the Birdsongs have a boy or a girl? I am pleased to announce the baby was a boy. Are you ready for this, ladies and gentlemen? I am the baby that is writing this story. My name is James Charles Birdsong, Jr. and I approve this message. I am known as "Junior," by family members and close friends. Mama named me after Daddy. She always wanted a daughter. God had His reason for my mother to have three sons. I learned a mother with sons is protected. I was born at Richmond Hospital on 23rd Street. The hospital was renamed East Bay Hospital. As of today, the hospital is no longer in operation. I stayed at Richmond Hospital with Mama for six days. My mother returned home with me on May 21, 1980. Our house was occupied with visitors from everywhere. This becomes essential as a baby is born. God has already ordained our Kingdom calling assignment before the foundation of the world.

One of my former professors, Dr. Kent Branch, expresses the role of our kingdom assignment in *A Kingdom Calling: How to Identify Your Divine Assignment*. The most important goal or assignment that you can accomplish in life is the one assigned by God (Branch, 2010). When we are born into this world there is a purpose to be fulfilled. Our journey on earth is not done by accident. As a child is born, they are associated with a story in their purpose. Our children are the dreamers and achievers of tomorrow. For instance, if you would ask them, "What do you want to be when you grow up?" They will have the guarantee answer of a future career field.

We are also born to be visionaries in our purpose. "For the vision is yet for an appointed time, but at the end it shall speak, and not lie: though it tarry, wait for it; because it will surely come, it will not tarry." (Habakkuk 2:3). Parents are aware of their children's gifts, talents and abilities to be productive adults. I always encourage people never to say discouraging words to your children. They will reflect on those words as adults. Charlene Walton-Birdsong was my grandmother. If you go back and read the first two chapters of this book, I already shared her story. I never had the opportunity to know my grandmother due to her sudden death five months before my birth.

You may be wondering, "What about your grandmother, Mildred?" She was my mother's mother and, after I was born, Grandmother Mildred was still respected in Richmond as a Civil Rights leader. She was in her mid-sixties by this time. I did have two grandfathers by the time I was born. I mentioned Jim Birdsong in Chapter Two of this book. He was residing in Shreveport, Louisiana, with his wife, Pearl. Otis Germany was my mother's father. He does have an interesting story. I will share this in another chapter. Children are a gift from God and they should be always treated with love and compassion. We attended Sunday morning services at Elisabeth Missionary Baptist Church. Reverend Johnson was one of the prominent pastors in Richmond. For those of you who were born and raised in Richmond, I know you remember this group of Baptist pastors. They were respected in our city. Reverend Johnson was among this elite association. I remember these pastors very well and they had a heart for God's people.

he other pastors in this elite association were Reverend Orenzia Bernstine of New St. James Missionary Baptist Church, Reverend A.H. Newman of Bethlehem Missionary Baptist Church, Reverend C.H. Richardson of Pilgrim Rest Missionary Baptist Church, and Reverend C.W. Newsome of North Richmond Missionary Baptist Church. They have transitioned to be with the Lord. My father knew those pastors personally. Those pastors were the Civil Rights leaders of Richmond. I am going to talk about the notables of my hometown later in this book. Parents' love for their children is unconditional. It builds a framework between childhood, for the child, and parenthood, for their parents. Success preparation is the key in this agenda. My parents were determined their son was going to become a successful person in life.

William and Martha Sears share practical steps in *The Successful Child: What Parents Can Do to Help Kids Turn out Well*. Parents begin to give their children the tools they need to succeed as adults before they were born (Sears & Sears, 2002). There is an old saying, "Charity begins at home." Before a child is born, their parents have already made the adjustments of the family foundation. This is exactly what my parents did in preparation of parenthood, with me. Daddy made the decision to name Paul Logan as my Godfather.

I addressed him as Uncle Paul. He died in 2001, after a battle with cancer. Not only was he a dedicated husband and father, Uncle Paul was very comical. He would have you laughing. Uncle Paul was a native of Boston, Massachusetts and relocated to Richmond, California, before my parents met in 1979. On January 20, 1981, President Reagan was inaugurated as President of the United States. In Chapter Two, I mentioned the 1980 Presidential Election, between him and his opponent, former President Jimmy Carter. As you are aware, President Carter was not reelected to a second term as the thirty-ninth President of the United States and conceded the race to Governor Reagan. Parents' love for their children is unconditional. It builds a framework between childhood, for the child, and parenthood, for their parents. Success preparation is the key in this agenda. My parents were determined their son was going to become a successful person in life. William and Martha Sears share practical steps in *The Successful Child: What Parents Can Do to Help Kids Turn out Well*. Parents begin to give their children the tools they need to succeed as adults before they were born (Sears & Sears, 2002). There is an old saying, "Charity begins at home." Before a child is born, their parents have already made the adjustments of the family foundation. This is exactly what my parents did in preparation of parenthood, with me.

Daddy made the decision to name Paul Logan as my Godfather. I addressed him as Uncle Paul. He died in 2001, after a battle with cancer. Not only was he a dedicated husband and father, Uncle Paul was very comical. He would have you laughing. Uncle Paul was a native of Boston, Massachusetts and relocated to Richmond, California, before my parents met in 1979.

On January 20, 1981, President Reagan was inaugurated as President of the United States. In Chapter Two, I mentioned the 1980 Presidential Election, between him and his opponent, former President Jimmy Carter. As you are aware, President Carter was not reelected to a second term as the thirty-ninth President of the United States and conceded the race to Governor Reagan. That same year, my parents decided to engage in a business opportunity to generate financial revenue.

A woman named Luzan Graham persuaded them to be distributors for the Amway Corporation. Luzan is my Godmother and she is very special to me. She lived across the street from us on Maine Avenue. Her daughter and my God sister, Kitara, was 9-years-old when I was born. The Amway Corporation sells a variety of products in health, beauty and home care brands, in multi-level marketing. The company was founded in 1959, by Jay Van Andel and Richard DeVos, and headquartered in Ada, Michigan. My parents were salespersons for their products. They did not continue in this activity for a long time. Their main priority was raising me and being a family, as Charlene Walton-Birdsong desired. God's Word gives instructions to parents on how to raise their children from the Biblical perspective.

This familiar passage reads, "Train up a child in the way he should go: and when he is old, he will not depart from it" (Proverbs 22:6). Parents are ordained and anointed by Jesus Christ to be the leaders, motivators, encouragers and directors in the lives of their children.

Parenting is a ministry and creates influential values. Integrity becomes our gold mine for the goal. Between nine to fifteen months old, my parents knew something was not normal with me. A baby in those stages begins to speak words. I had a different situation. The Lord had a calling on my life for ministry and service.

I was being spiritually attacked by the devil. This influenced my parents. Daddy already faced his situations. He said one day, "I am blind, mother is dead, and now Junior cannot talk."

The Lord will place tests upon us in our faith. James and Belinda Birdsong were challenged in this situation. They had many questions without immediate answers. "My brethren, count it all joy when ye fall into divers temptations; Knowing this, that the trying of your faith worketh patience. But let patience have her perfect work, that ye may be perfect and entire, wanting nothing" (James 1:2-4).

This is where God tests our faith. Abraham is a perfect example of how faith becomes tested. The Biblical writer quotes, "And it came to pass after these things, that God did tempt Abraham, and said unto him, Abraham: and he said, Behold, here I am. And he said, Take now thy son, thine only son Isaac, whom thou lovest, and get thee into the land of Moriah; and offer him there for a burnt offering upon one of the mountains which I will tell thee of" (Genesis 22:1-2).

Can you imagine Abraham's reaction as God spoke to him for Isaac as a sacrifice? I am sure he had questions. Why would I want to sacrifice my own son? How can this happen? What is the purpose of this sacrifice? A father's love for his son is a blessing. He prepares him to carry on his legacy after he transitions from this world. This becomes standard in the family tradition. Abraham knew Isaac would carry on his legacy, as I reflect on this scenario. God tests our faith to see how we are going to handle situations that approach unexpectedly.

If you read the entire chapter of Genesis 22, the Biblical writer explains the account. Abraham believed his Isaac was the sacrifice. This scripture declares, "And he said, Lay not thine hand upon the lad, neither do thou anything unto him: for now I know that thou fearest God, seeing thou hast not withheld thy son, thine only son from me" (Genesis 22:12).

Abraham passed the test and offered a Ram for a sacrifice. God ordained him to be a father to many nations. His descendants were blessed from this legacy, as his faith sustained him. God knew exactly what He was doing in this situation, regarding the developmental disability. Yes, my speech has been affected. Amid tests and trials, Mama and Daddy were in preparation to be elevated higher in the Lord.

A miracle happened to be in the horizon for the Birdsong household. I believe there were intercessory prayer warriors on their knees praying for James Charles Birdsong, Jr. to be healed. James and Belinda Birdsong continued to search for answers for their son's dilemma. Not too many people in Daddy's inner circle became aware of this situation. I am referring to the noted figures he developed friendships and associations with throughout the years. He had to overcome the death of his mother, grandparents, three uncles, cousins and friends, prior to my birth. This became shocking to him as a father, who had a son with a developmental disability. He also had to be strong for his wife in this process.

One of the most prominent figures of the Civil Rights Movement, Reverend Jesse Jackson, always said, "Keep hope alive" in his speeches. As believers of Jesus Christ, our faith and trust in Him becomes the voice of hope being alive in our walk. A miraculous deliverance occurred in my life. I am here to share the goodness of Jesus Christ in this testimony. The next chapter is going to become the voice of this transformation. I am not finished.

CHAPTER FOUR

Miracle at Three Years Old

The challenges of my speech impediment became a primary concern at home. Parents that have children with a form of disability encounter fears. I tried to speak. The only thing I can do is hum. Throughout the years, this testimony has touched the hearts of people. Please let me reverse the cassette for a moment.

Attending church services became the standard in our household. Daddy still had his status as a predominant figure in our city. Either in 1981 or 1982, Mama and Daddy scheduled an appointment at the Richmond Pediatric Group on Cutting Boulevard near John F. Kennedy High School and Easter Hill Park. One of the pediatricians, Dr. William Morris Jenkins, Jr., was among the icons and trailblazers. The most prominent pediatrician in Richmond, he was the man. If you were born and raised in Richmond, I know you remember Dr. Jenkins. He died on August 12, 2012, at 83-years-old. This man had compassion for children and their families.

Dr. Jenkins practiced medicine for more than 50 years. He worked alongside Dr. Robert Mines, Jr., at this prominent practice in pediatric care for children. The Richmond Pediatric Group is no longer in existence. Today, the building is now a Hispanic church. Majority of patients at the Richmond Pediatric Group were predominantly African-American and Latino.

He noticed my parents' worries about my struggle to speak. He told them, "Mr. and Mrs. Birdsong, I am going to make a recommendation at Children's Hospital for additional tests."

The problem began at 13-months-old. I had one leg shorter than the other. Mama and Daddy observed this very closely. A television show, *Fear Factor*, aired from 2001 to 2006. The production revived five years later. The contestants on Fear Factor had to decide if they had determination to face their fears in competition. As my parents were facing a dilemma of my developmental disability, the willingness of their sacrifices became a test of faith in hope.

The Word of God becomes our declaration on how to overcome our fears. I am going to share some scriptures in this perspective. "Fear thou not; for I [am] with thee: be not dismayed; for I [am] thy God: I will strengthen thee; yea, I will help thee; yea, I will uphold thee with the right hand of my righteousness (Isaiah 41:10)." This brings forth and sets the tone as our faith is being tested. "For God hath not given us the spirit of fear; but of power, and of love, and of a sound mind" (II Timothy 1:7).

Rick Warren speaks about our purpose on earth in *The Purpose Driven Life: What on Earth I am Here For?* He writes, "Long before you were conceived by your parents, you were conceived in the mind of God." Can a person that has been diagnosed as disabled be destined to be successful? The answer is yes. A disabled person can attend college and pursue a career as anyone else in our nation. Society has a unique perspective of disability. Daddy was blind and had no vision.

He migrated from the south, and made his journey to California for greater opportunities. I had the opportunity of meeting men and women that have a disability and established themselves as achievers. Reflect on Stevie Wonder, Ray Charles, Albert Einstein, Helen Keller and others, for a minute. Now, you can see the point of this in-depth conservation. With the recommendation of Dr. Jenkins, we drove to Children's

Hospital in Oakland near downtown for the appointment. Per the report, I had been born with motor delays that escalated my speech being affected. The doctors suggested for American Sign Language. Mama and Daddy had more worries on their hands. I began to attend Knolls Language Center, a daycare school for children that have disabilities. Located in Richmond near Hilltop Mall, the teachers were specialists. The school was affiliated with the Richmond Unified School District on Bissell Avenue. In the early nineties, the district changed their name. Today, they are known as the West Contra Costa Unified School District.

The school district made transportation accommodations for bus service. Mondays through Fridays, a bus driver picked me up. I boarded the bus for Knolls. I returned home in the afternoons. There were only a handful of children in the class that were special education students. At the same time, I met a boy named Ian Spath and we became best friends. I have so much to say about this young man. I am sure he feels the same way. We were classmates at three schools throughout the eighties.

As long God allows me to live, Ian will always be my best friend. Nobody can take that from us. Several years ago, I told Mama, "When I get married, I desire for Ian to be the best man in the wedding."

He lived in Kensington, California with his parents, David and Linda. Kensington is located east of Richmond, in the hills between El Cerrito and Berkeley. Our teacher was a woman named Sandy. She worked in the special education program as a specialist. There is one person I will never forget, Joan Albers. She taught at Knolls and visited different schools in the district as a specialist. The teachers made us feel comfortable and treated us fairly. Toys and games set the tone for learning. Dr. Jenkins and Children's Hospital worked collectively together alongside Knolls Learning Center in this effort.

We began to visit various churches in Richmond. I believe Mama and Daddy were searching for Divine intervention. Reared in the Baptist church of southern tradition, Daddy never abandoned his roots. In Mama's case, she did attend church services with her parents and siblings. Belinda Birdsong did not have this upbringing as my father did. She visited Bethel Temple Pentecostal Church in Richmond, where the late Elder Joseph Turner was the pastor.

Her childhood friend, the late Zelma Turner, was a preacher's kid. Elder Turner was Zelma's father. Bethel Temple is an apostolic church on Cutting Boulevard. The late Dr. Betty Hendricks became the pastor following Elder Turner's death. She and her husband, Deacon Clinton Hendricks remember me as a child.

The Georgia Mass Choir recorded a song that is one of their hits. Titled, *Hold On, Help is On the Way,* it declares encouragement in situations. Whitney Houston recorded the song with the Georgia Mass Choir for the motion picture, *The Preacher's Wife*. It becomes our reminder God is our help in the time of need. "I will lift up eyes unto the hills, from whence cometh my help. My help cometh from the LORD, which made heaven and earth" (Psalm 121:1-2). Our testimonies are birthed from tests and trials.

Clim knew about our situation. His children were adults with families of their own. He has a grandson that is two months older than me. I graduated high school with one of his granddaughters. Our families were close and had a special bond. Those memories will forever be cherished. How many of you remember Dottie Peoples hit song, *He's an on Time God?* He is on time during storms. A preacher named Elder

Robert Lee Crawford and his wife, Betty, came to Richmond. The Crawford's were living in Joliet, Illinois. He was invited to conduct a revival in 1983, at Now Faith Church of God in Christ, on Nevin Avenue and 2nd Street.

A man that was saved, sanctified, and Holy Ghost filled, Elder Crawford believed in the doctrine of Pentecostalism. We attended the revival service. Clim and his family were present. Elder Crawford eventually became the pastor of Now Faith. God revealed my condition to Elder Crawford. He immediately approached Mama. "Sister Birdsong, the Lord told me to tell you He is going to heal your son," he said. Mama stopped and listened to the Man of God.

"If you receive Jesus Christ in your life and be filled with the Holy Ghost, then James is going to talk. Before he goes to bed at night, anoint his head with oil and pray for him." The Crawfords knew God placed a Calling on Mama's life for ministry.

In the eighties, Pentecostalism became a powerful outpouring throughout the United States and abroad. World renowned pastors and evangelists, such as, Billy Graham, Kenneth Hagin, Sr., Oral Roberts, Robert W. Schambach, Jimmy Swaggart, and others, were respected and admired by millions. These Men of God were not in the ministry for money and fame. For the African-American church in Pentecostalism, we had Bishop Gilbert Earl Patterson.

I watched his television broadcast, Bountiful Blessings with Bishop G.E. Patterson, which was filmed at his church, Temple of Deliverance Church of God in Christ, in Memphis, Tennessee. In 2000, he was elected as the sixth Presiding Bishop in the Church of God in Christ. Bishop Patterson served in this office until his death in 2007. There is a difference being in the ministry for real purpose and those in their status of prosperity gospel. As the preachers, I mentioned came on television and radio, people listened to them as the Word of God was ministered to masses.

We eventually turned out to be members of Now Faith. Daddy and Clim were appointed on the deacon's board and serve faithfully. The Church of God in Christ was founded in 1907, by the late Bishop Charles Harrison Mason, in Memphis, Tennessee. It is the largest African-American Pentecostal denomination in the United States, as the membership has become 6.5 million people worldwide. Now Faith was a storefront church, which is common among inner-city neighborhoods. The largest church in Richmond happened to be Hilltop Community Church on Shane Drive. I passed by this church every day in route to Knolls Language Center.

Parents desire the best for their children. Mama and Daddy wanted more. She began to decorate the living and dining rooms of our house on Maine Avenue. Mama loves interior decorating. Visitors loved the work she had done, from family members to friends, dignitaries, pastors, church members and others. There were times church services were held in the living room. Deliverance will come in our situations. I am going to give the testimony. My parent's third wedding anniversary was approaching. Usually married couples celebrated by having a special dinner or vacation. This did not happen among Mama and Daddy. The Lord had something else in store.

Prior to the wedding anniversary, the saints at Now Faith constantly prayed for a miracle in my life. I am sure Elder and Mother Crawford were on a fast and consecration.

"And when the day of Pentecost was fully come, they were all with one accord in one place. And suddenly there came a sound from heaven as of a rushing mighty wind, and it filled all the house where they were sitting. And there appeared unto them cloven tongues like as of fire, and it sat upon each of them. And they were all filled with the Holy Ghost, and began to speak with other tongues, as the Spirit gave them utterance" (Acts 2:1-4). The Crawford's and our church family gathered on Maine Avenue.

Shall we resume Acts 2:1-4? The presence of God was amid the service. Someone placed me on the coffee table. Then suddenly, the Holy Ghost came upon me. I began to speak in tongues. The people began to give thanks unto the Lord. God filled me with the Holy Ghost, on this day, in our living room. Mama continued to seek the salvation of God. She eventually became Holy Ghost filled and delivered on March 8, 1983, at Now Faith. Mother Crawford had to attend some business in Joliet. She heard about Mama's deliverance. God answered her prayers.

I am going to resume to the experience on Maine Avenue. Daddy held me at my feet. He told me years later, "Son, I had to let you a loose." I heard the older saints say, "You have to let go and let God have his way." This is the truth. Are you ready for this? I received my calling to preach the Gospel of Jesus Christ, at three years old. I began preaching to my stuff animals. They would be lined up as though they were sitting in the pews at church. I had a black toy Corvette. I loved playing with that car. It had snap on wheels. They were removed to be a microphone. My room previously belonged to Grandmother Charlene. Every night before dinner, I preached so hard Mama and Daddy stood by the door and listened to their son having church. This gave me the platform of humble beginnings, in ministry and the gospel music industry. It began right there on Maine Avenue. I am grateful to God for the healing. Hallelujah.

The doctors and others could not believe what happened. I was on the verge of learning American Sign Language. Instead, they made recommendations for speech therapy. I did this for two years. My speech began to improve as time progressed. Moses becomes an example. "And Moses said unto the LORD, O my Lord, I am not eloquent, neither hereto after, nor since thou hast spoken unto thy servant: but I am slow of speech, and of a slow tongue" (Exodus 4:10)

God had chosen Moses to lead the Israelites into the Promised Land. They were in bondage for four hundred years as slaves in Egypt. He listened to the voice of God through the burning bush. "And the LORD said unto him, Who hath made man's mouth? or who maketh the dumb, or deaf, or the seeing, or the blind? Have not I the LORD?" (Exodus 4:11).

Moses is instructed by the Lord to tell Pharoah, "Let my people go." Aaron accompanied his brother to Egypt. "And he shall be thy spokesperson unto the people: and he shall be, even he shall be to thee instead of a mouth, and thou shalt be to him instead of God" (Exodus 4:16). Despite Moses speech difficulties, the Lord had a plan for his life in leadership. Society judges people that have disabilities.

They are going to say, "This person cannot do tasks as their non-disabled counterparts." Do not listen to negative stereotype thoughts.

Sometimes, I stutter in speaking. The Lord has blessed me to speak more clearly through the years. The power of prayer does works. I have been teased and made fun of, in this area. Mama always said, "If anyone makes fun of you about your speech impediment, tell them about Moses and have scriptures as a providing point."

I never realized this concept, until the age of ten, in fifth grade. Before that, I viewed myself as a normal child. Mama and Daddy never denied me as their son. They acknowledged the gift God had blessed them to have. My parents did the best they could to raise me right and to make me happy. For the rest of my life, I will always be grateful for the sacrifices they made for me, regardless of how situations may have occurred in our household. Most the Birdsongs did not know this until now.

Mama and Daddy continued to work with Dr. Jenkins, Children's Hospital and Knolls Language Center. I became a client of Regional Center of the East Bay, a private non-profit organization under contract with the California Department of Developmental Services. The center specializes in services and support to individuals that have developmental disabilities. There are twenty-one regional centers that work in partnership, with individuals, families, community leaders, and agencies, by implementing and coordinating services throughout Alameda and Contra Costa County.

The Regional Center of the East Bay helped me throughout childhood and early adolescence. They have offices in Concord and San Leandro, California and continue to operate today in the Bay Area. I would like to publicly acknowledge Regional Center of the East Bay for their faithful service among men, women, and children of all ages and nationalities with developmental disabilities.

From the time, I became a client of the center, the programs went into effect for me immediately. The case workers created a success plan for their clients. The case workers at Regional Center for the East Bay had regular communications between Dr. Jenkins, Children's Hospital, and Knolls Language Center, of their services. One of the key components of the services they offered was job placement skills and counseling. This became a standard at that time. I remember assisting my parents in obtaining a playset, for our backyard, for me. It consisted of swings and a slide. I remember going to our backyard with Mama. She placed me on the swing and did the pushing.

I will continue to say this, until the Lord calls me home to live in heaven. Mama and Daddy knew they had a miracle baby and acknowledged the Calling of God upon my life. They wanted me to be happy and content during my developmental disability. James and Belinda Birdsong had seen beyond their son's obstacles and knew of greatness in his life.

You are reading the chapter of a miracle child that can testify of God's healing in life. This scripture becomes a reflection. It reads, "Heal me, O LORD, and I shall be healed; save me, and I shall be saved: for thou [art] my praise" (Jeremiah. 17:14). I had been saved, delivered, and set free at 3-years-old. Sometimes I reflect on this testimony of God's deliverance. A certain thought comes to center focus for me. The enemy tried to block me from speaking. God had a purpose in my life even before Mama conceived me.

I remember a song that one of gospel music's best artists and songwriters, Kurt Carr, recorded on his 2004 album, *One Church Project*. This album featured the single, *God Blocked It*. If you listen to this song, it will bless your spirit. He sings, despite circumstances, the Lord has not failed us. For me, I can relate to the song for my healing and deliverance, at the tender age of three. When the enemy tries to block us, the Lord intervenes and turns our situations around for the greater. Mama shared something with me as an adult.

One day at home, she said, "James, the enemy tried to attack you from speaking. He knew God had a Calling on your life." I love the song Fred Hammond wrote and recorded in the mid-nineties. If you remember this song, I am referring to *No Weapon*. It is one of the most recognized songs in gospel music and has become a major hit. The Word of God declares, "No weapon that is formed against thee shall prosper; and every tongue that shall rise against thee in judgment thou shalt condemn. This is the heritage of the servants of the LORD, and their righteousness is of me, saith the LORD" (Isaiah 54:17). The story does not conclude here. I am now going to share the foundational structure as the community knows you, in this tradition.

JAMES C. BIRDSONG, JR.

CHAPTER FIVE

The Community Knows You

Every man that has a good woman as his wife, and children, is abundantly blessed. I often tell people, "Families are a gift that has been ordained by God." The focal point in this chapter covers the community. I am going to give insight into this presentation. Mama and Daddy had a new chapter in the lives.

They were grateful to God for healing their son from a speech impediment. Knolls Language Center gave me the opportunity to interact among my peers of different ethnicities. Like me, they were in the same boat of special education. I am a product of the inner-city reared on Maine Avenue, in Richmond, California. Growing up, I had friends that lived in the neighborhood and few blocks from me.

Clim's grandchildren are around my age. I mentioned in Chapter Four about his grandson. His name is Danny. We have a two-month age difference. His sister, Shameka, is four to five years older than us. Mama was very close to their mother, Sheree. We were all members of Now Faith Church of God in Christ. In the neighborhood, Daddy and Clim were the patriarchs. As Clim's children, grandchildren and in-laws came over to visit, they made sure to come and see about us. He was married to Bobbi Jean at the time. If you go back and read Chapter Four, I also mentioned his granddaughter who graduated high school along with me.

Her name is Chanelle, and her youngest sister, Amber, was born in 1985. Danny, Shameka, Chanelle and I played together. I am smiling as I reflect on those memories. Clim had a grandson, Mondrel, who was eight years older than me. He was known to us as "Mooch." This young man played the drums at Now Faith. Clim's children had the opportunity to know Grandmother Charlene. They respected her to the upmost.

Alongside Clim and his family, Luzan and Kitara, I remember this one woman named Minnie. She lived on 9th Street with her grandchildren, Hylisha and Lovell. Our connection goes back to childhood. Minnie knew Grandmother Charlene, Daddy, and Uncle Roosevelt for years. She was one of matriarchs in the community. I cannot forget Hazel Dunn, the babysitter. Mrs. Dunn was a family friend of ours, since they settled in Richmond.

Mrs. Dunn lived on 2nd Street near Maine Avenue. From my house, you must walk nine blocks towards the west. A person with a loving, caring heart, she worked for Jodi and Friends in Vallejo, a program for children that provides babysitting services for them. Mrs. Dunn died in the late 2000s, after a lengthy battle with diabetes. She had to take dialyses three times a week during her final years. I remained in touch with Mrs. Dunn. Her grandson was one of my classmates in elementary school. This woman loved the children of Richmond, and encouraged them to succeed in life. That is the kind of person Hazel Dunn will be remembered for. She was from the old school, in her Louisiana roots.

On the corner of Florida Avenue and Harbour Way South we had Johnny's Diner, the most predominant restaurant in Richmond. I need the young people of my hometown to read this historical presentation. For those of us raised in Richmond, who cannot forget about Johnny's Diner.

Originally located at the corner of MacDonald Avenue and 4th Street in downtown Richmond, in the fifties, Johnny's Diner became the premiere spot in the restaurant industry. The

4th Street Market was across the street. Later, the diner moved to Harbour Way South, at the corner of Florida Avenue. My parents knew the owner, manager, and the main cook himself, Big Man. The manager was a woman named Betty. She lived on 9th Street with her children. They were Minnie's neighbors.

Big Man knew how to prepare the diner's Deluxe Hamburger, the star attraction. You could not find a hamburger nowhere in the city like the Deluxe. Johnny's Diner began to serve grits for breakfast. Do you want to know who introduced this idea? A lot of people in Richmond don't know this. They are going to find out now.

My grandfather, Otis Baby Germany, suggested for Johnny Diner's to include grits in their breakfast menu. Thanks to Grandpa Otis, it gained the public's attention in Richmond. Johnny's Diner was an old-fashioned mom and pop's restaurant. There were times the children in the neighborhood had a free meal, if they did not have any money. Our elders had southern hospitality in the community. The reason for this hospitality is very simple. They never abandoned their upbringing in the old south.

Grandpa Otis was Mama's father and Mildred's husband. He served our country in World War II, as a United States Army drill sergeant. I will share this story in Chapter Seven, titled, "Strength of a Praying Mother." Johnny's Diner continued to remain in business until the early-mid nineties. The owner decided to close the diner due to the violence in Richmond, of gangs and shootings. I missed Johnny's Diner. The memories will forever live on in the hearts and minds of those that remember this popular restaurant. The building that was once Johnny's Diner still exists on Harbour Way South. It is now a Dairy King.

Behind Johnny's Diner, we had Willie Crutchfield as the

neighborhood barber. He and his wife, Nancy, lived on Florida Avenue. His barbershop in his backyard adjusted to the garage drawn customers from the community. Mr. Crutchfield was one of those old-school barbers. The Crutchfields lived into their nineties. I remember the garden in their backyard that had vegetables, such as, greens, cabbage, and tomatoes. A native of Louisiana, Mr. Crutchfield migrated to California for greater opportunities. As a child and preteen, I would go to his shop on Saturdays for haircuts. This is where barbers generated most of their revenues. Daddy, Demetrius, and Alonzo also had their haircuts done by Mr. Crutchfield.

Mrs. Burke lived on the corner of Maine Avenue and 9th Street. We knew her and her husband very well. This woman established herself as one of the elders in the community. Blind and disabled, I admired the fact she did not allow her disability to become a stumbling block. She is now deceased.

On Harbour Way South and two houses behind us, Mrs. Gill and her husband were our neighbors. Every morning she would always be raking in her front yard. She was already a senior citizen. If you walked south of our house on Harbour Way South near Virginia Avenue, Novelean's Beauty Salon is right there. I cannot forget about her and the family. Across the street on Harbour Way South, you had the Martin Luther King, Jr. Community Center and Nystrom Elementary School. The King Center was our place for recreational activities and events, such as, banquets, community awareness meetings, basketball games, and tutoring for the children. Daddy became a member of the NAACP, the oldest Civil Rights organization in the United States. The acronym is the National Association for the Advancement of Colored People.

The Richmond NAACP Branch was located on MacDonald Avenue in downtown. During the eighties, Mama and Daddy attended the meetings as the president of the local branch and executive committee chairpersons discussed issues affecting African-Americans in Richmond.

We had tragedy in our midst. This became a major shock for the Now Faith Church of God in Christ family. Elder Crawford suffered a heart attack. He died in 1984. This Holy Ghost filled anointed Man of God transitioned to be with the Lord. Mother Crawford had her husband buried in Joliet, Illinois. The elders, ministers, and members of Now Faith had a difficult decision to make, since our pastor had died. I was almost four years old when Elder Crawford died. Should the church continue and obtain a new pastor or close its doors? I am not sure of the results of their decision. Mama and Daddy decided to depart Now Faith and search for another church. Someone invited us to Faith Tabernacle A.O.H. Church of God on MacDonald Avenue and 36th Street in Richmond. The late Bishop George Washington Ayers was the pastor. He and his wife, the late Mother Verley Ayers, were among the icons and trailblazers in the city. A man of integrity, Bishop Ayers received numerous degrees. In 2000, he was elected third in succession as Presiding Prelate of the Apostolic Overcoming Holy Church of God. The international headquarters is in Birmingham, Alabama.

This Man of God was highly respected by the clergy and dignitaries throughout Richmond. As a young man, Bishop Ayers served our nation in World War II, in the United States Army.

A believer of Pentecostalism, the Apostolic Overcoming Holy Church of God believed in the baptism based on the scripture. "Then Peter said unto them, Repent, and be baptized every one of you in the name of Jesus Christ for the remission of sins, and ye shall receive the gift of the Holy Ghost" (Acts 2:38).

We eventually became members of Faith Tabernacle after two

visits, for Sunday morning services. Daddy joined the deacon's board. The church addressed him as Deacon Birdsong. Faith Tabernacle loved my parents. I am going to address my father's musical talent, for a moment. Daddy had been professionally trained to sing as a child, for nine years, in Greenwood, Louisiana. During the Golden Era of gospel music in the 1950s and 1960s, he had the opportunity to make his big break. I believe the Five Blind Boys of Alabama or Mississippi wanted Daddy to become a member of their quartet group. He could have recorded, performed, and toured with them nationally.

This did not happen, unfortunately, in his lifetime. Mama decided to place him on the spot. One Sunday morning at Faith Tabernacle, Bishop Ayers approached the podium in the pulpit. Before he brought forth the sermon, he made a request.

"Saints, I am going to ask our own Deacon Birdsong to bless us with a solo," he said.

Shocked and speechless, I can imagine Daddy saying, "How Bishop Ayers know about my singing?" Mama told Bishop Ayers about my father's singing abilities.

He wanted to observe this for himself. I guess he came to one thought, "Deacon Birdsong is going to sing next time he comes."

Someone came and assisted Daddy to the front of the church. The microphone was handed to him. Facing the congregation, Daddy began to sing *The Last Mile of the Way* recorded by the late Sam Cooke and the Soul Stirrers. A famous gospel-recording artist of the Golden Era, Sam Cooke transitioned to R&B music and recorded songs, such as, *A Change is Gonna Come*. This is a beautiful song that is still performed today. Daddy loved Sam Cooke and the Soul Stirrers. He incorporated his own style of singing. The entire church was stunned once Daddy finished singing. He continued to sing solos.

My father had four more years until his fiftieth birthday. The American dream does come into light in this aspect. Daddy made significant accomplishments. He completed high school, obtained a college degree, found himself to be a respected figure in the city, and became a devoted family man. For the first time in her life, Mama entered the foundational structure of a family. The Lord still allowed me to engage in preaching. I continued to have church in my room, as the stuff animals were the congregation.

In June 1984, I finished the program at Knolls Language Center, along with Ian and our classmates. They went on to attend other schools in the district. Meanwhile, Ian and I enrolled at Sheldon Elementary School on May Road in El Sobrante, for preschool. Our new teacher was a woman named Lynn Frantz. She worked collectively alongside her assistant Sandy. I continued my participation in the special education program. The principal at Sheldon was a gentleman named Robert Cone. He was very kind and had compassion for the students. I learned later he became the principal of Crespi Middle School in El Sobrante.

Once a week, I had to meet with the speech language therapist at nearby Murphy Elementary School.

Demetrius and Alonzo had departed from home and moved to Los Angeles. They lived with us on Maine Avenue, until I was almost three years old. In 1988, Demetrius and his wife at the time, Vanessa, drove from Los Angeles to visit us, at the house. She is the mother of my two eldest nieces, Giselle and Geminese. Alonzo returned to Richmond in the late eighties.

Tragedy happened again in the Birdsong family. Just image you are at home, together with your parents, on December 25, 1984, and the telephone rings. Christmas day is a time to spend among family. You are unwrapping gifts. Your father answers and finds out one of his cousins had died. Now you see the point.

Bishop and Mother Ayers learns of the news. The Faith Tabernacle family uplifted us up in prayer. Albert's second eldest brother, Robert James Birdsong, Sr. of Los Angeles, died after a battle with cancer, at 55-years-old.

Albert tells Daddy, "We will have Robert James funeral in Los Angeles."

My father immediately made a telephone call to one of our cousins, the late George Fields, Jr., for lodging. He and his brother, Lee Arthur Fields, Sr. were reared in Greenwood, Louisiana. They owned and operated the Fields Barbeque Ribs in Long Beach, California. The following day, after Christmas, Clim took us to the Greyhound Bus Terminal in Oakland.

Three things come to mind for this scenario. First, this became the first time going to Los Angeles. Second, I have never attended a funeral service and, finally, this was the first road trip for me. The distance between Oakland and Los Angeles is approximately 371 miles, in five hours and 23 minutes. Later, in the evening, George picked us up from the Greyhound Bus Terminal in downtown Los Angeles. Lee Arthur waited for us at the restaurant. Who remembers the Polaroid 640 Land camera? It made successful sales. Daddy purchased one at JCPenney's at Hilltop Mall. Mama used this camera for family photos.

Upon our arrival, at Fields Barbeque Ribs, Lee Arthur greeted us. Daddy was happy to reunite with his cousins from childhood. The family loved their James Charles. I remember the smile Daddy had during that moment. We stayed at George's apartment in Long Beach during the funeral.

I propose this question to you. Can a 4-year-old child who is diagnosed with a developmental disability remember this adventure? Yes, the Lord bring things to our remembrance. The family gathered together for Robert's wake on the evening of December 28, 1984, at the historical Angelus Funeral Home on South Crenshaw Boulevard in Los Angeles. In 1925, the mortuary became the first African-American owned and operated business to be incorporated in California. Angelus Funeral Home was listed on the National Register of Historical Places in 2009. Uncle Sidney's funeral was held at Angelus Funeral Home.

There were numerous Birdsongs in attendance at Robert's wake. My parents and I approached his open casket in the chapel, for the viewing.

Mama picked me up to view my cousin. "Robert James is sleeping," I said to Mama. I really thought he was asleep. Children at this age do not understand about death, until they begin to develop in their growth stages. We returned to Angelus Funeral Home the next day on December 29, 1984, for the service. I still have the photos of family to this day.

The funeral concluded and our family proceeded to Inglewood Cemetery, in Inglewood, California, for Robert's interment. Mama and Daddy decided not to go to the cemetery. We waited for the family at a church for the repass. Once they departed from the cemetery, Robert's surviving siblings accompanied their mother, Ola Mae Birdsong, to the church. There were so many people there among my family. Aunt Ola Mae was my great aunt-in-law who lived in Shreveport.

She was the wife of the late Deacon George Birdsong, Sr. Aunt Ola Mae was from the old school. She wanted the best for her children. Robert was her second oldest child. Uncle George and Aunt Ola Mae had thirteen children. There are only seven remaining today. They were very happy to see us at the funeral and repass.

Aunt Ola Mae was particularly glad to see Daddy again. He

was always treated like a superstar in the Birdsong family. I am not able to keep up with every member of our family due to the large capacity nationwide.

It became time for us to depart Los Angeles on December 30, 1984, for the five-hour road trip on Greyhound, to Oakland. Daddy had business affairs at Faith Tabernacle and the community to conduct. Sheldon resumed classes after our Christmas break. Enthusiasm came upon me, as Ian and our classmates could not stop conversing about our Christmas gifts.

I am a child of the eighties. Every opportunity that approaches, allows me to share stories to the young people of today. I tell them about the toys, cartoons, video games, and music of this decade. Reflections of video game consoles come to mind. Before Sony introduced PlayStation, and Microsoft presented X Box on the market, there was Atari and Nintendo.

For me, I never had possession of the Atari or Nintendo. Pac Man turned out to be the most prominent game for Atari and arcade centers. Super Mario Brothers became prominent for Nintendo Entertainment System. Friends and classmates had these consoles in their homes. I had Tyco race car, and model trains, Hot Wheels cars, and Lego sets Action cartoons were on demand for television. Every week, *He-Man* and *She-Ra* were broadcast alongside their counterparts. There were Transformers, G.I. Joe, Silver Hawks, Bionic Six, and others. I am a fan of the vintage Warner Brothers cartoons. I am referring to Bugs Bunny, Daffy Duck, Yosemite Sam, Porky Pig, Tweety Bird, Sylvester and other characters. Thankfully, we have the Cartoon Network, DVDs, and YouTube to watch these productions from the past.

The popular children's television series, *Sesame Street*, reflects to my upbringing. I watched this program every afternoon on KQED Channel 9, a Bay Area television affiliate of the Public

Broadcasting Service (PBS). There were three books I had from the Sesame Street series. They were *Don't Cry Big Bird* by Sarah Roberts, *My Doll is Lost!*, and *Ernie's Little Lie* by Dan Elliott. The books were based on the characters of Sesame Street. Debuted in 1969, this television series was created to educate our children in preschool settings.

Ernie was a favorite character of mine on Sesame Street. I reflect on Big Bird as the star of the production. The children of today are fans of Elmo. He has been featured on major day time television talk shows. Sesame Street has been fortunate to showcase celebrities and dignitaries as special guests, throughout the years.

Mama and Daddy were focused on developing their role as noted figures in Richmond. The people began noticing my mother as the wife of a respected community activist that advocated rights for the disabled. My parents have stories of their beginnings. The next following chapters will showcase their stories as children, and how they overcame challenges along the way.

One of my favorite experts in leadership, John C. Maxwell, gives practical principles in his book, *The 360 Leader: Developing Your Influence from Anywhere in the Organization*. "The better you are at making sure you're doing what you should be doing, the better chance you have for making an impact for others" (Maxwell, 2005). My parents were my role models and provided foundational building. We shall proceed to my father's roots in Louisiana

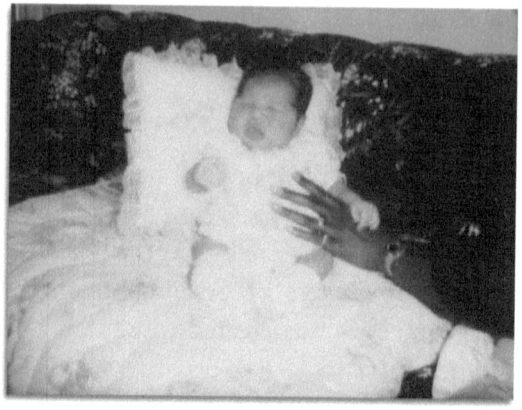
James as a baby

Christmas photo at Montgomery W

Celebrating his 6th birthday

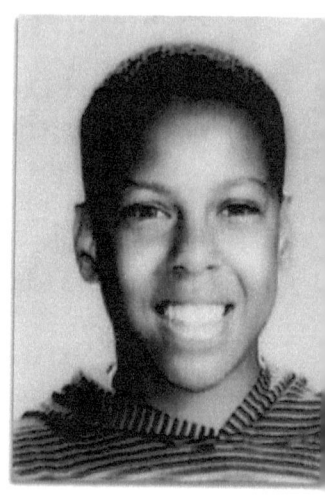
Eighth grade class photo at
ams Middle School in Richr
California

Having lunch with frien
during a school field tri
in Berkeley, California

CHAPTER SIX
Daddy's Roots in Louisiana

Our parents, grandparents, and great grandparents have their stories explained as if you were going to read a history book in class. James Charles Birdsong, Sr. earned his place in the family historical archives. Daddy was born on July 19, 1938, in Greenwood, Louisiana. Franklin Delano Roosevelt was the 33rd President of the United States.

A man of excellence, he was the first and only president to serve four consecutive terms. The thirties were defined as the decade of depression, by historians. At the beginning of the 1930s, more than 15 million Americans–fully one-quarter of all wage-earning workers–were unemployed (History.com, 2016). The Great Depression became a national crisis in the history of the United States. This had a significant effect on our nation's economy in the thirties. Millions of people worldwide were observing the Great Depression of the United States.

The American people had lost their faith and hope as this crisis impacted them. President Roosevelt had to plead his case to the American people so their faith could be restored. The nation needed a leader they could trust to bring them out of this crisis. He brought hope as he promised, prompt, vigorous action, as he asserted in his Inaugural Address, "the only thing we have to fear is fear itself." (Whitehouse.gov, 2016).

Babies are born and delivered in hospitals of modern times. The children of Daddy's generation, and his parents, were born either at home or in the church. If a woman of that era went into labor, the men would have to leave so a midwife could be present to help deliver the baby. We are talking about decades, prior to my birth.

Daddy was a southern man from Louisiana surrounded by his parents, grandparents, uncles, aunts, and cousins. Charlene was married to Jim Birdsong when she conceived Daddy. Uncle Roosevelt was my father's only brother. He was born on September 6, 1933, in Greenwood, Louisiana. His father was Roosevelt Daniel, Sr., my grandmother's first husband. Jim Birdsong was Uncle Roosevelt's stepfather. They lived on Greenwood Waskom Road. Daddy attended school with Uncle Roosevelt and his cousins, as children.

Shreveport is the third-largest city in Louisiana and the 113th-largest city in the United States. They attended services with his parents and Uncle Roosevelt, at Greenwood No. 1 Baptist Church. This is an historical church that opened in 1866. The late Reverend Samuel Price was the pastor of Greenwood No. 1 Baptist Church. He watched the children in Greenwood grow up.

In the old south, everyone knew each other and the elders believed in discipline. The scripture reads, "He that spareth his rod hateth his son: but he that loveth him chasteneth him betimes" (Proverbs 13:24). The elders of Daddy's generation applied practical Biblical application on raising their children to be productive citizens in life. The older generation of family attended services at the original church, before the current sanctuary was dedicated in 1973. Just image yourself in a small southern country town where there were no street lights, transit buses or paved roads, before modern technology was invented.

Located north on Springridge Road in Greenwood, this became our family church for the Birdsongs. Allow me to mention Greenwood No. 2 Baptist Church and Mt. Olive Baptist Church. The three churches united together and fellowshipped on special occasions, such as, anniversaries and revival services. Allow me to mention Greenwood No. 2 Baptist Church and Mt. Olive Baptist Church. The three churches united together and fellowshipped on special occasions, such as, anniversaries and revival services.

I am going to elaborate on the family connection of Greenwood No. 1 Baptist Church. My great uncle, the late George Birdsong, Sr., was a member of the deacon's board and served faithfully in this role, until his health declined in his sixties. His two youngest brothers, the late Reverend Sidney Birdsong, Sr. and the late Clarence Birdsong, were members of a popular gospel quartet group called the Greenwood Four Jubilee Singers.

The other members of the Greenwood Four Jubilee Singers were the late Earnest Taylor and the late Tommy Wayne. They never had the opportunity to record and tour as their counterparts. Quartets became the catalyst in gospel music before choirs were introduced on the scene. We are going back in time more than sixty years. Daddy told me about the Greenwood Four Jubilee Singers. They knew how to sing and harmonize.

Daddy was raised during a time of racism and segregation in the south, before the 1960s changed the face of America. The Civil Rights Movement was headed by Martin Luther King Jr. He delivered his most famous speech, *I Have a Dream*, on August 28, 1963, at the Lincoln Memorial in Washington, D.C. The children of Daddy's generation and their elders had endured racism and prejudice every day in the south, by white supremacist groups.

Before the name African-American was defined, blacks were known as Negros. African-Americans in the old south had stories to capture your attention on how the Lord blessed them with strength. The stories of my ancestors and elders have touched my heart. I can only say, "Wow, this is a testimony of survival in the storm." Tramaine Hawkins recorded a song, *I Never Lost My Praise,* from the title of her album. Written by Kurt Carr, this song continues to be a blessing and inspiration to the nation. She sings about enduring situations and never loses her praise to God. Those people depended on Jesus Christ as they were being oppressed during segregation. The south has changed since the days of oppression.

According to family members and friends, Daddy was charming, popular, and outgoing. He was certainly blessed with both sets of grandparents, on his mother and father's side, during his childhood and adolescence. Ed and Ida Birdsong had eleven children. The elders of those times believed in large families.

Born on October 1, 1911, Grandpa Jim was the eighth child born from this union. Employed as a helper in Shreveport, Jim was a truck driver. He did not complete school. Charlene's highest level of education was graduation from high school. A dedicated housewife, she stayed at home while her husband worked. His income did not generate much revenue. We are talking about the forties, as World War II made global headlines. By the time Daddy was born, Uncle Roosevelt was 4-years-old.

Charlene had relation in the Collins and Walton's due to her parents, the late Charlie and Fannie Walton. They were my great grandparents. Born in 1892, Charlie Walton was employed as a presser in a pressing shop. He married Fannie, at the age of 21. This was common in those times when couples married young, before they reached twenty-five. Charlie died in 1953 at 61-years-old. Ed Birdsong was born on September 15, 1881, in Greenwood, Louisiana. Prior to his death, on April 24, 1953, my father was 14-years-old when his grandfather died.

Ida Birdsong died 15 years after, on May 15, 1969, at Willis-Knighton Hospital in Shreveport, at 83-years-old. I researched her records.

My great grandmother was born on May 5, 1884, in Greenwood. Ida was fond of her grandchildren. I am sure you heard of the statement, "A picture is worth a thousand words." I find this to be true. Ida was mulatto and worked as a farmer. The fourth grade became her highest education. The descendants of my great grandparent's generation were former slaves in the south as slavery became abolished. Since the historical account of my grandparents and great grandparents has been shared, we will resume Daddy's story.

Daddy attended Greenwood Elementary School, located by the church. His classmates were on both sides of the family. One of his cousins, Henry Durden, lived in Greenwood. Henry was Charlene's cousin. Greenwood Elementary School no longer exists. Daddy enrolled at Oak Hill Junior High School in Shreveport. Once he completed junior high school, he attended Booker T. Washington High School. Daddy also attended school with Henry's wife and our cousin-in-law, Dorothy Jean Durden. For the duration of the forties, in Shreveport, there were no schools for African-Americans, at that time. Booker T. Washington High School was the first high school built for African-Americans in the city. It is named after the famous African-American educator himself.

Have you heard of the saying, "That person is nothing but a trouble maker?" Daddy had numerous cousins in the neighborhood. Lee Arthur told me a story of an incident involving Daddy and two of his cousins, in Greenwood. James Charles had a close bond with his cousins, Lewell Birdsong and Linzy Fields. Lee and Linzy's father was George Fields, Sr., the husband of my great aunt, Mary Birdsong-Fields.

Something made Uncle George very upset. James Charles, Lewell, and Linzy stole gasoline from his truck for a motor scooter. Why did he and his cousins do such a thing? Okay, I will explain. The boys placed a hose in the gasoline tank, to release in a metal can. A person from the old- school generation, Uncle George did not play games. I mentioned previously that the elders believed in discipline.

When children did something wrong during that era, the community became aware of their actions. The child received a whipping from an adult, and you were sent home to your parents for further discipline. This became standard in the old south. Times have changed.

Daddy's life changed forever. I will tell the story of how he lost his vision. Four months prior to Thanksgiving Day of 1956, he was a popular student at Booker T. Washington High School. Still living at home, Daddy spent time among family and friends. An avid sports fan, he played basketball in high school. On Thanksgiving Day, Charlene knew her son had basketball practice. She immediately enforced the law of old school discipline on Daddy.

"Now, James Charles, you go to basketball practice today, okay," she said. Charlene was very strict.

"Okay mother, I will go today and come back," he tells her.

Throughout the years, Daddy claimed he was in the woods with his cousins, Eugene Coleman and Albert Wyandon, as they were hunting. He disobeyed his mother and proceeded with other plans. My father did not go to basketball practice. Mama figured out the truth of his accident during their marriage. She told me what really happened. The 18-year-old James Charles joined Eugene and Albert for a ride, in the woods of Greenwood, in a pickup truck. They portrayed themselves as cowboys and Indians, imitating Westerns on television, such as,

Gun smoke and *The Rifle Man*. The three young men began to play cowboys and Indians. A rifle in Eugene's possession fired a round as James Charles hid behind a tree.

Eugene pulled the trigger of his rifle and unaware of James Charles surroundings, he turned around. The rounds from Eugene's rifle struck my father in both of his eyes. The two cousins immediately ran over to Daddy.

"James Charles, you are alright?" Eugene asked.

Unbelief and despair came upon Daddy, as his life changed in a sudden minute. He cried, "I can't see, I can't see."

They immediately got into the pickup truck. Daddy knew he was supposed to attend basketball practice. He disobeyed his mother.

"I am already in trouble," Daddy said. "I just want to go home."

They pulled up in front of the house. Jim and Charlene were very devastated. Charlene asked, "What happened to you, boy? You need to tell or I'll whoop your ass."

Eugene and Albert explained to her what happened in the woods. Daddy did not know how to react. This has never happened in the Birdsong family. A towel over his eyes, Jim and Charlene were worried. The news of Daddy's injury spread throughout Greenwood and Shreveport.

In the old south, the doctors made house visits. A physician came and examined Daddy in the living room. The doctor made his observation and broke the news to Jim and Charlene. He said, "Mr. and Mrs. Birdsong, I am going to place a patch over his eye. There may be hope for him to regain his vision." This became a sigh of relief.

The doctor gave a warning, "If he removes the patch and rubs his eyes, then it will damage where he cannot regain his vision again."

James Charles did not listen to the doctor's orders. The next week, he returned to the house and did a second examination. Disappointment came for James Charles as the doctor gave Jim and Charlene Birdsong devastating news.

"I am sorry, Mr. and Mrs. Birdsong. Your son will not be able to regain his vision. He is now completely blind," the doctor said. "The best thing you can do is to make him feel comfortable, and be supportive as a family."

Daddy now had to live his life as a blind disabled man. I can imagine Eugene's reaction after hearing the news. He felt guilty, despite this incident being an accident. Things had changed for the household now that he was disabled. I can imagine Eugene's reaction. He felt guilty. It was an accident what happened in the woods. Daddy spent ten years of his life in Greenwood, after losing his vision. He began listening to news broadcasts of sport teams on the radio. My father did not attend college due to his blindness. The Civil Rights Movement made headlines as Dr. King proclaimed his message of non-violence. He led marches throughout the south. African-Americans continued to battle racism and segregation.

Daddy did not participate in the marches. He did remember the Civil Rights Act of 1964. The Voting Rights Act of 1965 went into effect during the administration of President Lyndon Johnson. Jim and Charlene Birdsong had marital differences, while their son dealt with blindness. Uncle Roosevelt and Aunt Annette migrated to Richmond, California in the early sixties, for greater opportunities.

African-Americans born and raised in the south, of my father and grandparent's generation, made their migration to the north, eastern and western United States, for escape. They faced oppression, racism, and segregation every day. Times have changed for African-Americans since Jim Crow and the Civil

Rights Movement.

The tables have turned for African-Americans, in a modern-day migration. They are departing California and other states in the northern, western and eastern regions. Guess where this great migration is captivating? We have made the return to our southern roots. The states of Alabama, Arkansas, Florida, Georgia, Kentucky, Louisiana, Mississippi, North Carolina, South Carolina, Texas, and Tennessee are considered Bible belt states. The older generation is going home to the south. It has been in existence, since the late nineties and into the 21st century.

Daddy heard stories and studied about California being the land of opportunity. He decided to take the opportunity for a change in his life. Our family began their migration to California, in the fifties, to Los Angeles, as Uncle Sidney paved the way for us.

Uncle Roosevelt became aware of the marital crisis between their mother and the man who raised him as his own son. Daddy called his brother and said, "I do not want to continue living here in Greenwood."

"I know, James Charles," Uncle Roosevelt said.

"You know mother and Daddy are having marital difficulties, and I am blind."

My father was very frustrated, and he was almost 30-years-old. This occurred in 1967, a year before Dr. King and Senator Robert Kennedy's assassination during the Civil Rights Movement. He loved his family. At the same time, Daddy desired to have a new direction and advancement, with greater opportunity.

My uncle gave him news as a sign of relief. "I tell you what, James Charles, you and mother come live here in California," he tells his brother. "When you are ready, call me, and I will make the necessary plans. I need you and mother to stay with us."

I am sure many of you can identify. Uncle Roosevelt and Aunt Annette gave the encouragement to Daddy and Grandmother Charlene to leave Greenwood. My father had never ventured outside of his hometown before. Aunt Gladys relocated to Oakland, prior to Chicago. She still lives there today. The Birdsong family resides throughout the United States.

As Uncle Sidney made the step of faith to Los Angeles, he was selected to pastor Solid Rock Baptist Church. His inspiration established the tone for our family to build a foundation in California, by our Louisiana roots. Grandmother Charlene desired a new direction in her life. She knew her marriage to her husband was on the rocks. The elders of this generation did not believe in professional counseling.

This is what I believe in this scenario. If the problem had occurred today, Jim and Charlene Birdsong would have obtained counseling from a psychologist. She could not handle the situation any longer. I am sure this series of events led to her departure from Greenwood. She and Daddy boarded a Greyhound bus from Shreveport and headed on a three-day journey to Richmond, in 1967. Daddy and Grandmother Charlene arrived in California to begin a new chapter in their lives. He immediately went forth with his plan and enrolled at Richmond Union High School. My father became a student in their adult school program. He earned his high school diploma in 1970, and pursued undergraduate studies at Contra Costa College. In 1974, Daddy graduated Contra Costa College with an Associate of Science degree in Social Studies. He began to become active in the community as an advocate for Civil Rights and the disabled.

He became a client at Center for Independent Living, in Berkeley, on Ashby Avenue. This is an organization in the Bay

Area that provides services for the blind and disabled, from job placement to counseling services.

The West County Times began to write and publish articles about Daddy, throughout the seventies and eighties. He developed himself as a leader, in his own right. My father eventually enrolled at the University of California at Berkeley, in 1975, to obtain a Bachelor degree. He never completed the program.

One of his classmates, at Contra Costa College and University of California at Berkeley, Lucille Allen-Killingsworth, became the first African-American woman to enter the political race for mayor and city council in Richmond. She knew my father very well. She worked in the administration for the West County Toxic Coalition on MacDonald Avenue.

In the seventies, disabled people in California began to fight for their civil rights, to be accepted and treated fairly. Daddy helped and assisted people in Richmond that were blind and disabled. In the early eighties, he and Mama went to Sacramento to advocate for the rights of disabled people in California. He was a native son of the south that remembered the oppression of African-Americans fighting on the front lines for freedom and justice. A man that was knowledgeable, my father knew African-American history thoroughly.

After the assassination of Dr. King on April 4, 1968, Daddy had someone on his behalf to write a letter to Mrs. King. I cannot remember what the letter was about. She responded back to him. James Charles Birdsong, Sr. wrote Coretta Scott King and received a letter from her. This was an honor to the Birdsong family. I never had the opportunity to see the letter.

He had this book about noted African-Americans, with the biographies of Richard Allen, Harriet Tubman, Charles Richard Drew, Matthew Henson, and others. I read this book as a child.

Later, he understood it was time for him to be a married man as I explained in Chapter One. Daddy may have moved away to California, but he had always taken time to call family members. I witnessed this firsthand. Our family in Louisiana wanted him to return home. Daddy had made up his mind not to relocate back. He loved Richmond and the State of California.

Daddy sang solos on Sunday morning services, at Elisabeth Missionary Baptist Church, before Reverend Johnson preached the sermon. This was the first church he established himself as a member, for thirteen years. Daddy and I attended a funeral service at Elisabeth for Travis Williams, a former professional NFL football player that once played for the Green Bay Packers. The funeral service was held in 1991, prior to my eleventh birthday.

My father certainly was a people's person. He conducted himself as a businessman when it came to certain issues. There were times Daddy remained on the telephone for hours in our living room assisting people that needed his help. Daddy had taken a huge step of faith and migrated to Richmond, California. The Lord already knew this, before the foundation of the world. The strength of a praying mother is ordained by God. We will now proceed to Mama's story.

...ad during a family visit in Benicia, California

Dad with his mother, the late Charlene Birdsong

...m and Dad with the late Bishop ...ge W. Ayers and his wife, the late Mother Verley Ayers

Dad with my great aunt, the late Ruby Birdsong-Jackson and her husband, the late Foster Jackson, Sr.

Dad with my great aunt-in-law, the late Ola Mae Birdsong

JAMES C. BIRDSONG, JR.

CHAPTER SEVEN

Strength of a Praying Mother

Proverbs 31 explains a beautiful poem of the virtuous woman, in the role as a wife to her husband. Belinda Birdsong has the characteristics of a Proverbs 31 woman. An overcomer of obstacles, her story begins on how symbols of hope build strength. She is one of the nicest people you can meet and have a conservation with. This chapter has been a challenge for me. The world needs to know her story.

Born on July 28, 1947, at Highland Hospital in Oakland, California, her parents were Otis and Mildred Germany. World War II made headlines in the forties. Japan surrendered to the United States on August 14, 1945. On September 2, 1945, representatives of Japan signed the official statement of surrender aboard the U.S. battleship Missouri, which lay at anchor in Tokyo Bay (World Book, 2015). World War II ended on this day.

She is the second of six children. Otis and Mildred had four daughters and two sons. Mr. Germany enlisted in the United States Army and served our country in World War II, as a drill sergeant. A man with southern roots, Grandpa Otis was born on September 14, 1922, in Monroe, Louisiana, to Henry Germany and Malisse Hollingsworth-Floyd. His ancestry consisted of African-American and Native American. Grandmother Mildred's parents were Joseph and Susie Carter.

A native of Tennessee, she was born in 1919 and had southern roots. Grandpa Otis made the newspaper during World War II, as he rescued his platoon of troops during an ambush in the South Pacific of Asia. Mama told me her father built roads as his soldiers were stationed in the Philippines. The military drafted soldiers of World War II, in their twenties, for combat

In the case of Grandpa Otis, he was 19-years-old when the newspaper published the article of his heroic efforts. After serving our nation in the United States Army, Grandpa Otis decided to not further his career in the military. In my honest opinion, he could have worked his way up the ranks to be a ranking general, such as, Colin Powell, Wesley Clark, George Patton, and Dwight Eisenhower, who later served as the thirty-fourth President of the United States from 1953 to 1961.

Grandpa Otis went to Beale Army Base near Marysville, California, for his discharge in 1944. He worked as a truck driver at Treasure Island near San Francisco, until the sixties. I do not know that much about Grandpa Otis. As a child in Richmond, I would see him occasionally. The week of my high school graduation in 1998, he died, at 76-years-old, in Richmond, at a hospital.

Unfortunately, I never had a close relationship with my grandfather. You may be asking, "Did you attend his funeral?" Neither I nor Mama attended the funeral. I am not going to comment on the details. There is more to this story.

If you read the first chapter, Grandmother Mildred is mentioned. She served the community in Civil Rights and charitable organizations. Mama spent the first nine years of her childhood in Berkeley. In 1956, the family settled in Richmond. Each of us has a childhood that is not the same as others. In Mama's case, hers was different from Daddy's. No child should ever be mistreated by their parents and siblings.

They are precious gifts from God. "Every good gift and every perfect gift is from above, and cometh down from the

Father of lights, with whom is no variableness, neither shadow of turning" (James 1:17). Desiring a family bond, Mama experienced sadness in her childhood. I am going to take a moment to talk about parents having favoritism for one child over others. This is morally wrong in God's sight and modern day society. Regardless of how many children are born in a union, parents should love them all the same way. It grieves my heart when I hear stories about children in these situations.

My mother became the black sheep of her immediate family. Stories of incidents between her and her siblings escalated into fights, at home. When we reflect on fights, they are usually started by a person. In the case of Mama, she became an innocent bystander. Her siblings would accuse her of doing certain things.

"Why they hate me so much?" she would ask herself.

Belinda had her moments where she cried. When Mama tried to tell her parents of how her siblings had mistreated her, they ignored the plea. I hope the mothers and fathers of today are reading Mama's story. You have a responsibility from God as parents, to your children. When they are crying out for help, do not ignore them.

I am very disappointed in the fact that her parents did not take matters seriously in resolving this problem. They should have listened to their daughter's plea for help. In one incident, Mama had been accused of stealing money out of a wooden box that belonged to one of her siblings. You are familiar with the words, "What's go around comes around." The truth always comes to fruition. She learned the truth as an adult from another sibling. Mama confronted her mother and told her who stole the money. Grandmother Mildred was shocked. I am not sure what happened afterward.

There will always be a family member you develop a close

relationship with. This is ordained by God Almighty. Mama was very fond of her grandmother. A woman of character, audacity, and nobility, Malisse Hollingsworth-Floyd dedicated her life to the family. My great grandmother wanted to raise her granddaughter as her child. Mildred learned about her mother-in-law's request. She did not approve of her daughter being raised by the grandmother. By the time Mama reached adulthood, Malisse told her the story of how she was conceived. "Belinda, you were born out of rape," her grandmother said.

Can you imagine the devastation that news brought? Mama did not have a good childhood due to the problems at home, between her parents and siblings. As her son, it saddens me this happened to her. I am not going to disclose the details of what occurred in this situation. She and Daddy taught me early in life about the importance of having respect for myself and others.

After the family became settled in Richmond, Mama began to attend Peres Elementary School on Pennsylvania Avenue near Standard Oil Refinery and the Santa Fe Richmond Rail Depot. Peres continues to be in operation today by the local school district. The oil refinery is now owned and operated by Chevron.

Mama met this Hispanic girl name, Adela. They became childhood friends. From Peres, Mama and Adela went to Roosevelt Junior High School on Barrett Avenue, Once the eighth grade finished, the two best friends enrolled at Richmond Union High School on 23rd Street. A child of the fifties and sixties, Mama remembers the western shows, *The Lone Ranger*, *Gunsmoke*, and *The Rifleman*. The children of that generation watched the original production of The Mickey Mouse Club on television.

A fan of the Doo-wop music scene, this achieved mainstream popularity among African-Americans in the fifties.

Mama can tell you about the artists and songs of Doo-wop. Mama and her siblings would visit their grandparents, uncles, and aunts. They traveled to Modesto, California near Fresno and as far as Columbus, Ohio on road trips. As a child, Mama attended church services at Bethel Temple Pentecostal Church in Richmond. Mama became close friends with Zelma Turner when they were children. Zelma died, between the late eighties and early nineties. Grandmother Mildred was a faithful and dedicated member of North Richmond Missionary Baptist Church. She served on one of the main auxiliaries at the church. Grandpa Otis did not attend church services. I mentioned in this chapter of his work as a truck driver.

The problems continued to escalate at home for Mama. She realized, at 16-years-old, that there were two options. She can either continue to endure the situation or do what any child does. I am referring as a runaway from home. Mama went to San Francisco and remained there for four months. She met my brother's father and they married when Mama turned 18-years-old.

Before her eighteenth birthday, the authorities learned of her location. She had to stand before a judge at the Contra Costa County Juvenile Hall in Martinez, California. Mama did not want to return home due to the problems she endured with her immediate family. Grandpa Otis and Grandmother Mildred attended the hearing in Martinez. Mama returned to San Francisco and lived there for two years.

A young wife and mother, for the first time, Mama had to learn principles from the university of the streets. God knows our strengths and weaknesses.

"There hath no temptation taken you but such as is common to man: but God is faithful, who will not suffer you to be tempted above that ye are able; but will with the temptation also make a way to escape, that ye may be able to bear it. (I Corinthians 10:13)."

Demetrius and Alonzo's father was born and raised in Louisiana. I never met him. While I was living in Atlanta, Georgia, pursuing my Bachelor of Arts in Biblical Education, at Beulah Heights University, Demetrius called me one day.

"Little brother, I just found out my father is dead," he said. I asked him, "Demetrius, when did this happen?"

"He died sometime in 2006," my brother told me. "I will share the news with Mama," I said to him. Married to their father for four years, she endured marital problems and filed for divorce. A single mother with two sons, the journey was not easy for her. Mama knew her parents and siblings did not demonstrate the love she always desired to have as a child. The only family member that showed her love was Malisse.

When I reflect on her story, I think about Joseph in the Bible. God blessed Joseph to be a dreamer. His brothers expressed hatred and jealousy towards him. Their father, Jacob, gave him a long coat of many colors. When he was 17-years-old, Joseph had two dreams that made his brothers plot his demise. The brothers saw a camel caravan carrying spices and perfumes to Egypt, and sold Joseph to the merchants. His brothers lied to their father about Joseph being dead. The brothers painted goat's blood on Joseph's coat and showed it to Jacob. The Lord had a divine plan for Joseph's life. If you read Genesis, the Biblical writer explains a series of events that occurred for this young man.

The older saints of the church always say, "What the devil meant for evil, God turned it around for my good."

The Lord elevated Joseph as Prime Minister of Egypt. His faithfulness and obedience to God Almighty allowed him to be second in power next to Pharaoh. Joseph's brothers came to Egypt during the second year of famine. The brothers stood before Joseph. He recognized his brothers and decided to test them. When the brothers found out the second most powerful man in Egypt was indeed Joseph, devastation came upon them. They thought Joseph was going to have them imprisoned due to their jealousy.

A man of love and compassion, Joseph did not have his brothers sentenced to prison. Their father learned about his son's position in Egypt. The Lord allowed him to reunite with his family after the brothers sold him into slavery. He embraced his brothers and offered forgiveness to them. God had a calling on my mother's life for ministry. She would have dreams and visions during her childhood. Mama's prayers were answered when she met Daddy. She admired the bond and closeness of the Birdsong family. Even to this day, they continue to claim my mother as a family member, after thirty-seven years, from the time she and Daddy first met. She is still known today as Belinda Birdsong, especially in the church, the gospel music industry and among prolific noted figures.

My mother married Daddy and the community knew her as Sister Birdsong. The lessons of example setting become essential in our lives. When God prepares us for our journeys to the next level in destiny, there are questions to be asked. I am sure Mama had questions. She had to learn how to be a strong person.

Do I have a close relationship with my mother's family? From the time I was born to today, I have never developed a close bond with her immediate family. I am going, to be honest. There is only one person in my mother's family I developed a close relationship with. I am referring to my cousin Breanna Ford. Malisse came over to the house when I was a baby. Her death on January 16, 1984, affected my mother. Grandmother Mildred had health issues and made her transition on December

22, 1985, at 67-years-old. Her funeral was held at Sunset View Cemetery and Mortuary in El Cerrito.

I remember attending the small private funeral service with my parents. Her siblings were in attendance. She is buried at the cemetery, along with Grandpa Otis, Malisse, and other members of her family. The public attended a memorial service at North Richmond Missionary Baptist Church, for Grandmother Mildred. Mama continued to focus on her role as a wife, mother, ministry in the church, and Richmond, at large. The West County Times published an article about Grandmother Mildred and her work in Richmond.

Breanna is Mama's only niece. She was born and raised in Richmond. My cousin is a year older than me. Her two sons, Joshua and Jeremiah, are my younger cousins. They love their Aunt Belinda. A week before Mama relocated to Atlanta, for the second and final time, Breanna, Joshua, and Jeremiah visited her for the day. My mother was living in Berkeley at the time. This made me smile as Mama shared the news. I had departed California two years prior. I am closer to Breanna than the others. She has been very supportive to me in my endeavors. My cousin is a regular follower of mine on Facebook.

After much thought and prayer, I made the decision not to mention the names of my mother's siblings and their children in this book. Mama is almost 70-years-old and still looks young.

Conversations about her childhood have been discussed among us, throughout the years. There is still no closeness among Mama and her siblings. She accepted this and has moved on. Breanna and Mama have a close aunt-niece bond. I am grateful to God for this blessing.

One day, I told Mama, "You do have a family. They are the Birdsongs."

In her heart, she knows this. People always inquire about the

Birdsong family. My focus will continue to remain on Mama, my brothers, Breanna, Joshua, Jeremiah, my beautiful nieces, Giselle, Geminese, Demetria, Rolonda, and my great-niece, Tory. Their parents are included in this position. As long they are alright, healthy, and doing well, this gives me joy.

God ordained Mama with the gift of discernment. I have witnessed and observed the Holy Spirit use her. She is an intercessory prayer warrior and has been considered a mentor to younger women. On June 4, 2004, Nystrom Elementary School honored her as the first former parent to be the recipient of the Blue-Ribbon Honorees Award. She received congratulations from elected officials, from the City of Richmond to United States Senators, Barbara Boxer, and Dianne Feinstein, for her service to the community.

I presented the award to her during the ceremony. My mother was surprised about the news of her receiving the recognition. The accolades continued to be bestowed upon Mama. All Nations Community Church of God in Christ, in Oakland, honored her during an appreciation service on March 8, 2013, as their church mother. My family and my girlfriend, at the time, attended the appreciation service.

Breanna and her boyfriend, Leon, came and surprised her at the church. I wanted Mama to feel special. We were living in Berkeley at the time. I called the pastor and requested limousine service for Mama. He reached out to the owner. It was a beautiful white Lincoln Town car; ten passenger stretch limousine. Mama received an award from the church, recognizing her as their church mother.

This became her first time being appointed as a church mother. It was thirty years ago, on that day, she gave her life to Jesus Christ. The Jurisdictional Prelate, the late Bishop Jessie Dickens and their Supervisor of Women, Mother Valor Herring of the Church of God in Christ, California Western Jurisdiction, were notified about Mama's appreciation. They were unable to attend due to prior commitments. The Richmond City Council and then-Congressman George Miller of the United States House of Representatives issued proclamations and citations to Mama.

She has met friends and sources of mine in the gospel music industry. We met Dr. Bobby Jones, of Bobby Jones Gospel, at the 2010 6th Annual Agape Gospel Awards, in Decatur, Georgia. He hosted *Bobby Jones Gospel* on BET for thirty-five years. Mama attended the awards ceremony, alongside me and members of the gospel music industry, in a limousine. Dr. Jones knows about the Birdsong family. The two of us took a photo with the legendary Ambassador of Gospel Music.

My friends and classmates at Beulah Heights University were very fond of Mama. They did not hesitate to assist her. If she needed a ride to the grocery store, they made themselves available. To those friends and former classmates of mine, at our alma mater, thank you so much for assisting Mama in any way you could. Twenty-two years later, after her attendance in college, Mama was accepted at Chattahoochee Technical College in Marietta, Georgia. The news came in August 2016. My mother will not be able to attend classes until the fall 2017 semester. She plans to do her undergraduate studies in Business Technology. I have been encouraging my mother to resume her studies for years.

Two weeks before Mama's birthday on July 28, 2016, I purchased her a 2002 Buick Century Custom. You should have seen her happiness of joy. She desires to own the last generation of the Lincoln Town Car and, later, a Cadillac Escalade as her favorite sports utility vehicle. The Lord placed in my spirit to assist her in the enrollment at Chattahoochee one month after her relocation to Atlanta. Once she completes the program, Mama will graduate with a Business Technology Diploma. Her desire is to learn church administration and management, from a business perspective in ministry. She is currently reading books on church administration and leadership.

Mama currently serves on the board of Gospel Outreach Tabernacle Church in Marietta, Georgia, where I am the founder, senior pastor, and overseer. She has been appointed to spearhead the Community Services Department, a ministry that specializes in services for children, seniors, families, and homeless individuals in the six cities of Cobb County, Georgia. They are the cities of Acworth, Austell, Kennesaw, Marietta, Powder Springs and Smyrna.

They will obtain assistance, such as food distribution, personal care items, and referrals to case managers, social workers, and other services. Her background and experience in public relations prepared Mama to work closely alongside her assistant and volunteer staff in this role. She has a compassion for the less fortunate. Her favorite hobbies are cooking and interior decorating. There are people that have been anointed and ordained by God, with His strength, as prayer warriors. Triumphs of victory have been inspired by a living testimony. She is a woman of class, dignity, strength, and integrity.

Me and mom at Beulah Heights University in Atlanta, Georgia during a gospel concert to raise money for the homeless

Me and mom Beulah Heights University Atlanta, Georgia during gospel concert to raise money for the homeless

CHAPTER EIGHT
Mid-Late Eighties

We will take an examination of the mid-late eighties. You have read stories of my parents in the last two chapters. Let's move forward to this presentation. Michael Jackson continued to make headlines as the biggest selling artist, of all time, worldwide. The success of *Thriller* will forever be recorded in music history.

The Jacksons embarked on the Victory Tour, featuring Michael and his brothers, Jackie, Tito, Jermaine, Marlon and Randy. This tour was based on their 1984 album of the same title. This became the final album Michael collaborated with his brothers, as he pursued a successful solo career, with the release of his next album, *Bad*. It was released in 1987, and became his second best-selling album.

I remember Bad, and the world tour. Songs, such as, the title song, *The Way You Make Me Feel, Smooth Criminal*, and *Leave Me Alone*, dominated the charts worldwide. The King of Pop has been imitated. Michael Jackson can never be duplicated and you can agree with me on that.

The Victory tour reportedly grossed approximately $75 million and set a record for the then-largest grossing tour. The 1984 Victory Tour showcased Michael's single decorated glove, black sequined jacket, and moonwalk, which captivated audiences around the world early in 1983, just about a year prior (ipetitions.com, 2016). President Reagan decided to obtain a second term in office during the 1984 Presidential campaign. As the incumbent Republican candidate, his opponent was former Vice President Walter Mondale. A Democratic candidate, in the campaign, he served with President Jimmy Carter as his Vice President for four years. President Reagan was declared as the winner. His inauguration was held on January 20, 1985, at the White House, in Washington, D.C.

My mother's birthday on July 28, 1984, became the opening ceremony for the 1984 Summer Olympics in Los Angeles, California. This was the second occasion Los Angeles hosted the games; it subsequently hosted in 1932.

The HIV/AIDS epidemic made headlines in the eighties. I remember this very well. I am going to explain the definition of HIV/AIDS and the effects of this disease. HIV stands for human immunodeficiency virus. If left untreated, HIV can lead to the disease AIDS (acquired immunodeficiency syndrome). Unlike some other viruses, the human body can't get rid of HIV completely. So, once you have HIV, you have it for life (AIDS. gov, 2016).

The treatment of HIV medications has advanced more today than almost forty years ago. I remember stories of people with HIV that developed to AIDS. They died from the disease. My heart goes out to these people and especially the children.

The mid-late eighties produced popular television sitcoms, such as, The Cosby Show, A Different World, Punky Brewster, Full House, Family Ties, Growing Pains, The Golden Girls, Benson, Night Court, Alf, Perfect Strangers, Head of the Class, Amen, 227, and Mr. Belvedere. I remember watching these sitcoms, throughout the week, alongside cartoons. These shows promoted essentials of family structure. Today, there are reality shows, dramas, and sci-fi on television. They have taken over sitcoms. Have you heard of CSI, Empire and Scandal? It established themselves as the modern-day trend of 21st century television. In the sixties, the original Star Trek series starring William Shanter, Leonard Nimoy and DeForrest Kelley paved the way for Star Trek: The Next Generation. Mama is a fan of sci-fi shows. I watched Star Trek as a child.

My parents established themselves as respected leaders and icons in Richmond. Our pastor, at the time, Bishop George Washington Ayers, appointed my parents to the board of trustees at Faith Tabernacle A.O.H. Church of God. The members of the church respected James and Belinda Birdsong. They loved Daddy's singing.

Mama and Daddy attended meetings at Faith Tabernacle. They were actively engaged in their son's academic progress as a special education student. During that time, special education students in public school districts throughout California were placed on IEP. Yes, I said the initials. This stands for Individual Educational Plan. Allow me to explain this in detail. The parents of the child meet with their teacher and specialist, in the special education program, once a year. The specialist is assigned to the child by the school district.

It is designed to create alternatives for a child to improve in their academics. A plan would be developed as the guidelines are followed. Out of respect, I cannot publicly comment on my IEP records. They are now in my possession. I made the decision not to have them disclosed.

However, mathematics became a struggle for me in school. God blessed me to overcome this problem. The special education program of my childhood is different compared to today. I believe in organizational skills and structured development. The teachers treated us the same as non-special education students. Race did not become a factor in this perspective. I am sharing with you about the status of special education in my childhood days. This young man lived and witnessed this ordeal.

Mama began attending meetings at Richmond City Hall, with Daddy, as the mayor and city council members had dialogue about issues pertaining to Richmond, its residents, and businesses. Ian and I completed pre-school at Sheldon in June 1985. The first year at Sheldon became enjoyable for us. I did not begin to receive awards until kindergarten. When a child is in pre-school and kindergarten, they are only in class for half of the day. They are the first to depart school before first to sixth graders. For instance, if a preschooler and kindergartner leave at 12:00 PM, their older peers in elementary school do not depart until 2:00 PM, depending on the itinerary. For middle and high school students, it is very different. I remember us leaving to go home between 12:00 and 12:30 PM, in the afternoons.

Not too long afterwards, Daddy received an emergency telephone call from one of our family members in Shreveport.

"James Charles, Uncle Jim had a stroke," the family member said. Grandpa Jim was 72-years-old. "He has been admitted at Willis-Knighton Hospital."

Daddy informed Mama about his father's stroke. He already knew he had to do a visit in Greenwood. After he and Grandmother Charlene migrated to Richmond in 1967, our family on the Birdsong and Durden side, in-laws and loved ones, had constantly asked him about visiting his birthplace.

Now, for the first time in eighteen years, God opened the door for Daddy to visit his father. He had to put his differences aside. The family always knew him as James Charles. This created a reunion between father and son. For me and Mama, this became our first visit to the southern United States. My mother always wanted to visit the south.

Daddy called Albert and told him about Grandpa Jim.

"Albert, Daddy had a stroke. I am going home to visit him. I need you to take us to the airport."

"Okay, James Charles, I will be over there," Albert said.

Three years earlier, Albert went to Greenwood and visited

the family. He had taken some photos of Grandpa Jim and Pearl. I have a photo of my grandfather in this book, along with other family members. On the morning of our departure, Albert drove his Volvo 740 GL and picked us up from the house. I remember us going on Interstate 80 towards the Bay Bridge toll plaza in San Francisco. Albert dropped us off at the terminal, at San Francisco International Airport near San Mateo, California. This is one of the major airline hubs in the United States. San Francisco International Airport handles domestic and international flights. There were two airlines that became popular in the eighties. I am referring to Pam Am and Trans American Airlines (TWA). Pam Am and Trans American are no longer in existence.

We boarded the first flight on Trans American, from San Francisco to Los Angeles International Airport, the second major hub in the United States. In the State of California, Los Angeles and San Francisco are the only two major hubs that have international flights. The three of us had to do a layover for the next flight to Dallas/Fort Worth International Airport in Dallas, Texas.

Delta Airlines is my preferred carrier in the airline industry. Within two hours of our layover in Los Angeles, it was time for us to board the second flight on Delta Airlines for two hours. We arrived and waited for the final flight to Shreveport, which lasted for one hour. Prior to the landing at Shreveport Regional Airport, I remembered spilling my peanuts on the floor.

This happened as I said, "Airplane crash."

Daddy turned around and said, "Boy, stop it."

You must understand, as a 5-year-old child this became the first commercial flight for me. I loved aviation and automobiles as a hobby. The passengers exited to the terminal. My 77-year-old great aunt, Ruby Birdsong-Jackson and her husband, Foster, waited for us. They were happy to see Daddy again.

The second eldest sister of Grandpa Jim, Aunt Ruby was from the old school. We stayed at their house in Shreveport. I still have the photos today. Uncle Foster and Aunt Ruby raised chickens for their eggs. I would go to the backyard and try to play with them. Mama observed me from the kitchen and came outside.

"You can't play with the chickens," Mama said.

Aunt Ruby smiled and thought it was cute. I am a pet lover and this has not changed.

Numerous phones calls and visits to family became a heart touching moment for Daddy. I finally had the chance to see Eugene Coleman and Albert Wyandon, the cousins that were present alongside Daddy on Thanksgiving Day of 1956. If you go back and read Chapter Six, I told the story of how father never regained his vision.

We visited Grandpa Jim, at his house in Shreveport, upon his discharge from the hospital. He was still married to Pearl at the time. The reunion of James Charles Birdsong, Sr. and Jim Birdsong became inspirational to us. I will never forget the moment Daddy was overcome with emotion. This became their first time in eighteen years being in each other's presence. At 72-years-old, Grandpa Jim had health issues. I climbed on the bed and kissed him on the forehead. We visited him when he was hospitalized. My last surviving great uncle, Ed Birdsong, Jr., came to Willis-Knighton.

Still active at 77-years-old, Uncle Ed walked over to me and gave me a bank with approximately seven dollars. Known as "Uncle Buzz," he was not your typical senior citizen. He was very hip for his age. He married Maggie Bell Birdsong. She was Grandmother Charlene's cousin.

We departed Shreveport and returned home to Richmond.

Daddy loved road trips. He wanted his wife and son to enjoy sceneries of landscapes. We traveled 1,916 miles throughout three states on a Trailways Bus. The opportunity to visit Texas, New Mexico and Arizona were breathtaking to me. Trailways was founded in Chicago on February 5, 1936. The three-day road trip became a wonderful time in my life.

Clim waited for us at the Greyhound Bus Terminal in Oakland. Once the four of us arrived on Maine Avenue, I walked into the house with Mama and Daddy. My father continued to remain in contact with family in Shreveport about Grandpa Jim's progress. My parents continued to be active members at Faith Tabernacle and served on the board, by Bishop Ayers' appointment. In September 1985, Ian and I begin kindergarten at Sheldon. Our teacher again was Mrs. Frantz.

Faith Tabernacle provided my parents the opportunity to develop themselves as leaders in ministry and the community. The congregation loved and respected them. We were neighbors of the Rankin family. They lived on the corner of Maine Avenue and 9th Street. I am the same age as the two younger Rankin brothers. We were right there as children in the same community and at Faith Tabernacle. Grandmother Charlene made her transition five years earlier. The death of my grandmother influenced me as a child. I never had the opportunity to know her. Friends of mine had their grandmothers. The Lord allowed me to have a bond among the mothers of the church. Nobody could replace Charlene Walton-Birdsong. I visited her grave site throughout the years.

The minute class completed, I rode the bus to Contra Costa College for their early childhood development program. Mama and Daddy had to enroll in a course at the college, for me to participate in early childhood development, a component in special education the Richmond Unified School District decided. Ms. Albert played a key role in the process.

I inform young people today, "The teachers I had pushed me to strive for excellence, and knew the gift placed in an African-American boy from the inner-city of Richmond, California, with a developmental disability."

James and Belinda Birdsong did not raise their son to be a failure. I'm grateful to God for that. This reflection allowed the transformation of a journey as a strong voice. As you continue to read this book, there is a chapter that speaks to the children. God does things for a season. The time had come for us to depart Faith Tabernacle A.O.H. Church of God, after being faithful members for two years. My parents resigned from their roles on the board. We transitioned to another church in 1986.

Greater Faith Pentecostal Church in Jesus Name became our new church home. Located on 9th Street, the pastor was Elder Jesse Ary. Daddy continued his friendships with the members of Faith Tabernacle. The deacon board respected Daddy and his leadership abilities. Deacon Earl Palmer served as the chairman of the deacon board for many years. He and Daddy remained in contact. In addition to Deacon Palmer, Daddy established a friendship with Deacon John Taylor. Both gentlemen were lifetime members of Faith Tabernacle. I admired the fact that they were dedicated to their families. Deacon Palmer died in 2016. His daughter, Kimberly, worked in marketing and sales at KDYA 1190 AM "The Light" during the new millennium.

She is no longer on staff at the radio station. I remain in touch with Kimberly. During our conversations, I always inquire about Bishop and Mother Ayers, her father, and the older saints at Faith Tabernacle. A high school student, at the time, she sang every Sunday morning in the youth choir. Faith Tabernacle had a children's and adult choir.

They established themselves as one of the most respected

churches in Richmond. Bishop Ayers believed in the doctrine of Pentecostalism, and the anointing of the Holy Ghost. He and Mother Ayers settled in the Bay Area during the late fifties. Bishop Ayers once served on the city council in the San Rafael, California area. This man was well educated, received numerous degrees and was respected in the city among dignitaries. He traveled throughout the United States.

My parents had compassion for others. This became an influence for me, by example. I may have been very young at Faith Tabernacle; however, I observed my parent's abilities up close. This was truly amazing. NASA made headlines throughout the world on January 28th, 1986, with the Space Shuttle Challenger. Just 73 seconds into mission STS 51-L, a booster failure caused an explosion that resulted in the loss of seven astronauts, as well as the vehicle (NASA.gov, 2013). The highlight of STS-51-L became a teacher named Sharon Christa McAuliffe. She was planning to conduct experiments and teach two lessons from Challenger. NASA investigated. All the space shuttle missions were on hold, until Space Shuttle Discovery made a return to space flight on September 29, 1988, with the STS-26 mission.

The Challenger explosion occurred four months prior to my sixth birthday. Sharon Christa McAuliffe had been the first teacher aboard a space shuttle mission. President Reagan issued a statement expressing his condolences to the families of STS 51-L crew. The media reported this story around the world.

I graduated kindergarten on June 18, 1986, along with Ian and our classmates. Mrs. Frantz gave us certificates of completion. The following September, Ian and I began the first grade at Ellerhorst Elementary School on Pinole Valley Road in Pinole. Our teacher was a woman named Jean Mahrt. A veteran in teaching, she taught in the special education program. Ms.

Albert worked closely with her and made visits to me on campus.

Before the first grade began, Mama and Daddy purchased a blue 1984 Lincoln Town Car from Mira Vista Lincoln-Mercury, at the Hilltop Auto Plaza, in Richmond. The Lincoln Town Car became the most famous full sized luxury car in America. Ford Motor Company discontinued production of the Lincoln Town Car in 2011. Grandpa Jim died on August 18, 1986, at 74-years-old. This would have been Grandmother Charlene's seventy second birthday. We made our second visit to Shreveport for his funeral. Mama, Daddy, Uncle Roosevelt and I took a three-day road trip in the Lincoln Town Car, from Richmond to Shreveport.

Daddy's cousin and one of Aunt Ruby's daughters, Ruth Ella Jackson, lived in Los Angeles. Once we reached there, she joined us on the road trip to Shreveport. Mama and Uncle Roosevelt each had their turn to drive. A woman that knew our family for years, named Clearne Norman and her husband, opened their home to us. Mrs. Norman was from the old school, in her traditional Louisiana roots. She died two years later in 1988.

The family joined friends and loved ones for Grandpa Jim's funeral on August 23, 1986, at Benevolent Funeral Home in Shreveport. When the Birdsongs plan a funeral service, it is going to be well attended, with class and grace.

His last four surviving siblings, Ed Birdsong, Jr., Ruby Birdsong-Jackson, Myria Birdsong-King and Gladys Birdsong-Murray, attended the funeral of their brother. Aunt Myria was born in 1914. She lived in Denver, Colorado. I have a photo of my great aunts during the repass. It was held at Uncle Foster and Aunt Ruby's house. I tried again to play with the chickens. Being in the presence of my great aunts became a lifetime memory for me. This is an historical milestone for me as a Birdsong.

One month after Grandpa Jim's funeral, Uncle Ed died, at

79-years-old. We were unable to attend Uncle Ed's funeral.

I desired to have a puppy. A woman that was a dog breeder placed an ad in the West County Times newspaper. She sold different breeds of puppies from her home in San Pablo. Daddy thought about it and wanted to me happy. The three of us drove to the woman's house. In her backyard, she had about four to five puppies for sale. The puppy that captured my attention was a German Shephard mixed male. A cute, innocent baby, I named him Tony. We brought him home.

"Son, Tony is you and your mother's responsibility," Daddy said.

Mama and I became very attached to him. He eventually became the guard dog in our backyard. On a personal note, he became an early Christmas gift for me. Mama and Daddy made the local headlines in the West County Times. They developed a food pantry program, alongside a deacon and his wife. This became the agenda of giving back. The food pantry was being operated from the church and our home on Maine Avenue. Mayor George Livingston was a friend of Daddy's. He and the Richmond City Council honored their efforts. They received the City of Richmond Distinguished Service Award. This became the first award for my parents.

Our season had finished its course at Greater Faith. In 1988, we became members of Apostolic Temple of Truth, a church on South 13th Street in Richmond, where the late Elder Vernon Robinson was the pastor.

My parents were licensed and ordained as ministers by World Christianship Ministries, in Fresno, California, on February 29, 1988. Maple Jones made this possible for them. She hosted a popular Bay Area radio broadcast on KDIA 1310 AM in the late eighties. Ms. Jones lived in Berkeley at the time. I remembered us going to her house one time.

A series of events in 1988 and 1989 were reported by the media. Ian and I continued our attendance at Ellerhorst, for the second and third year. We became best friends, beginning at Knolls Learning Center. I made a promise to Mama that this young man would be mentioned. Our parents developed a close bond. Ms. Mahrt and our classmates observed our friendship. I felt secure at Ellerhorst. The principals, teachers and facility were very dedicated, faithful, and professionals in their occupation. Ms. Mahrt remained our teacher until her retirement. This school became my comfort zone for four years. Believe me, the academic experience became excitement and memorable for me. I know the students of today, at Ellerhorst, are going to read this book.

They are going to say, "Wow, he attended our school. That is so cool." I have the awards and records to prove it.

There is always a person related to a celebrity. Yes, this is the truth. The story of my three famous cousins will be told in the next chapter. You have made the request. Ladies and gentlemen, may I present Cindy, Edwin and Otis Birdsong.

The King of Pop himself, the late Michael Jackson and my cousin who is a legend, the one and only Edwin Birdsong

The late Bob Marley and my cousin, Edwin Birdsong

Mick Jagger, Edwin Birdsong and Stevie Wonder

CHAPTER NINE
Cindy, Edwin and Otis Birdsong

People always asked this one question, "Are you related to Cindy, Edwin and Otis Birdsong?" They are the famous cousins. This chapter will describe their story and how they turned out to be celebrities. God has smiled upon the Birdsong family, for more than 100 years. Our family loves the Lord. We value the beliefs of foundational structure.

Daddy made his contribution to me in the family legacy. "Neither shall thy name any more be called Abram, but thy name shall be Abraham; for a father of many nations have I made thee. And I will make thee exceeding fruitful, and I will make nations of thee, and kings shall come out of thee" (Genesis 12:2).

A decade ago, I had an interesting telephone conversation with my cousin, Angela Birdsong, of Inglewood, California. She is the daughter of Edwin Birdsong and the granddaughter of Reverend Sidney Birdsong, Sr., my late great uncle. During the conversation, she mentioned something that is so true.

"Cousin James, our great grandparents were our Abraham and Sarah." I had to agree with her.

The three cousins in this chapter consists of a world-renowned R&B legend, a Grammy Award winner and talented songwriter, producer and keyboardist, and a former NBA four-time All-Star basketball player. The Birdsong family is very large. We reside in various cities nationwide. To this present day, I am not able to remember most of their names. We are a very down to earth, family oriented people that are not materialistic.

Music and preaching are embedded in our DNA. It's been in existence before and after James Charles Birdsong, Jr. was born. I've known about my cousins since childhood when Daddy talked about them.

Cindy Birdsong

Cindy Birdsong is an original member of Patti LaBelle and the Bluebells, one of the most successful R&B female groups in the 1960s. Born on December 15, 1939, in Mount Holly, New Jersey, she joined the group in 1961. Her full birth name is Cynthia Ann Birdsong.

The group scored their first hit with *I Sold My Heart to the Junkman*, in 1962. After performing at the famed Apollo Theater in 1961, the group became regular headliners at the world-famous venue earning the nickname, "Sweethearts of the Apollo." Cindy toured with Patti and the group from 1963 to 1967, when they found success on the music charts. After another hit for Patti LaBelle and the Bluebells, *Down the Aisle (The Wedding Song)*, fans noticed Cindy's high soprano voice as a background singer. They also recorded *You'll Never Walk Alone* and *Danny Boy*. During Cindy's tenure with Patti LaBelle and the Bluebells, they were signed to Newtown Records and transitioned to two other labels in the music industry.

The 1960s produced some of the greatest artists in the history of gospel and secular genres, such as, Aretha Franklin, James Brown, Ray Charles, The Temptations, Chuck Berry, Mahalia Jackson, Brother Joe May, Sam Cooke, Dionne Warrick, Reverend James Cleveland, The Caravans, Dorothy Norwood and others. I must also mention Ike and Tina Turner, Rou Rawls, Gladys Knight and the Pips, Bobby "Blue" Bland, Nancy Wilson, Stevie Wonder and B.B. King.

One of the most successful record labels, Atlantic Records,

signed Patti LaBelle and the Bluebells in 1965. The group recorded two albums, *Over the Rainbow* and *Dreamer,* gained success on the music charts. Subsequently, Patti LaBelle pursued her solo career in the 1970s. In the nineties, she re-recorded *Over the Rainbow* for her two live albums, *Patti LaBelle Live!* and the Grammy Award winning project, *Live! One Night Only.* They were recorded from New York City, in front of a large audience. Patti is at her best in a live setting. Cindy eventually began to appear as a stand-in vocalist for the Supremes. This happened in 1967. The Supremes is one of the most popular R&B groups of all time. She performed with Diana Ross and the Supremes. Cindy made her departure from Patti LaBelle's group to join the Supremes as Florence Ballard's replacement.

From 1967 to 1970, Cindy toured with the Supremes. She had already established herself in the music industry. Diana Ross left the Supremes to become a solo artist, and Jean Terrell replaced her as the new lead singer. Cindy Birdsong, Jean Terrell and, original member, Mary Wilson became the Supremes. My cousin retired from the Supremes in 1976.

From there, Cindy worked at the UCLA Medical Center in Los Angeles and later joined Suzanne de Passe at Motown Records. They hosted a television special, Motown 25, in 1983, celebrating twenty-five years in the music business. Cindy joined Diana Ross and Mary Wilson on this special occasion. This is the same television broadcast Michael Jackson debuted his famous moonwalk during his performance of *Billie Jean.* She recorded a single, *Dancing Room*, in 1987, on Hit-Hat Records. I remember watching Cindy on the Motown 45 television special in 2004. This embarked forty-five years of Motown Records founded by Berry Gordy in Detroit, Michigan.

She was joined on stage by Mary Wilson and Kelly Rowland, of Destiny's Child, as they performed a medley of hits made famous by the Supremes. As of today, Cindy is a minister in the Los Angeles area. Cindy, if you are reading this book, I want you to know our family loves you very much. Your sacrifices and contributions in music will forever be recorded in history. I pray you will eventually record a gospel album soon. I would love to see that happen. I believe our family feels the same way. A friend of mine, Pastor Jerome Bell, of Washington, D.C., is one of Cindy's biggest fans. He is the former manager of Tramaine Hawkins.

Edwin Birdsong

I am now going to share the story of Edwin Birdsong in this chapter. He was the eldest son of Reverend Sidney Birdsong, Sr. and Daddy's first cousin. Edwin is one of the most talented organists, keyboardists and songwriters in the music industry.

Like me, Edwin is very family oriented and believes in supporting our endeavors. I told him about this book. I called him one day and said, "Edwin, I am going to have a chapter about you, Cindy and Otis. The public wants to know more about our family."

"That's good, cuz," he said.

He recorded a total of five albums, from 1971 to 1981, in his more than forty-five years in music. Raised in Los Angeles, his father had already begun to gain respect all throughout the city as the pastor of Solid Rock Baptist Church. His mother was Josephine Birdsong, my great-aunt-in-law and Angela's grandmother.

Edwin joined the Los Angeles Community Choir, for a brief period, prior to serving our country in the Vietnam War. He played at clubs in Germany. As a young man, he moved to New York City and pursued his music career. This is one of the major cities in the country for actors and singers pursuing big breaks.

Are you familiar with the Manhattan School of Music and the prestigious Julliard? My cousin attended those institutions as a music composition major. Edwin eventually signed a record deal in 1971, with Polydor Records. They released his first two albums, *What It Is* and *Supernatural*.

This allowed him to move forward in the music industry. Edwin is close friends with Stevie Wonder, and they worked together for several years. Stevie is family to the Birdsongs. He traveled to Chicago with Stevie for an episode of *The Oprah Winfrey Show*, where he did a performance. The legendary Roy Ayers co-produced three albums for Edwin during the seventies. Mama remembered the radio stations in the Bay Area playing Edwin's music on the air. This happened before she met Daddy. Who remembers the talented pianist and keyboardist Billy Preston? Edwin knew and worked alongside him during his early years in the music industry.

During the late nineties, African-American television comedy sitcoms were still on demand. The UPN Network had a show, titled, *Good News*. Broadcast for one season, Billy Preston made appearances as the organist of the Church of Life, in Compton, California, where David Ramsey portrayed an acting pastor named Reverend David Randolph. In 1975, Edwin released his third album, *Dance of Survival*, on Bamboo Records. He and Roy Ayers came together and wrote the songs, *Running Away* and *Freaky Deaky*. His popularity continued to expand throughout the United States and abroad, with a passionate fan base. One of the top record companies at the time, Philadelphia International Records, offered Edwin a recording contract. Patti LaBelle was once signed to this label during the early years of her solo career.

Founded by music icons Kenneth Gamble and Leon Huff, Edwin released his fourth album, *Edwin Birdsong*, in 1979. This album produced the singles, *Cola Bottle Baby* and *Phiss-Phizz*. My cousin recorded one more album that was released in 1981 on Salsoul Records, titled, *Funtaztik*. He has not recorded any more albums since Funtaztik.

He also worked as a producer and songwriter for other artists. If you are familiar with his music, Edwin is an instrumental artist. He would sing on some songs. The seventies were a decade of disco and funk music. Edwin is in that category, along with Donna Summer, George Clinton, Gloria Gaynor and Candi Staton, before she became converted as a born again Christian and gospel singer. My cousin has been blessed to meet and know famous names in the music industry, such as, Michael Jackson, Miles Davis, Mick Jaggar and many others.

Edwin even knew Reverend James Cleveland and visited his church, Cornerstone Institutional Baptist Church, in Los Angeles. His largest achievement came when Kanye West sampled *Harder, Better, Faster, Stronger,* by the French house duo Dalf Punk, for his Grammy Award winning single, Stronger. Dalf Punk featured a re-worked instrumental of Cola Bottle Baby. I made a visit to one of the college gospel choirs, at a popular university in Atlanta, as the 2008 50th Annual Grammy Awards was televised in Los Angeles. Stronger won the Grammy Award for Best Rap Solo Performance.

I knew the song would be nominated for a Grammy. I called Edwin and he said, "Cuz, we won the Grammy tonight."

This made Edwin the first member of our family to be recognized by the Grammys. The trophy went to Kanye West. Edwin received a Grammy Award participation certificate from the National Academy of Recording Arts and Sciences. Edwin attended the Grammy Awards throughout the years. He is a voting member of the Recording Academy. He went on to receive additional Grammy Award recognitions for his work in the music industry.

One of my former college classmates is a fan of Edwin and told me, "I want to meet Edwin Birdsong." I want him to know he still has fans and admirers around the world.

Otis Birdsong

Born on December 9, 1955, in New Haven, Florida, Otis Birdsong had a successful career as a professional basketball player in the NBA for twelve years, from 1977 to 1989. Otis attended Winter Haven High School, in New Haven, Florida. Upon his high school graduation, he enrolled at the University of Houston, in Houston, Texas. Prior to being selected by the Kansas City Kings, with the second pick of the 1977 NBA Draft, Otis played basketball as a college student.

The Kings was his first time playing as a professional basketball player. A height of 6'3", Otis played four seasons with the Kings. They remained in Kansas City until the NBA moved the team to Sacramento, California in 1985. He averaged a career high of 24.6 points per game during the 1980-1981 NBA season. His contributions to basketball allowed Otis to appear in four NBA All-Star Games.

Following his stunt with the Kings, Otis played seven seasons with the New Jersey Nets. Mama told me a story about Otis during his professional basketball career. He and his team mates would come to the Bay Area during the NBA season. Daddy and Otis talked on the telephone on many occasions. My father loved sports. If Otis and his team lost a game to their rivals, Daddy became his own sports critic.

As a child, Michael Jordan and Earvin "Magic" Johnson dominated the game of basketball. As former players, they continue to be symbols as icons in the NBA. Otis is among the NBA greats, such as, Michael Jordan, Earvin "Magic" Johnson,

Larry Bird, Julius "Dr. J." Earvin, Kareem Abdul-Jabbar and Dominque Wilkins. These men paved the way for today's players in the NBA.

The abbreviation for NBA stands for National Basketball Association. His tenure with the Kings became a highlight of his career. In 1980-1981, he shot 5440% from the field, and 2860% from behind the arch, short of his career high mark of 3640% from three-point range. He is a career 5060% field goal shooter (www.basketball-players.pointafter.com, 2016).

I was born in 1980, and my cousin had his best season in the NBA that year. Otis joined the Boston Celtics during the 1988-1989 NBA season. He participated in four NBA All-Star Games, in 1979, 1980, 1981 and 1984. When you hear about the Boston Celtics the first thing that comes to mind, "This is the team twelve time NBA All-Star Larry Byrd played for and was named the Most Valuable Player." As a child, I watched the games on television as Larry Byrd, Michael Jordan and Earvin "Magic" Johnson dominated the league.

Please allow me to share an example in professional basketball. Michael Jordan comes to mind as the Chicago Bulls. Earvin "Magic" Johnson and Kobe Bryant come to mind as the Los Angeles Lakers. Stephen Curry comes to mind as the Golden State Warriors. Charles Barkley comes to mind as the Phoenix Suns. LeBron James comes to mind as the Cleveland Cavaliers. Shaquille O' Neal comes to mind as the Orlando Magic.

This is based on famous players in basketball from past and present times. Otis Lee Birdsong comes to mind as the Kansas City Kings and New Jersey Nets. Some of these players had been traded to other franchises more than once. Otis played one season for the Celtics before he retired in 1989. The nineties had approached and the players of that era were rising stars. Following his 12-year career in the NBA, Otis returned to

Houston and served as a member of the Cougars broadcasting team for several seasons, before moving to Dallas, Texas. Otis never forgot about his roots as a member of the Houston Cougars, a college basketball team from the University of Houston. I met people who remembered Otis playing for the Kansas City Kings, New Jersey Nets and Boston Celtics.

He has been honored as a Hall of Famer on three occasions. In 2000, the University of Houston inducted Otis into their Hall of Honor. Polk County, Florida also wanted to honor my cousin for his achievements in the NBA. They inducted him into the Polk County Hall of Fame in that same year.

On October 20, 2014, Otis was inducted into the Southwest Conference Hall of Fame in Fort Worth, Texas. Presented by the Texas Sports Hall of Fame, they acknowledged him as a legend and icon in professional basketball. He did not receive the endorsements of major corporations marketing their products, such as his counterparts, Michael Jordan and Earvin "Magic" Johnson. He dedicated his life for twelve seasons and made his investment on the court. Otis Birdsong certainly has not been forgotten. I want the young people to know about him.

I am not referring to the fact that he is my cousin. The young men of today that play basketball in high school and college are aware of Michael Jordan, Earvin "Magic" Johnson, Shaquille O' Neal and most recently, Kobe Bryant, Lamar Odon, LeBron James and Stephen Curry. They are not aware of the legends that once played on the court. Michael Jordan, Earvin "Magic" Johnson, Larry Byrd and the others in this group are retired now.

They worked hard and I can say that about Otis. When those players had a game, they believed in teamwork and building unity as brothers. As a child of the eighties and nineties, I know what I am talking about. Michael Jordan, Earvin "Magic"

Johnson, Otis Birdsong and their counterparts believed in the value of a college education. They were drafted in college. I believe in building that legacy for future generations.

The Inspiration Continues to Impact Others

Cindy, Edwin and Otis inspired me. Yes, they have given me inspiration. I have been told, "You are the next Birdsong to be famous." A smile comes to my face. I am grateful for their compliments.

All honor, glory and praise belongs to Jesus Christ. The Bible speaks about gifts and how they can elevate us to higher depths. One example is found in Proverbs 18:16, where it reads, "A man's gift maketh room for him, and bringeth him before great men."

You have read the story of Cindy, Edwin and Otis Birdsong. There has never been a book authored about them, to my knowledge. People around the world are aware of them, and what they have done in their careers. The Birdsong family are very down to earth people, who believe in being humble and steadfast to the Lord. Our ancestors and forefathers had a dream for their descendants.

I refer to the conversation between myself and Angela about our great grandparents being the Abraham and Sarah of our family. The heritage transcended before Ed and Ida Birdsong. My famous cousins are joint-heirs in the lineage of our ancestors. The lineage consists of preachers, singers, and musicians. There are entrepreneurs, teachers, community leaders, attorneys, law enforcement officials and health care professionals in the Birdsong clan.

Forthcoming artists, musicians and athletes will now recognize the contributions made by Cindy, Edwin and Otis Birdsong in their professions. The development of this book fulfills the promise I made to the public. They requested me to include my cousins in this memoir. The Lord has blessed me with many followers on social media, such as, Facebook and Twitter.

I reflected on their accomplishments. They are now senior citizens and continue to be active. Challenging work does generate benefits of success. Predominant people from Richmond and the Bay Area of those times inspired me to move forth as a dreamer. They are celebrities and noted names that have built a catalyst in my childhood.

Trials and tribulations becomes the test of our faith in Jesus Christ. Cindy, Edwin and Otis had a dream starting in childhood to become somebody in life. Our goals of achievements do not happen overnight. They are thoughts in our mind, "Process becomes hard and difficult." Determination produces investment for lifetime benefits. Our outcome to the benefits establishes creativity in success patterns. God will give us the desires of our hearts. We must first submit to His Will and Purpose.

The influence of Cindy, Edwin and Otis Birdsong has become a legacy in and of itself. Sometimes in this journey, I often reflect on my legacy for future generations to carry forth. A few years ago, Edwin and I were speaking on the telephone. He desired to record another project in the future. The moment gospel music came up, he said, "I want to do a gospel album." I pray that he pursues this goal. This would be a blessing to our family. I believe this project will become successful and will introduce him to a gospel audience in traditional and contemporary genres.

In 1995, Stevie Wonder did a concert at the Paramount Theater in Oakland. Edwin toured with him for this performance. My father and Stevie had conversations on the telephone throughout the years. School concluded for the day. I returned home and Daddy passed the phone for me to speak with Edwin. He and Stevie invited me to the concert. I was 14-years-old and was unable to go. Luzan and Kitara attended in my place. They took a photo with Stevie backstage. The concert happened on a school night.

The Lord blesses those that are humble and steadfast. Cindy, Edwin and Otis Birdsong are examples as it relates to patience of dreams being fulfilled. I did not come to the full realization of their contributions, until I became old enough to understand. This is an historical moment in the legacy, and the glory belongs to God for blessing the Birdsong family.

For those of you that are closest to me, I acknowledge the fact that your encouragement granted this opportunity to share the story of their humble beginnings. They did not allow negative aspects to hold them back. I am sure Cindy, Edwin and Otis Birdsong had influential figures as role models. Someone had to pave the way for their journey of dreams. My experience in this path has allowed God to place the right people to guide me along the way.

This concludes the story of Cindy, Edwin and Otis Birdsong in this chapter. History had recorded a document for future generations to learn the contributions and sacrifices they made in their careers. My cousins are examples of how our children can become the dreamers and achievers of tomorrow. One thing for sure, Cindy, Edwin and Otis Birdsong established themselves as visionaries. It started in their youth. I can attest to this in my life. I publicly acknowledge them for building a strong legacy.

Who remembers the afternoon of October 17, 1989? Everything came to a complete standstill on this day. Series of events leading to the Loma Prieta Earthquake becomes our compass in the next chapter.

CHAPTER TEN
1989

I will never forget 1989. The last year of the eighties, there were a series of events that have been recorded in history books. Vice President George H.W. Bush won the 1988 Presidential Election, after he defeated his Democratic opponent, Massachusetts Governor Michael Dukakis. President Reagan served as our fortieth President of the United States for eight years, and his vice president was elected to succeed him.

On January 20, 1989, President Bush was inaugurated as the forty-first President of the United States, in Washington, D.C. Janet Jackson released her best-selling album, *Rhythm Nation 1814*. The youngest sister of Michael Jackson, she became a major star in her own right. Three years prior, the world had already taken notice of her with the album *Control*.

Critics began to compare her with Michael and his success of Thriller. Whitney Houston, Madonna and Prince were popular and in their highlight of music. Who remembers a pop group in the late eighties called New Kids on the Block? Before N'Sync, that launched Justin Timberlake's solo career and the Backstreet Boys, there was New Kids on the Block.

For me, I completed the third grade at Ellerhorst Elementary School in June 1989. Two things happened at that time. First, Ian had transferred to Tara Hills Elementary School in Pinole for his fourth-grade year. The second thing is the retirement of Jean Mahrt, our teacher for the last three years. She decided that time had come, after teaching for more than twenty-five years. Ms. Mahrt was 62-years-old. She loved to travel and play tennis. We were saddened about her departure. The entire Ellerhorst family loved and respected Ms. Mahrt. I made two visits to her beautiful home nestled in the El Cerrito hills. Never married and had no children, Ms. Mahrt had a brother that died and one surviving sister. She had nieces and nephews. I still have a photo of Ms. Mahrt from our first-grade class photo session.

She loved to travel and play tennis. We were saddened about her departure. The entire Ellerhorst family loved and respected Ms. Mahrt. I made two visits to her beautiful home nestled in the El Cerrito hills. Never married and had no children, Ms. Mahrt had a brother that died and one surviving sister. She had nieces and nephews. I still have a photo of Ms. Mahrt from our first-grade class photo session.

I had so much fun at Ellerhorst. I attended more field trips there than at any other school in my lifetime. During the first and second grades, Ian and I attended summer classes for six weeks at Ellerhorst. My parents and Clim were concentrating on building a church. The services were held in our living room and outside at the carport, in front of a vacant apartment building. Clim's family and the neighbors gathered for the services. They knew about the vision God had revealed to Daddy and Clim, to launch a church in Richmond.

Here were the plans for the leadership in this proposed church. Clim was going to serve as the senior pastor, while Daddy occupied the assistant pastoral position. My father continued to be a noted figure in Richmond, among dignitaries and the residents. The West County Times published more articles on Daddy.

This chapter will cover the 1989 Loma Prieta Earthquake. If God allows me to live, I will always remember exactly what had taken place on the afternoon of October 17, 1989. Before

I proceed with the story, tragedy happened once again in my family. I loved my Uncle Roosevelt very much. We were close and I wanted to visit him. He lived in San Pablo with his children, son-in-law and grandchildren. I attended church services along with Mama and Daddy on the Sunday morning of July 26, 1989, in Emeryville, California. Clim and JoEvelyn were already there by the time we arrived. Located on San Pablo Avenue near Oakland, it was a typical storefront church. Inner-cities nationwide have storefront churches as well large sanctuaries. Uncle Roosevelt rested heavily on my mind. I had not seen him recently.

He had a profound sense of humor. If you had the chance to know Uncle Roosevelt, he reminded you of George Jefferson on *The Jeffersons*. Comical and playful, my uncle was very special to me. Once services concluded, Clim and JoEvelyn came over to greet us.

As we were leaving, I broke the ice. "I need to go see Uncle Roosevelt," I said to Mama and Daddy. They knew how important this was to me. Mama drove the Lincoln Town Car on San Pablo Avenue.

Going north, it passes through the cities of Emeryville, Berkeley, Albany, and El Cerrito. It briefly turns on Cutting Boulevard, before entering Richmond at its northern terminus, under Interstate 80. Upon the arrival at Uncle Roosevelt's house, he greeted us at the door. His children, son-in-law and grandchildren lived there also.

The three of us sat in the living room as he and Daddy talked. Their bond as brothers was special to them. Grandpa Jim and Grandmother Charlene were no longer around. Uncle Roosevelt's biological father lived in Los Angeles.

The two-hour visit was spent very well. Daddy knew it was time for us to return home. We said goodbye to Uncle Roosevelt.

On the following morning of July 27, 1989, the two brothers spoke on the telephone, as usual. Daddy and Uncle Roosevelt never had a day when they did not call each other. I observed their brotherly bond.

Before the conversation ended, Daddy told him, "I will call you this evening."

"Okay James Charles," Uncle Roosevelt said. "Tell Belinda and my nephew hello." Later, in the evening, I played a Bible study cassette on the stereo system as I laid in my bed. Mama began to receive free King James translation New Testament Bibles, magazines and correspondence from world-renowned ministries, such as, Oral Roberts, Kenneth Hagin and Peter Popoff. The Bibles were donated to the people of the community and our food pantry program.

Then the doorbell rang. Mama and Daddy answered the door. It was one of Uncle Roosevelt's daughters. I immediately got out of the bed as they were taking. His daughter was crying. "What is going on here," I wondered. She gave Daddy the distressing news no one wanted to hear.

"Uncle James, Daddy had a heart attack. He is dead," she said.

Shocked and distressed, Daddy said, "What, Roosevelt is dead? I just talked to him this morning, and now he's gone."

Uncle Roosevelt died that evening, at 55-years-old.

Our phone service was interrupted later in the day. We walked across the street to Clim and JoEvelyn's house. Daddy could not believe his only brother had died. I remembered the reaction on his face as Mama guided him. They answered the door.

"Clim, Roosevelt is dead," he said to him and his wife.

They could not believe the news either. Daddy began to call family members in the Bay Area, Los Angeles, and even

Shreveport, to inform them about Uncle Roosevelt's death. Mama sat there speechless. Moments later, Daddy broke down and started to cry. I had never seen him in this state before.

Daddy lost three of his immediate family members during this decade. First his mother, followed by his father. Now, his only brother that he loved dearly and shared a bond with was gone. While the phone calls resumed, I went into the kitchen and walked toward the microwave oven. I broke down and cried.

JoEvelyn walked in and hugged me. "It's going to be alright," she said.

His death hit me like a ton of bricks. I could have asked God, "Why did this happened?" Those thoughts never came across to me. I was grateful to God for allowing me to visit Uncle Roosevelt on that Sunday afternoon. There are lessons for experience as loved ones become involved.

I did not realize that July 26, 1989 would be my last time with Uncle Roosevelt. His death had a major effect on me for the entire summer. This was the truth. More than twenty-five years later, I still miss him to this day. One thing I know for sure, this man never denied me as his one and only nephew. Reflecting and writing this story is very emotional. I loved my uncle very much, and the memories will never die.

We spent time together. Our road trip to Grandpa Jim's funeral in Shreveport reflected on the closeness Uncle Roosevelt and I shared. He was very playful with me. Daddy had so much on his mind. He felt alone in this process, and I observed with close attention.

One day, he said, "Junior, you are the only one I have now."

At 9-years-old, I had friends, school and childhood to focus on. He had a good wife and son in his life. My father asked Clim and JoEvelyn to accompany him to Fuller's Funeral Home on Cutting Boulevard in Richmond, with Uncle Roosevelt's daughter, to plan arrangements.

The arrangements were for Uncle Roosevelt's funeral. I remained at home as I played with friends in the neighborhood. I told them about the death of my uncle. Mama was in the house the entire time. The funeral arrangements were finalized for a service on August 5, 1989, at the Fuller's Funeral Home chapel. This was not going to be our first time attending a funeral service there.

African-American owned, the Richmond chapel and the second location in Oakland on 14th Street, the founder of Fuller's is a gentleman named Paul Fuller. I remembered Mr. Fuller as a child in Richmond. On the day of the funeral, Daddy delivered his first eulogy as a licensed ordained minister. Albert and Barbara attended the funeral. We were joined by his sisters, Mary Lou, Josephine and Myria. They were raised in Greenwood, Louisiana, alongside Daddy and Uncle Roosevelt.

Josephine and Myria sang solos at the funeral. To be honest, I wished they could have recorded and toured nationally in the gospel music industry. Wearing an all-white suit, Uncle Roosevelt laid in an opened beige casket, at the chapel of Fuller's Funeral Home. Held near the grave site of Grandmother Charlene, Uncle Roosevelt's interment at Rolling Hills Memorial Park became very emotional for us. The funeral was well attended.

After the interment of Uncle Roosevelt, we held a small repass at the house. It consisted of myself, my parents, Albert, Barbara, Mary Lou, Josephine and Myria. Daddy wanted to have a small gathering with his wife, son and members of the Birdsong family only. Weeks later, Daddy tried his best to cope. He accepted the death of his only brother. Daddy resumed his duties in ministry and his activism in Richmond.

In September 1989, I began the fourth grade at Ellerhorst. My new teacher that year, Laura Johnson, transferred from a previous school. Our new principal was an African-American woman named Irene Kirby. I am smiling right now. Purpose driven and determined to be a leader, she never allowed any obstacles to intervene in her way. I still was in grieving over the sudden death of Uncle Roosevelt. Mrs. Johnson and her two assistants became aware of this situation.

"I am so sorry to hear about your Uncle," one of the assistants said to me. God eventually gave me strength to endure. The bus routes were still in service for special education students and the disabled. Now, I am going to discuss the Loma Prieta Earthquake. The week before October 17, 1989, my father was rushed to Brookside Hospital one morning while classes at Ellerhorst were in session. Years earlier, Daddy had been diagnosed with diabetes. His blood glucose level escalated one morning. He had not remained on his diet as prescribed by the doctor.

On San Pablo Avenue, we made purchases of bread and pastries at the Wonder Bread store. Daddy began to eat honey buns. This dessert triggered his glucose level. A diabetic should maintain a heathy diet. Coming home from school, I exited off the bus and walked up the stairs of our porch to enter the house.

Mama opened the door and greeted me. "How was school today?" she asked.

As always, I told her, "It was fine, Mama."

I noticed Daddy was not sitting on his chair in our living room. I turned around and said, "Mama, where is Daddy?" She did not say a word. I asked her again, "Where is Daddy?" She still did not answer my question. I began to become worried about him.

"Let's go, James," Mama said.

I followed her outside to the garage and she drove to Brookside Hospital. We walked into his hospital room. Can you believe my mother surprised me at the hospital, by visiting Daddy? A week after being hospitalized, he was discharged on the afternoon of October 17, 1989. Mama and I returned to the hospital as we accompanied him to the car. I was very happy my father had finally come home. On this same day, the San Francisco Giants and Oakland Athletics played at the 1989 World Series, at Candlestick Park. Once home to the Giants and the San Francisco 49ers, this popular sports arena is no longer in existence. Just minutes before the start of the third game, a magnitude 6.9 earthquake struck the Bay Area causing considerable damage to both Oakland and San Francisco. The game was interrupted.

    I had a childhood friend that lived three houses from me. His name was Troy. He came to visit me, and the two of us sat on the front yard porch. Before he came to visit, I was already outside. I decided to walk in the house to see how Daddy was doing. He had the television turned on in our living room. Guess what he was doing? My father loved sports and he was listening to the World Series between the Giants and Athletics. I immediately returned outside to the porch.

    Mama went outside to the front of the house. She had a conversation with Clim and JoEvelyn about the Lord. Then, suddenly, I felt a strong shock on the front porch, at 5:04 PM.

    "James, what are we going to do," Troy said.

    The both of us looked towards Mama, Clim and JoEvelyn as they were praising God during the midst of the earthquake. Troy had a puzzled expression on his face. He said, "I am going home right now."

    I went inside the house to see about Daddy. I went upstairs to the room. On every channel that I turned to, the media reported on the Loma Prieta earthquake throughout the afternoon and evening. Sixty-seven people were killed and it caused more than five billion dollars in damages. Though this was one of the most powerful and destructive earthquakes ever to hit a populated area of the United States, the death toll was quite small (History.com, 2016).

The Loma Prieta earthquake even made the world news on major networks, such as, ABC, NBC and CBS. I grew up watching the three respected news anchors of all time. These men are legends and icons in journalism. Tom Brokaw of NBC Nightly News, Peter Jennings of ABC World News Tonight and Dan Rather of CBS Evening News dominated the evening news on television. They reported on the Loma Prieta earthquake.

For the Bay Area, our local anchors and reporters on KTVU 2, KRON 4, KPIX 5 and KGO 7 were busy around the clock broadcasting the damages of the Loma Prieta earthquake. I remembered Dennis Richmond and Elaine Corral of The Ten O' Clock News on KTVU engaging with their colleagues on around the clock updates on live television. I am going to provide accounts of this day in history.

Caused by a slip along the San Andreas Fault, the quake lasted 10-15 seconds and measured 6.9 on the moment magnitude scale, or 6.9 on the open-ended Richter scale (Nist.gov, 2011). It left an estimated 3,000 to 12,000 people homeless. Oakland had the highest number of fatalities due to the Cypress Street Viaduct on the Nimitz Freeway of Interstate 880. The double deck portion of the freeway collapsed, crushing vehicles on the lower level. A section of the San Francisco-Oakland Bay Bridge eastern span's upper deck collapsed onto the lower deck. The bridge was then closed for a month-long repair. At that time, it was determined that the bridge needed a long-term solution, which resulted in the retrofit of the West Span and replacement of the East Span (Baybridginfo.org, 2016).

A woman driving on the upper deck of the bridge, falls into

the lower deck, and died instantly. Recognized as BART, the Bay Area Rapid Transit System is a national renowned public rail system that delivers service to Alameda, Contra Costa, San Mateo and San Francisco counties.

On the day of the Loma Prieta earthquake, the Transbay Tube located in San Francisco Bay was virtually undamaged and only closed for post-earthquake inspection. BART hauled commuters between the East Bay and San Francisco daily.

With the closure of the Bay Bridge, due to damages, the Transbay Tube became the convenient way into San Francisco via Oakland for a month. The Marina district in San Francisco suffered extensive damage. Built on an area where there was no underlying bedrock, the liquefaction of the ground resulted in the collapse of several structures (History.com, 2016). I remembered the fires in San Francisco as journalists reported this tragedy.

The earthquake caused significant damages in San Jose, California and surrounding areas of the South Bay. Another hard-hit area was Watsonville, located several miles from the quake's epic center. More than 30 percent of Watsonville's downtown and 1 in 8 houses were destroyed (History.com, 2016). San Francisco and other communities began to retrofit buildings, following the afternoon of the earthquake. That evening I remained outside of the house on Maine Avenue as friends, parents and the community gathered.

Thankfully, the earthquake did not cause damage in Richmond. I remembered this young African-American woman in her twenties. She had a baby. The woman rang the doorbell.

"Can you please pray for my baby," the young mother said.

Mama began to pray for her baby as paramedics gave medical attention. Clim joined in the prayer. I will never forget her and the beautiful baby. The schools throughout the

THE BEST IS YET TO COME

Richmond Unified School District held classes the next day on October 18, 1989. At the campus of Ellerhorst, the students, facility and teachers had conversations about the Loma Prieta earthquake. I constantly prayed for the victims and the families affected.

It has been more than twenty-five years since the Loma Prieta earthquake. There is one conclusion that comes to mind. I could have been in any one of the areas widely affected. The last major earthquake in the Bay Area took place on April 18, 1906, in San Francisco, with an estimated magnitude of 7.8. This earthquake has been described as one of the worst and deadliest natural disasters in our nation's history.

When the opportunity presents itself, I will share the story of Loma Prieta to the young people of today. They were not born when this tragedy occurred. This generation heard about Loma Prieta in history books, documentaries and published articles. Young people can now hear from someone who witnessed this life changing situation as a child.

I thought about the woman who drove her car on the upper deck of the Bay Bridge and fell to the lower level. She had a family as the other victims that died did. I thought about the homeowners that lost their homes in San Francisco as fires erupted in downtown. I thought about the commuters that were driving their cars on Interstate 880 of the Nimtiz Freeway. The sad part of this tragedy are the people that became homeless. John P. Kee recorded a song, *It Could Have Been Me*, on his 1994 solo album, *Colorblind*. The song had the nineties New Jack Swing beat to it. There is a message in this song. When I think about this song, Loma Prieta comes to mind.

What does God say about earthquakes? "And great earthquakes shall be in divers places, and famines, and pestilences; and fearful sights and great signs shall there be from heaven" (Luke 21:11). God is always, and will always remain, in control. There have been more earthquakes in California, since Loma Prieta. Some were not as severe as this one. Eighty-three years and seven months after the 1906 earthquake in San Francisco, the Loma Prieta earthquake occurred in the Bay Area.

This chapter concludes the eighties. Memories of this decade will forever live in the hearts of children such as myself. Everything from President Reagan's legacy to Michael Jackson and his counterparts, the Apple Macintosh computer, Hot Wheels, Matchbox and Tyco, Teddy Rumpkin, Lego sets, Barbie and Ken dolls, Power Wheels, Nintendo and others have made history. I missed the eighties. If there was a time machine in real life, I would step inside and take a journey back.

We will now enter the nineties. How are things going to be different? Will there be a new fashion trend? Will the Birdsong household on Maine Avenue remain the same? A decision has been made for this perspective. We will now transcend to this new decade. I am ready for a road trip.

About to go down the slide while playing with my friends

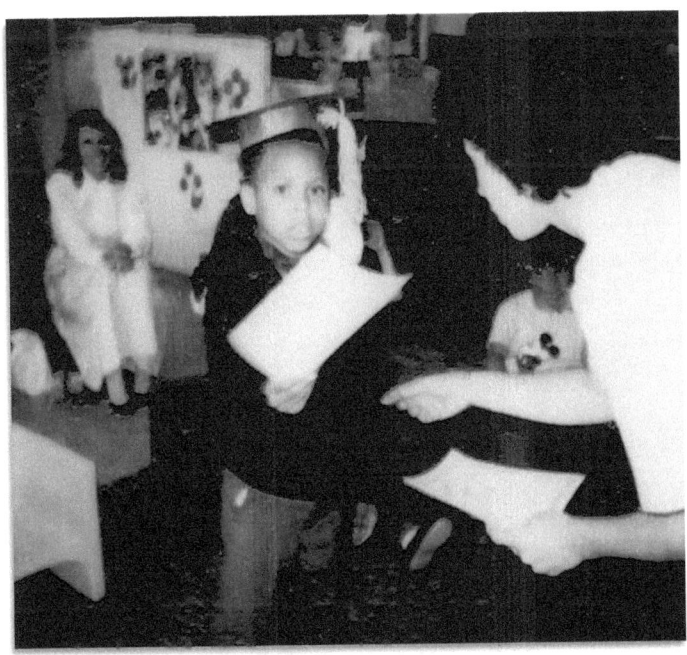

Graduation from kindergarten at Sheldon Elementary School in El Sobrante, California

JAMES C. BIRDSONG, JR.

THE BEST IS YET TO COME

CHAPTER ELEVEN

Welcome to the Nineties

Merriam-Webster defines triumphs as the very happy and joyful feeling that comes from victory or success (Merriam-Webster, 2016). Transition into the new decade indeed brings forth both triumphs and tests for redemption. The 1990s became a time of trials and tribulations for me. Observations of changes in our home and family life became the factor.

I am going to reflect on memories of this decade, in society.

Janet Jackson embarked on the Rhythm Nation World Tour, from February 27 to November 16, 1990. The tour was based on her 1989 album, Rhythm Nation 1814. The eighties babies, such as myself, can speak about her and Michael Jackson. As brother and sister, Michael and Janet broke barriers as African-Americans in the music industry.

They were the most famous artists in the Jackson family, throughout my childhood and adolescent years. Rhythm Nation 1814 was produced by multi-Grammy Award winning producers, Jimmy Jam and Terry Lewis. The album produced songs that dominated music charts, such as, *Rhythm Nation, Alright, Miss You Much, Escapade, Come Back to Me, Black Cat, Love Will Never Do (Without You)* and *State of the World*. I remember watching the music video of Alright on television.

The video featured a cameo by legendary jazz singer Cab Calloway. It went double platinum by the end of 1989, and went on to become the best-selling album of 1990, sending seven singles to the top five, including four number ones. All told, Rhythm Nation 1814 has sold nearly 20 million copies worldwide (Ew.com, 2014). The popularity of hip-hop music in the nineties made the impact of this genre. As a boy raised in the church, I remember the artists. M.C. Hammer was my favorite among hip-hop music. Often described as the "golden age" of hip-hop and rap, the 1990s introduced many rappers and rap groups that would go on to become the best rappers of all time (Ranker.com, 2016).

The beginning of the decade, artists, such as LL Cool J, Ice Cube, Tribe Called Quest and Public Enemy led the charts. They established their careers in the eighties. Their female counterparts, Queen Latifah, MC Lyte and DaBrat, broke barriers for women in rap and hip hop today. There were rap artists that recorded songs based on racism, drugs, police brutality and gangs in Los Angeles. Dr. Dre recorded an album, *The Chronic*. Released in 1992, this album became one of the best-selling rap albums of all time. He and Snoop Dogg represented the West Coast of the United States, alongside Tupac Shakur and the rest of the Death Row Records family. On the East Coast, you had Sean "Puff Daddy" Combs and the Notorious B.I.G. These two sides were crucial in the East-West Coast rap rivalry that not only produced some of the top rap music of the decade but also ultimately ended the lives of 2Pac and Biggie, as both were tragically murdered (Ranker.com, 2016).

I did not listen to hip-hop as a child. The songs had to proclaim a positive message, without profanity. Before the nineties, we had Run DMC, The Sugarhill Gang, Kurtis Blow, Grandmaster Flash, DJ Jazzy and the Fresh Prince.

On February 11, 1990, Nelson Mandela was released from prison in South Africa after serving 27 years. A leading anti-apartheid campaigner, he was convicted of treason and sabotage in June 1964 and sentenced to life imprisonment (BBC.co.uk, 2016). Frederik William de Klerk served as the President of South Africa, at the time of Nelson Mandela's release. A celebration of Nelson Mandela's path to freedom was observed worldwide. He is another person I have admiration for, alongside Martin Luther King, Jr., Coretta Scott King, Rosa Parks, Ambassador Andrew Young, Maya Angelou and Bishop Gilbert Earl Patterson. Over the course of his imprisonment, Mandela's fame rose as the spiritual leader stamping out apartheid. He became known for staging protests and radicalizing other Black prisoners at Robben Island (Newsone.com, 2012).

Nelson Mandela made a visit to the United States, giving speeches about racism and injustice of blacks in South Africa, and his imprisonment. Four years later in 1994, he was elected South Africa's first black president. He served five years in office. Reflecting on his life, I consider Nelson Mandela as the Martin Luther King, Jr. of South Africa.

He had friends that were legends and icons of the Civil Rights Movement, such as, Ambassador Andrew Young and others. Nelson Mandela died on December 5, 2013, in Johannesburg, South Africa, at 95-years-old. Throughout the years, I would see paintings of Martin Luther King, Jr., Malcolm X, and Nelson Mandela, at beauty supply stores and businesses that are African-American owned.

At the beginning of 1989, KTVU 2 announced a news broadcast for children in the Bay Area known as Kids town. It debuted on television. Recorded at the KTVU Studios, at Jack London Square in Oakland, the anchors and reporters were children. The broadcasts were taped once a week. The first segment of Kidstown engaged me so much.

"This is so cool. I want to be a part of this," I said.

There is no way I would pass this opportunity. I began to write letters inquiring about the auditions. A woman named Kim Richardson responded to three of my letters for the auditions.

She worked at KTVU as the coordinator for Kidstown. She wrote me a third letter for an open audition on January 28, 1990. I unsealed the envelope and read the requirements for this audition. A smile came upon me. This became an opportunity for my big break in Bay Area television broadcasting. I still have the letters from Kim to this day.

Most of the anchors and reporters on Kidstown resided in Oakland and San Francisco. There were no other children in Richmond and the surrounding cities in West Contra Costa County, to my knowledge, auditioning for this popular news broadcast for children. I had family, friends, and classmates that lived in Richmond, El Cerrito, San Pablo, Pinole, and Hercules. None of them told me of their interest in auditioning.

Prior to the audition, I practiced my news broadcasting skills on Mama and Daddy. I used my father's audio cassette recorder.

On the morning of January 28, 1990, we attended Sunday services at Apostolic Temple of Truth. The excitement came upon me for the audition. At the very same time, I was feeling nervous. Several thoughts ran through my mind. You must remember this, I was 9-years-old and a fourth grader at Ellerhorst. This could open doors for me in speech, communication, and building an audience.

Not knowing what to expect, I thought, "Am I going to broadcast live on television?"

After Elder Robinson gave the benediction, we immediately exited the church and proceeded to the audition at the KTVU studios in Oakland. Wearing a light gray suit and a dark blue poker dot tie, we arrived there within twenty minutes, from Interstate 80 to Interstate 880 in Jack London Square. Mama did the driving during her marriage to Daddy since he was blind.

Kim informed me to be there at about 2:00 PM PST, for this audition. KTVU had a long history of television news in the Bay Area. This became my favorite news station as a child. In that era, KTVU was not affiliated with any major news network, since it was independent. Today, the station is a FOX Network Bay Area affiliate. My mind thought on Dennis Richmond, Elaine Corral, Faith Fancher and all the popular names at KTVU. They were icons of the Bay Area news scene. I grew up watching them reporting breaking news and other stories. I could not believe this 9-year-old boy from Richmond, California was inside the KTVU studios, where Dennis Richmond, Elaine Corral, Faith Fancher, Rita Williams, Pat McCormick and the sportsman himself, Mark Ibanez, worked throughout their careers as journalists.

Most them are either retired or pursued other careers. Dennis Richmond retired in 2008, after a 40-year career. Who cannot forget about Faith Fancher? Her legacy continues to live on through her foundation, Friends of Faith. Upon our arrival, we waited for Kim in the lobby. The first thing I thought, "Am I going to see any of them at the studio today?" Then I said, "Will I see the main man of the Bay Area news himself, Dennis Richmond?"

Sitting with my parents, I read a document to guide me for the audition. About ten minutes later, Kim came and greeted us. I remember her smile.

"It is nice to meet you, James," she said. Kim told my parents, "Thank you for coming today."

Daddy said, "It is our pleasure, Ms. Richardson."

The four of us walked to the studio where the Ten O' Clock News, with Dennis Richmond and Elaine Corral, is broadcasted live every evening. Worried and not sure what to expect, Kim must have discerned this from me.

"James, you are going to be reading in front of the camera," Kim told me.

My question to her was, "Will I be on television?"

She smiled and said, "No, you will not be broadcasting on live television. The only thing you will be doing is reading in front of a camera."

I walked to the news desk of the studio and began the audition. Kim observed as the camera person proceeded. My parents were watching the entire audition process. It lasted for about five to ten minutes. Afterward, Kim told me she would notify me with the decision. As my parents and I were leaving, I became star struck when I noticed a familiar face in the newsroom. Did you see Dennis Richmond? The answer is no. Was the person his co-anchor Elaine Corral? The answer again is no. I am referring to Faith Fancher.

She was speaking to someone. I did not have the opportunity to meet her. For those of you raised in the Bay Area, Faith Fancher was beautiful, attractive and had that million dollars smile on television. Alongside Pamela Moore at KRON 4, Barbara Rodgers at KPIX 5, and Carolyn Tyler at KGO 7, they were the four African-American women in Bay Area news broadcasting.

I never received a response from my audition to be a reporter on Kidstown. I had to accept that and move forward. I continued to watch Kidstown until KTVU canceled the broadcast two years later. As of today, the Bay Area does not have a children's news broadcast on television. The experience of this audition will always be a treasured moment. I walked into a television studio for the first time in my life. The Lord blessed me to be on television for the new millennium.

I resumed the remaining five months of fourth grade at Ellerhorst. The certificates of awards continued to be bestowed upon me. The school hosted their annual science fair on March 29, 1990. Held inside our multi-purpose room, the students from first to sixth grade worked tirelessly on their projects based on science.

Prior to the science fair, I developed an interest in astronomy and aerospace. After completing the third grade, I began writing letters to NASA, at the John F. Kennedy Space Center in Florida and the Jet Propulsion Laboratory in Pasadena, California. They began to send me literature of Space Shuttle missions and exploration of planets in our solar system.

I still do not remember what my science project was based upon. I became one of the winners in the 1990 Ellerhorst Elementary School Science Fair. The award was on display in our living room. During my tenure at Ellerhorst, I had been recognized as Student of the Month six times. Two of the certificates were in the library with my photo. They were October 1987 and October 1988, from Ms. Mahrt. I was in second and third grade. I cherish all the awards and certificates God blessed me to receive throughout the years.

There is something very important to be discussed in this book. Each one of us will have tests of strengths. Mrs. Kirby had a test of strength. The first two months of 1990 became very challenging for the entire Ellerhorst family. She would always bring board games for the students to play during lunch time. One afternoon I was sitting in front of the multi-purpose room on campus. She walked up and told me something.

Our principal did not seem normal. Mrs. Kirby knew my parents were ministers and highly respected in Richmond. "How are you doing today, James?" she asked me.

Sitting there, I looked up to her and said, "I am doing fine, Mrs. Kirby."

Her facial expression appeared to be different. Something

was wrong.

"James, I have something to tell you," Mrs. Kirby said. I immediately stopped playing with one of the board games and listened to her. She was my favorite principal at Ellerhorst. I did not know what had been going on with Mrs. Kirby. I was just a 9-year-old boy in special education and enjoying childhood. Her words concerned me.

"I am going to be away for a while," she said. "A friend of mine is going to be the substitute principal in my absence."

Out of all the students, she told me this. I don't think Mrs. Kirby shared the same news with other friends and classmates on campus. Maybe I am wrong. The truth of the matter became lessons of understanding. God knew what He was doing as Mrs. Kirby told me the news about her leave of absence. She never indicated the reason. A few weeks later the students learned the truth. Mrs. Kirby had been diagnosed with breast cancer. I had never heard of breast cancer as a child. She had to take chemotherapy treatments for about two months. When I learned the news, I told Mama and Daddy. A lot of prayers went up for the principal at Ellerhorst Elementary School. She eventually returned to the school and resumed her role as our principal.

We loved her so much. The school was not the same while she was taking her chemotherapy treatments. Mrs. Kirby always smiled and fought to the end. She died two years later in 1992. A year before her death, I saw Mrs. Kirby and her daughter one Sunday afternoon at Scandia Family Fun Center in Fairfield, California. I went there with some friends of mine after church.

Irene Kirby never gave up being an encouragement to others striving to accomplish their dreams. She was very fond of me and my parents. Writing this story is very emotional for me. I had met people that were cancer survivors. Their stories of courage touched my heart.

On May 16, 1990, I turned 10-years-old. I decided to have a birthday party, again, in school. Mama baked me a homemade cake. Mrs. Johnson and her assistants made the preparations for the class to celebrate my birthday. Every year on my birthday, I had a party in the classroom. Those parties excited me. I value the memories.

I successfully completed fourth grade in June 1990. Two weeks later, I attended summer classes at Valley View Elementary School on Maywood Drive, in El Sobrante. By this time, seven years of my life had been spent in special education. The Richmond Unified School District continued with their budget for students in the special education program as it related to bus service. The racial makeup at Valley View was like Sheldon and Ellerhorst. Those schools had students of different ethnicities, such as Asian, Hispanic and Indian. What about the African-American ethnicity in attendance? I did attend Sheldon, Ellerhorst and Valley View with African-American classmates. They lived in the suburbs and nearby cities. Being a child of the inner-city, the children of my neighborhood attended Nystrom. I invested my time at Ellerhorst for four years. My friends in the neighborhood were pushing for me to attend Nystrom. They were not pleased with me attending predominantly white schools in the suburban areas of West Contra Costa County. They knew about the bus coming to pick me up every morning and bringing me home in the afternoons.

One day as I was outside playing with them, a boy told me, "You need to be at Nystrom with us. None of your friends at Ellerhorst come over and visit."

There is one thing I can say about this situation. Ian would come to the house and visit me. There were some weekends he and his parents picked me up to spend time with them. The four of us visited popular attractions in the Bay Area, such as Pier 39, Marine World Africa USA and the Oakland Zoo. Our parents always engaged in our school activities and participated in PTA meetings.

About the third or fourth week of classes at Valley View, one of the students became ill and stayed home due to a virus. Chickenpox (varicella) is a contagious illness that causes an itchy rash and red spots or blisters (pox) all over the body. Chickenpox can cause problems for pregnant women, newborns, teens and adults, and people who have immune system problems that make it hard for the body to fight infection (Webmd.com, 2005). The week this young man returned to class, I developed the symptoms of chicken pox. Believe me, I suffered the entire week. Mama made an appointment for me at the Richmond Pediatric Group on Cutting Boulevard. A new pediatrician on staff, Dr. Pauline Wilkins prescribed calamine lotion.

McMillan's Pharmacy, located next to the Richmond Pediatric Group, became popular in Richmond. African-American owned and operated, the pharmacy's owner was a gentleman named James McMillian. An elected member of the Richmond City Council, Mr. McMillian, and my father were friends. I had to go there to pick up the prescription of calamine lotion. In the eighties, my parents were regular customers at McMillian's Pharmacy as patients of Dr. Robinson. Comical and playful, Mr. McMillian would always ask Daddy to sing songs at the pharmacy. The people of our city loved Daddy's singing. Mr. McMillian served on the Richmond City Council, until 1995. He is now retired as a pharmacist and continues to serve the community in local organizations.

Mr. McMillian and others, in his caliber, could have become elected members of the United States Congress. Instead of a national elected office, they dedicated their lives to Richmond.

We may not have agreed on some of their politics. Contributions establish the legacy for future generations.

The elected officials of the Richmond City Council, of my childhood, inspired the message, "Never forget where you came from." Those values were instilled at an early age.

I honored and cherished the principles of my elders and teachers. Mr. MacMillian served on the Richmond City Council during the administration of Mayor George Livingston. Daddy knew so many people at City Hall on Barrett Avenue. John Marquez made history in 1985, as the first Hispanic elected to the Richmond City Council. He continues to make a difference today in Richmond.

I remember Richard Griffin and Lonnie Washington, Jr. on the council. Mr. Griffin and Mr. Washington were dedicated to our city. My father would speak to them. I was being raised during the time when Mayor Livingston and the Richmond City Council built Interstate 580, in Richmond, and created jobs for residents.

Mayor Livingston knew how to bridge and unite the community. He was defeated in 1992, for re-election as mayor. Rosemary Corbin served on the Richmond City Council. She declared her candidacy for the mayoral race against Mayor Livingston. Mayor Corbin knew daddy very well. I cannot forget about Donna Powers on the Richmond City Council, at the time. Irma L. Anderson once worked for the Contra Costa County Health Services. She made history as the first African-American women to be elected to the Richmond City Council in 1993. After the tenure of Mayor Corbin, the residents of Richmond elected Mayor Anderson, to succeed her.

The last senior member of the Richmond City Council was Nathaniel Bates. Daddy knew Mr. Bates for many years. These individuals are legends and icons in Richmond politics. They are all still living, except for Mayor Livingston, Mr. Griffin, and Mr. Washington. I cannot forget about these leaders. They were good people and I respected them to the utmost.

The lesson of never forget your roots has been a part of this foundation. Often, people can forget where they come from, regardless of economic and classification status. As this book was being planned, I made sure my hometown would be placed on the global map. My family roots had been birthed from Greenwood, Louisiana. Humble beginnings for me started on Maine Avenue, as a child of the ghetto. I love Richmond very much and the people, from the babies to the seniors.

There are more currents events of this decade, in the nineties. I have lived and have witnessed politics, disasters, music, television, motion pictures, and education, the rising of drugs, gangs and violence in ghettos throughout the United States. Poverty in third-world nations continued to escalate. While these events were on the horizon, changes began to take place in the Birdsong household on Maine Avenue. The next four chapters of this book are going to be difficult for me. Lord, give me the strength to write them.

The Greenwood Four Jubilee Singers from left to right: the late Tommy Wayne, the late Clarence Birdsong, the late Earnest Taylor, and the late Sidney Birdsong, Sr.

cousin and a man who was very special in our family, the late Albert Birdsong, Sr. holding me as a baby

Wearing my father's black hat at 3-years-old

JAMES C. BIRDSONG, JR.

CHAPTER TWELVE
Things Begin to Change

Marriage should last for life. I have stood on this principle since my upbringing and continue to believe this today. Things began to change in our home. There were issues that related to my parent's marriage. The nineties had the good and the bad. I had not observed this escalation until 1990. The same love for Mama and Daddy remains.

This chapter will outline a series of events in my life as a pre-teen and what had taken place at Maine Avenue. Mama and Daddy had a beautiful marriage in the eighties. Everyone from the family, to the residents of our city, knew this first hand. They were highly respected among pastors, dignitaries, teachers, politicians, city officials, administrators at our school district office, and the community.

I know you've heard this statement, "This couple is happily married, and they have the perfect marriage." There is no perfect marriage.

Before my parents met, Daddy had a breakdown due to his blindness. If you go back and read Chapter Six of this book, this explains his story in Greenwood, Louisiana and how his life changed forever. His physician had prescribed medication to calm his nerves. I began to observe arguments between Mama and Daddy. As a 10-year-old boy, with a developmental disability, lessons of strength before adulthood became a strong hand. Daddy had changed towards his wife and son. One situation comes to mind as this chapter is being written. I do not desire this behavior on any child or my enemy. The income of SSI monthly benefits through the Social Security Administration were offered to me, after my diagnosis. Classified as Supplemental Security Income, this program pays benefits to disabled adults and children with limited income and resources. SSI benefits also are payable to people 65 and older, without disabilities, who meet financial limits.

The first of each month, Social Security issues the benefits to thousands of recipients all over the United States with disabilities. Payees for children are usually parents, grandparents, legal guardians or foster parents that are legally dependent in their care. Daddy became the payee for my monthly benefits. At the same time, Daddy began to obtain services from a caregiver through Dr. Carter's approval.

After the lung cancer diagnosis on Dr. Robinson, he decided not to continue his medical practice on Cutting Boulevard. He focused on cancer treatments. The news of his diagnosis shocked the entire community. Dr. Robinson later joined the board of trustees at Brookside Hospital and became a mentor to numerous doctors. Dr. Robinson died in 1994, after a five-year battle with lung cancer.

For those of you born and raised in Richmond, there will never be another Julius Caesar Robinson and William Morris Jenkins, Jr. These gentlemen were admired, respected and trustworthy. They were two African-American doctors that made significant contributions in our city and the Bay Area, at large. My parents attained the services of Dr. Carter. He continued to practice medicine on MacDonald Avenue, near the Richmond Civic Center Plaza. The main branch of the Richmond Public Library, the former headquarters of the Richmond Police Department, and Richmond Police Department is located there.

Mayor Livingston was still in office at the time. I made

trips to the Richmond Public Library on Saturday mornings. I loved to read and research. With a height of 6'0", the person that provided his care services was Shirley. African-American and approximately between 5'1" to 5'2", she came to the house Mondays through Fridays. Her duties as caretaker consisted of cooking and preparing meals, taking Daddy to his doctors' appointments, giving him insulin for his diabetes, and other duties as assigned.

Lucky's had a grocery store on MacDonald Avenue, at the corner of San Pablo Avenue near El Cerrito. This is where Mama and Daddy would shop. One morning I went there with Daddy and Shirley. Strolling over to the cereal section, I saw a box of Cocoa Pebbles. Once I grabbed the Cocoa Pebbles, I politely asked Daddy, "Can I have another item in the store?"

"No, you cannot," he said to me.

He began to be selfish and declined my request. Facing a hunger situation is not healthy for the well-being of a child. There were already problems within James and Belinda Birdsong's marriage. I eventually approached Mama, and informed her about what was happening. My mother did not like the fact that the man she had fallen in love with began to change towards his wife and their son. He purchased food for himself, and that should never have happened. I only had a box of cereal.

Parents, I need you to listen right now. You are reading about a person who can relate to children in these situations. Hurt and upset, Mama had to take matters into her own hands. She made a visit to the Social Security Administration office on Barrett Avenue, to report what had happened to my monthly SSI disability benefits. They did their research, and Mama became the official payee. Once Daddy learned about what his wife has done, he was not pleased.

"James, our son has to eat and you have not been fair

towards him," Mama said.

An argument occurred between them concerning this situation. Daddy realized there was nothing he could do. Things still had not changed in the Birdsong household, and unhappiness came upon me. Not too long afterwards, Mama took me grocery shopping at the same Lucky's grocery store on MacDonald Avenue. Her first and main priority was food on the table for me.

Mama and Daddy even began to sleep in separate rooms. As a husband and wife, they shared the same bed. The second story of our house had three bedrooms. My parent's room, located in the east, with a view of Nystrom Elementary School, became their place of rest and comfort. My room was occupied by Grandmother Charlene during her lifetime. By 1990, Grandmother Charlene had been deceased for ten years and would have approached her seventy-seventh birthday in August. I believed she would not have approved of this behavior from her son. You had already obtained a description of her character in Chapter One.

With the deaths of Grandmother Charlene in 1980, Grandpa Jim in 1986, and Uncle Roosevelt in 1989, it took a mental toll on Daddy. He felt as though something had been taken from him, and turned on his wife and son. A person that specialized in mental health made their predictions in this matter. Daddy's mental status occurred due to his blindness as a young man in Greenwood, Louisiana.

Now, I will resume to my parents sleeping in separate rooms. Facing the south, Mama began to sleep in the front bedroom towards the north. Not too many people in Richmond knew what occurred in our home. There were only a handful in the inner circle. Arguments continued to escalate between my parents. Daddy even said something that hurt Mama's feelings.

"Belinda, you are not being a good mother to Junior," he said to her.

How could the man that married my mother say something very offensive? I could not believe this. The father-son bond began to change between us. Satan came and began to destroy the marriage of James and Belinda Birdsong. God ordains marriage, and Satan is against it. The Apostle John writes this position of how the enemy is on his mission to steal, kill and destroy, as he writes, "The thief cometh not, but for to steal, and to kill, and to destroy: I am come that they might have life, and that they might have it more abundantly" (John 10:10). When the Lord ordains a marriage, abundance of life is birthed into marital covenant. Married couples should remain prayerful and be observant, always. You are reading the story of a young man who learned the difference between right and wrong in this process.

The relationship between father and son became noticeable. In the eighties, the bond was positive. Now, the new decade arrived and things began to change. I admired fathers that spent quality time with their sons. He guides his son into manhood. In the case of my father, I did learn a lot from him. I am not here to speak negatively about him. Daddy had some good in him and the family knew this. He had physical blindness in the natural sense. However, spiritual blindness had overtaken him. Realization of God's blessings does not hit home until later. This includes relationships and marriages. I learned this lesson first hand in this stage of pre-adolescence. When the Lord blesses you with something precious, never allow any negative obstacles to intervene. Once that precious gift is gone, it's over for good.

There was a time I overheard Daddy saying, "I am not married to Belinda."

This even hurt Mama more. Believe me, I am not writing

this book as a fictional fairytale. I lived through and witnessed this ordeal. Can you imagine the hurt and frustration of my mother? The marriage began to take a mental toll on her. People noticed the changes, even the neighbors in our community and their families.

I was raised in the same neighborhood as their children on Maine Avenue and a few blocks away. We played together every day. They had Nintendo and Sega Genesis games, action figures, race car sets, board games, and the girls had Barbie and Ken dolls. Please allow me to say one thing, we were children of the inner-city that grew up together in the ghetto. I could not allow the problems of my parent's marital crisis to stop me from childhood and spending time with friends. In the latter part of 1990, the Birdsongs stopped attending church together on Sundays as a family. Daddy retained his membership at Apostolic Temple of Truth, as Clim and JoEvelyn were planning to open their church. As for Mama, she was invited to attend services, by Adella, one Sunday. She and her husband, David, were members of Prayer House Apostolic Faith Church on Foothill Boulevard in Oakland, where Bishop Presley Mobley was the pastor. A popular pastor and gospel-recording artist in the Bay Area, Bishop Mobley had a radio broadcast on KDIA 1310 AM. The Bay Area had numerous pastors that broadcasted church services, either live or pre-recorded. I am going back to the eighties and nineties, before modern day technology of internet live streaming and demand television. Prayer House had a mission ministry in the continent of Africa.

Mama had experience in public relations and outreach in various churches. She joined the choir at Prayer House and aided Bishop Mobley in missions. I attended services with Mama, Adella and David on several separate occasions. I am not sure if Bishop Mobley became aware of my parent's marital crisis.

Daddy visited the church once. He still claimed his traditional Baptist roots.

My upbringing was Church of God in Christ and Apostolic. This began at Now Faith when Elder Crawford was alive. Mother Crawford and Mama retained their friendship throughout the nineties and early 2000s.

I told Mama a long time of ago, "I wish Mother Crawford could have been a state mother in a Church of God in Christ Women's Jurisdiction Department."

Mother Crawford discerned Mama's situation. I knew she was not very pleased at Daddy's behavior. She was one of those old-school mothers of the church that believed in prayer, fasting and intercession of the Holy Spirit. Her education in nursing gave her a sense of Daddy's mental crisis. She would have been a great Jurisdictional Supervisor of Women, in my honest opinion. Those of you that were raised or still members of the Church of God in Christ can attest to this position. I still value my Pentecostal roots. My affiliation in church is currently non-denominational. The Lord has blessed me with friends and acquaintances in Church of God in Christ and Apostolic.

The problems of James and Belinda Birdsong's marriage turned out to be tales. You may be wondering, "Okay, please explain this position." Encounters of situations can either make or break you. The problems that have a breaking point become a roller coaster ride.

What made matters worse in the Birdsong household? Daddy did not want me to attend church services with Mama at Prayer House. There is so much a child can endure. He eventually became a controller. Mama experienced problems in her first marriage to Demetrius and Alonzo's father. My brothers lived in the house on Maine Avenue, until I was about three years old.

I am going to say this statement, until God calls me home. I loved Daddy very much. Yes, he was not a perfect man and made mistakes. Prior to his marriage, family and friends told Mama about his breakdown and diabetes. They knew about his singing abilities. He began to do certain things behind his wife's back, without her knowledge. When my mother married her husband, she no longer had communication with male friends. Mama believed in being a faithful wife. Daddy wanted to hold on to his female friends, and this is exactly what he did.

This preceded to the stage of divorce. When a man and woman enter the stage of marriage in their love account, they make a complete change in their personal and social lives. The Word of God talks about them being together as one. Never open the door of invitation for anything to hinder your marriage. Rates of divorces continue to be on the horizon. Marital problems did not allow them to stop being involved in my academics, with special education. My parents were serious about the IEP meetings, and had good relationships with teachers and school administrators. Daddy became selfish with our Lincoln Town Car. They purchased the car just before Grandpa Jim's death. I witnessed that moment at Mira Vista Lincoln-Mercury in 1986. He began to tell people, "I brought the Town Car." The only thing I can say is, "What in the world is he talking about?"

Mama found out and approached her husband. "James, our incomes combined together purchased the car," Mama said.

He knew she told the truth. He didn't care and wanted to have full control of the car. They had arguments in front of me. You are thinking, "What happened to your father? Why is he tripping?" Daddy had personality changes. Observations of patterns became noticeable. He became nice and calm one day, and then a different person entered the room for an episode.

You now have the picture.

Suddenly, Daddy stopped Mama from driving the car. This treatment made me more disappointed. She began to ride AC Transit, the most notable public transportation system in the Bay Area. Daddy had Shirley or other care providers drive it. His female friends would drive the car, and certain people he should never have had association with. They knew he had a disability and financial status.

My friends would say, "James and his parents are rich." The Birdsongs were not millionaires living in a large mansion and driving a Rolls Royce.

We lived in a two story Victorian house, with five bedrooms, two bathrooms and a Lincoln Town Car in the garage. The luxury cars were Buick Park Avenues, Cadillac Fleetwood's, Chrysler New Yorkers and Lincoln Town Cars. I would see these classy automobiles throughout the city. These were the large, six passenger American made luxury sedans among pastors, deacons, the mothers of the churches, and high profile figures in Richmond. They seldom drove BMWs and Mercedes Benz's, unless they were attorneys or physicians. Toyota had just introduced their Lexus brand on the market. My father did not believe in being broke. He was financially stable. My parents would purchase me brand new clothes and shoes at JCPenney's and Mervyn's, at the beginning of each school year. Mama loved interior decorating and household plants. If you visited our home, the living and dining room should've been featured in Better Homes and Gardens magazine.

I am going to go back and proceed to the role of marriage. Our young people need to be careful in choosing friends, potential relationships and acquaintances. These principles instilled in me as a child are valuable today, as it relates to the definition of friends and acquaintances. Married couples should develop their friendships with other men and women in marriage. There are going to be individuals that will not respect your marriage. Chapter Two explains the three stages of love growth. Please allow me to contribute another proposition in the stages. In the second stage of love growth, I explained the relationship level. There will be people that will come against your potential soul mate for marriage. Once they become husband and wife, these same people will be against the marriage even further.

Observations of this situation became a five-year dilemma. Behavioral patterns affected me mentality as a pre-teen. My father began to mistreat me. I could not understand, at this stage of my life. Questions came to mind on how to endure inside the situation. Allow me to address two specific points in this chapter.

First, the transition from early years to adolescence became concepts into adulthood. Puberty changed my voice from high pitch to deepness. Secondly, I experienced the change in my home between Mama and Daddy in their marriage. It seemed like a beautiful family life on yesterday, and then suddenly it changed the next day. I had to experience trials and tests. You must realize the position of an African-American boy, of the inner-city, born with a developmental disability, on the verge of communicating in American Sign Language based on diagnosis of speech, and being a special education student in public schools. This became the start of redemption.

The world knows about the Birdsong Family. People are aware of Cindy, Edwin and Otis. They are my famous cousins. I realized this as a child. My father became very well known throughout Richmond. My hometown knew James Charles Birdsong, Sr., as a man of his caliber. He settled in Richmond from Greenwood, Louisiana.

Noted dignitaries noticed his record of public service to

the community. The West County Times published articles about him, dating back to the seventies as he first began his activism in Civil Rights, and the advocacy for disabled people. Local organizations in our city knew of Daddy's leadership, and this included the NAACP Richmond Branch on MacDonald Avenue. He joined the Shepherd's Way in 1989, and served as their chaplain. He became close friends with a Caucasian gentleman named E.R. "Andy" Anderson. Mr. Anderson and I remain in communication to this present day. He and Daddy were also members of the Full Gospel Businessmen Fellowship International.

He served as President of the Shepherd's Way. A non-profit, Christian based organization, the Shepherd's Way dedicated their mission to help the homeless, drug addicts and families, for their lives to be changed in society. The board members were Christian based entrepreneurs and business professionals. They resided in the five cities of West Contra Costa County.

The Shepherd's Way has not been in operation since the early nineties. My father joined the organization in 1989, prior to my fourth grade at Ellerhorst. Mama had attended the meetings with him. They were still working on the food pantry program before the new decade. Mama tried to be a good wife to Daddy, despite their marital crisis. A person can only handle so much in their situations. Only God can only restore broken homes, marriages and families.

Mama had to apply for assistance through community resources. She became determined and motivated by enrolling for courses at Contra Costa College, in San Pablo, California, for the fall 1992 semester.

I will never forget when Mama said, "I am going back to school." This was Daddy's alma mater.

For the first time in her life, Belinda Birdsong developed into a college student. My mother remained there until the fall 1994 semester. Contra Costa College offered diplomas and Associate degrees, as a two-year undergraduate institution. Happiness for Mama's college enrollment placed a smile on my face.

As the company of friends and classmates seemed to be excited, I was hurting on the inside and frustrated. I became the innocent child, due to James and Belinda Birdsong's failing marriage. Daddy's behavior did not change for the better. Emotions are reality for children that make observations as their parent's marriage is on the verge of sadness.

CHAPTER THIRTEEN

Innocent Child in the Middle

Children are innocent and vulnerable. They are special in God's eyes and have a purpose on this earth. The Purpose-Driven Life, by Rick Warren, becomes a reflection. There had been a Kingdom Calling assignment before my mother conceived me at birth. God knew what I had gone through at Maine Avenue. It is not easy for a person to share what they have encountered in childhood.

The Lord is allowing me to write this book for a purpose. People dearest to my heart said, "James, the world needs to know your story."

This chapter is going to explain the trials and tests of an innocent child in the middle. What do you mean James as an innocent child in the middle?

If you take the time to read and analyze the whole concept of this situation, of James and Belinda Birdsong's marital crisis, will come to your undivided attention. Before I share common details of this identity, I am going to share the specifics of additional major headlines in the media. In the early hours of August 2, 1990, more than 100,000 Iraqi troops moved tanks, helicopters, and trucks across the border into Kuwait. Iraq maintained the world's fourth–largest military and had mobilized an overwhelming invading force. Within an hour, they reached Kuwait City, and by daybreak, Iraqi tanks were attacking Dasman Palace, the Royal residence (pbs.org, 2002-2011).

Saddam Hussein became the focus of this invasion of Kuwait.

The fifth President of Iraq, he served in this capacity from July 16, 1979, until April 9, 2003. The invasion proceeded to the Gulf War. President George H.W. Bush was the commander-in-chief during that time. The war began on August 2, 1990, and concluded on February 28, 1991, the operations leading to the buildup of troops and defense of Saudi Arabia.

Operation Desert Storm, in the combat phase, was a war by coalition forces led by the United States against Iraq, in response to the invasion and annexation of Kuwait. The war lasted approximately six months. There is a pastor I met that served in the United States Marine Corps during the Gulf War. He is now a veteran of the armed forces. I was 10-years-old when Iraq did the invasion of Kuwait.

The marital crisis of James and Belinda Birdsong, indeed, became many tales in my opinion. I always say children suffer the most in the situation. They are innocent bystanders and did not cause the marriage of their parents to fail. Children across the United States and abroad will read this book.

I can relate to them as it comes to parents being married and problems beginning to escalate. This had a mental effect on me. People would see me happy and sometimes smile. They did not know about my true feelings. I did not have anyone that I could talk to, for advice and counsel, outside of my circle of family and friends.

One evening, before I went to bed, I fell on my knees and prayed as always. This time things were different in the prayer. I said, "Lord, I am so tired of my parents fighting and arguing all the time. Daddy has changed and I don't know what else to do. Please take me, Jesus."

I am not speaking from a fictional tale. This is the 100% truth, and I am not ashamed to admit this to the world. A few days later, Mama walked downstairs and greeted me. Her expression notified there was a problem. "I have something to say, Mama," I said sadly. She stopped and listened.

"Mama, I want to die. I am tired of going through this."

No child should ever feel this way. I need every parent to listen and pay close attention to your children.

Sadness came upon Mama. In that moment, she tells me, "It is not worth it. If this happens, you will have missed out on so much in your life. This will hurt me for the rest of my life, and those that really do love you."

Mama's words gave me a change of heart. I had thoughts of suicide. I could have been dead and buried at Rolling Hills Memorial Park. Mama acted and called Dr. Jenkins. She informed him about the situation. He recommended professional counseling for me through a psychologist. Not aware of what Mama did, I learned about this later. Daddy never realized his only son had suicidal thoughts.

What made matters worse, Daddy never particularly cared for Tony. I had him since he was a puppy. I could never understand why my own father disliked our dog. He became well observant as a guard dog. Tony was kept in the backyard. I loved him so much and so did Mama. Tony was well taken care of, to the best of our ability. You can imagine the expression on Tony's face every time he saw me.

Dogs have senses just like humans. They know how to express their feelings and attention towards their owners. While dogs do possess emotions, they are not as complex as a human's. Dogs do, however, feel the emotions coming from humans. They feel our emotions as energy radiating from our bodies. The dog knows if you are sad, nervous, stressed, happy, calm, strong-minded, confident, passive, anxious, hyper, meek, etc. (dogbreedinfo.com, 1998-2016).

Tony remained in our lives for seven years, until the

morning of October 19, 1993. I will never forget this day. God gave me the strength to share this story. I walked to the bus stop on the corner of Harbour Way South and Virginia Avenue. I had classes that day at Adams Middle School, in Richmond. Tony would run from one corner of the fence to another in our backyard. He did this every time I departed for school.

That afternoon, I took my key and unlocked the front door. Mama had classes at Contra Costa College. The only person in the house was Daddy. I placed my backpack on the floor and proceeded to the backyard.

I opened the backyard door and called Tony. He was nowhere around. I began to get worried. This was not like him. About three minutes later, I stormed upstairs to Daddy's room. He and Mama shared this room when their marriage was beautiful. My parents were still sleeping in separate rooms. Can you imagine the anger I had in this situation? He was resting on the bed.

"Daddy, where is Tony? He is not in the backyard."

Being argumentative with me, he did not want to cooperate with me. "Junior, he was a naughty dog," he said. "He became a problem."

From that moment, the Lord revealed to me what happened. As much as I loved my father, despite the dilemma at our house, I became more disappointed in him. His words did not register well about Tony's whereabouts.

The week before this situation, Daddy went downstairs to the laundry room in the morning. His caregiver had already departed for the day. Home alone and no one to assist him due to his blindness, he placed his shoe brushes in the washing machine. Once the brushes finished washing, Daddy removed them and opened the backyard door. He placed the brushes on the porch to dry. Tony suddenly attacked him. I am not sure what happened that made Tony attack. One thing I know for sure, my dog never did that before to Daddy. I know what my father told me and Mama, after bringing Tony home as a puppy. The Contra Costa Animal Services were notified. Satan constantly attacked the Birdsong family household, from my parent's marital crisis to their son's suicidal thoughts.

My seventh-grade year, at Adams Middle School, became a time of unhappiness for me. For those of you that were my classmates, I had to go home to school and face the crisis all over again. This is what God revealed to me. Daddy contacted the animal services to remove Tony from the premises after I and Mama departed for our classes.

I believed this was revenge. It became a long time for me to heal over the loss of Tony. God does not dwell in anything that is unclean and unrighteous. The news about Tony spread in the community. Other situations at our home resulted, that I prefer not to disclose. You may be asking, "James, your father is blind. How can he physically abuse his wife?" Did you hear of the power structure? Since he never regained his vision, Daddy had individuals that demonstrated jealousy towards Mama. They wanted to do her physical harm. While I am not going to disclose the details of one event, at our home, this still made me an innocent child.

Encounters of nightmares affected my sleep at night. I did not reflect on this pattern during classes on campus. Mama became very aware of the nightmares. The marital crisis of Mama and Daddy reminded me of a time capsule. When you entered the time capsule, our imagination will take us either to the past or future events. It seemed like yesterday, a beautiful love story between James and Belinda Birdsong. The episode became a tragedy.

I watched comedy sitcoms and sci-fi episodes on television. They included a time capsule. If they desired to step back in past or predictions in future events, the person had their wish granted. You must remember time capsules are fictional and not actual. Explanation of this theory gives us a more in-depth knowledge and understanding. Standing as the innocent child developed the redemption stages. They are good in a time of crisis. Clim and JoEvelyn launched their church, Holy Mission Christian Center, on Nevin Avenue near the Chevron Richmond Refinery and the Santa Fe Rail Depot. The building, once belonging to Now Faith Church of God in Christ, was nearby.

Started as a non-denominational church, Clim decided to re-establish his affiliation in the Church of God in Christ, in the mid-nineties. He and JoEvelyn eventually were appointed in positions of their jurisdiction. Based on the bylaws and doctrines of the Church of God in Christ, they had to connect and serve under a jurisdictional bishop.

Even though I am no longer affiliated with the Church of God in Christ, I still have the official manual that had been in publication since 1971. If you read the manual, the constitution of the Church of God in Christ is listed.

The late Bishop Warren Wilson served as the Jurisdictional Prelate of the Church of God in Christ, California Valley Jurisdiction, in Fresno, California. He appointed Clim as a District Superintendent. For the women's department, Mother Blanche McGee led that role. She made the appointment for JoEvelyn to serve as a District Missionary. Today the California Valley Jurisdiction is presided by Bishop Samuel Doyle. I never had the opportunity to meet Bishop Wilson.

Mama remained a member at Prayer House. We had stopped church attendance as a family due to the marital crisis. Daddy and I rode with Clim in his Dodge Ram 15 passenger van from the eighties. We walked into the sanctuary. His family and in-laws were in attendance. The young people singing in the choir captured my undivided attention. I immediately recognized four girls that were members of the choir. They were JoEvelyn's granddaughters.

Two of the granddaughters, Jessica and Mercedes, were the lead soloists of the choir. They had the most beautiful, amazing voices. If they had pursued this opportunity, the record labels would have considered a contract for them to be recording artists. I remembered an interesting conversation with JoEvelyn about the music industry. She wanted her beautiful granddaughters to be discovered and go far in music. I totally agreed 100% in this position.

Clim preached on this Sunday and extended the invitation to discipleship. Tears began to come upon me. This had never happened to me before. Sitting in the pulpit alongside Clim, JoEvelyn and two ministers, Daddy already knew in his spirit Holy Mission was going to be his new church home. Besides, he and Clim's friendship extended to 1968.

Still crying, I approached the pulpit and walked over to Daddy. He hugged me. On this day, we became founding members of Holy Mission Christian Center. I joined the choir. Rehearsals were held on Saturday afternoons. I became active in the church, by attending Wednesday night Bible study, evangelistic services on Friday evenings, and the youth Sunday school class.

A few weeks after joining the church, I was baptized in the name of Jesus Christ, according to Acts 2:38. Daddy performed my portion of the baptism service as Clim and another minister was in the baptismal pool. The Lord called me to preach at three years old. Now, I was baptized at 10-years-old.

I continued to face problems at home, and how the enemy destroyed James and Belinda Birdsong's marriage. Effects of the dilemma caused me to be the innocent child.

Many years later, I asked my mother about joining Holy Mission. "The Lord never directed me to become a member," Mama said.

There is one thing I know about her. She is the kind of person that believed in abiding by the truth in God's Word and being honest. If something was not right, then Mama was strong enough to have a standpoint in her position. A few months at Holy Mission, Clim approached me and said, "You are the example to the youth." The understanding came to mind. He and Daddy must have had numerous conversations about my participation in the choir and activities. They believed more young people would begin to come and be part of the church. This 10-year-old African-American boy, born and raised in Richmond, California, encountered problems at home, arguments among my parents, suicidal thoughts, and our family members were not aware of the issues.

Albert's brothers and sisters continued their visits to him, Barbara and their two sons. They were Daddy's first cousins. Some of them lived in Los Angeles, while others were still living in Greenwood and Shreveport. Two of Albert's brothers, the late William Birdsong, lived in Phoenix, Arizona. His eldest brother, the late George E. Birdsong, Jr., moved to Fairbanks, Alaska many years ago. George served in the United States Army as a Staff Sergeant.

Every time they came to visit Albert and Barbara, they told him, "James Charles, we are coming to Richmond to see you, Belinda and Junior." He knew the dates of their visits. My father informed his female friends and the people that never cared for him not to visit while the family was present.

Daddy did not want the members of our family outside the Bay Area to know what occurred in our home. He knew they would be disappointed on how his wife was being mistreated.

I did not take notice of this pattern until the early nineties. They would have reminded him about Grandmother Charlene's discipline. She did not play games. It's hard to believe, isn't it? There is no reason for me to tell lies. Again, I loved my father very much, and yes, he taught me so much about the Birdsong family legacy. Daddy's knowledge of African-American history became valuable to me. He was born and raised in Greenwood, Louisiana during the late thirties, after the Great Depression.

I desired for things to be normal again with Mama and Daddy. Unfortunately, the marriage was failing. Despite what a person's character portrays, there's good inside of them. An unforgettable event in July 1991 originated. I had dreamed of going to Disneyland, a theme park in Anaheim, California. Famous to millions globally as "the happiest place on earth," this had stayed their motto for years. For me, I had continuously prayed for God to bring this to fruition. One afternoon, at home on Maine Avenue, Daddy wanted to speak to me.

"Junior, come here. I have something to tell you," he said.

I was in my room playing with the Hot Wheels Freight Yard train set I received for Christmas in 1983. I told him, "I'm coming, Daddy."

I walked in his room that he once shared with Mama. Daddy gave me the news I did not expect. We are going to Disneyland for the weekend," he said, with a smile on his face. The excitement became overwhelming for me.

A few weeks later, the choir at Holy Mission had to sing at Kingdom Land Baptist Church on Nevin Avenue, where Reverend Leslie James was the pastor. I departed the service before Reverend James finished his sermon. Upon returning home, I said goodbye to Mama. Daddy and I proceeded on the road trip to Los Angeles. He requested a member at Apostolic Temple of Truth to drive us there.

The following morning, we arrived in Los Angeles, after lodging at a rest stop adjunct to Interstate 5 near Bakersfield, California. The three of us proceeded to Lee Arthur's apartment at a senior citizen's complex. George had obligations. Daddy and Lee Arthur had their conversation about their childhood memories in Greenwood, Louisiana.

Four hours later, George arrived and greeted us. We followed him to his house in Long Beach. I could not stop thinking about Disneyland.

"This is amazing. My dream finally came true," I said. Everything from the parades to Space Mountain brought excitement to me. The commercials on television captured this young man's attention. Daddy had his moments during this journey. He wanted me to be happy. We had breakfast at George's fiancée's house on that Saturday morning. Her name was Cynthia. She played a documentary about the life and career of Mahalia Jackson. It portrayed the story of the World's Greatest Gospel Singer and her rise to fame. I listened to Mahalia's music early in life. The big moment had finally come. The five of us departed Cynthia's house for the drive to Disneyland.

Anaheim is located 26 miles south of Los Angeles, in Orange County, California. From Long Beach to Anaheim, we arrived in approximately thirty-five minutes. The entrance to Disneyland had an extensive line of people from different ethnicities, from children to senior citizens.

Once the tickets were purchased at the booth, Daddy said, "Son, what do you want to do first?" I immediately had the answer for him. "I want to ride the monorail train," I said, with joy and excitement.

We boarded the train and made a stop at the Disneyland Hotel station, before proceeding on the entire ride around the park. This 11-year-old boy could not believe he settled on

Disneyland soil. The feeling reminded me of a child running to open their Christmas gifts. Once the monorail train ride ended, I remembered us boarding a submarine. How many of you remember the Disney motion picture, *The Little Mermaid?*

On the ride on the submarine, the characters of the Little Mermaid were on display as if they were a reality. I was like, "Wow, this is so cool." Throughout the day, we continued to experience rides, such as the Space Mountain and Big Thunder roller coasters. Daddy and I even went to a popular attraction where they had race cars. I had to do the driving. Later in the evening, crowds of people watched the popular Disneyland parade.

Did I see Mickey and Minnie Mouse? This 11-year-old boy had seen them, besides other Disney characters. The five of us departed from Disneyland and returned to Long Beach.

Daddy told me, "We are going to Sunset Missionary Baptist Church, in Los Angeles, tomorrow." The pastor of the church at the time was my cousin, Reverend DeWayne Birdsong. He was Albert's nephew. I wanted to go home.

We packed our belongings later that evening. The following day Daddy, along with George, myself and his friend from Apostolic Temple of Truth, proceeded to Sunday morning services at Sunset. DeWayne and his father, Martin E. Birdsong, Sr., were glad to see us. Martin once served as a deacon at the church. He and his wife, Catherine, had visited us in Richmond throughout the years.

The four of us did not stay for the entire service. One thing I can say about my father, he believed in completing a task at a certain time. He was a man of order, in a business perspective. We said goodbye to DeWayne and proceeded with our journey on Interstate 5 back to the Bay Area. I knew this route between Northern and Southern California very well. I had traveled on Interstate 5 throughout my life. Once the car pulled up in the driveway on Maine Avenue, I walked into the house and hugged Mama.

My experience at Disneyland continues to be a reflection for me more than twenty-five years later. I do desire to visit there again. My niece Demetria worked at Disneyland about two years ago, for a brief time. The position of being an innocent child continued for me on Maine Avenue. The marital dilemma of James and Belinda Birdsong just would not improve for the better. This is a reality. How will my school life change for me? The next chapter will explain this very clearly. I am not done writing and explaining.

CHAPTER FOURTEEN
School in the Inner-city

The adjustments of environment comes to remembrance for me, in this particular situation. I listen to the concerns of our children. In the recent decade, the status of bullying has become worse than the last twenty-five to thirty years. Can I relate to the problems of young people being victims of being teased and provoked by their peers that portray themselves bullies?

Yes, I can relate to this topic.

This chapter is going to be the story about my school attendance, from the suburbs to the inner-city. I successfully completed the fourth grade in June 1990, at Ellerhorst Elementary School. The tenure at Ellerhorst became a comfort zone. I attended more field trips than at any other school. You are aware of the upbringing on Maine Avenue in Richmond.

Ian had transferred to Tara Hills Elementary School and our teacher we all loved so much, Ms. Mahrt, had already retired in June 1989, at 62-years-old. She continued to remain in contact with me throughout the nineties.

Ellerhorst conferred numerous certificates of awards upon me starting in first grade. I still have them to this day, more than twenty-five years later. I am a child of the inner-city that is considered by African-Americans as the ghetto. My cousins and childhood friends were right there in the same community. They lived three to five blocks from me. Anticipating the fifth grade, I truly believed Ellerhorst would remain my comfort zone again. Administrators at the Richmond Unified School District decided to make significant changes throughout the region.

First, the children had to attend the school nearest to their homes. There was one change that affected the special education students such as myself. I am referring to budget cuts for school buses as their transportation accommodations. The budget cuts happened in the early nineties. Bay Area journalists reported the story on television, radio and newspapers. The State of California had a Republican Governor in office.

My cousins and friends in the neighborhood were students at Nystrom Elementary School. If you go back and read previous chapters, this school has been mentioned. Nystrom is one of the oldest elementary schools in Richmond. The school has a history that extends to the 1920s. Daddy did everything he could for me to continue as a student at Ellerhorst, for the fifth grade. Unfortunately, that never occurred and fear came upon me.

Early in life, I became aware of stereotypes. Racism became the factor. When a person is raised around peers of diverse cultures, discrimination becomes one of the last things on your mind. Allow me to share the three identification models of this description.

First, I surrounded myself among the children in our circle. They attended an inner-city elementary school as James Charles Birdsong, Jr. went to class in the suburbs. Second, I am an African-American male born with a developmental disability and, third, I appeared to be different from my peers in the community. We classify the identification models as adults, once childhood and adolescence stages has acquired the course. I began summer school at Valley View Elementary School, for six weeks, in El Sobrante. I continued to ride the bus from my house as a special education student.

Minnie was our driver for this route. She previously worked as the bus driver in my fourth-grade year at Ellerhorst. This is not the same Minnie that lived on 9th Street. Who can forget about Minnie? She was very sweet and had compassion. Yes, she came from the old school. In those times, the bus drivers gave certificates of awards to students that demonstrated good behavior and character. Minnie gave me a certificate of award, by the end of summer school. I still have it today.

The next month in August, the administrators at the Richmond Unified School District made a telephone call to Mama and Daddy. They gave the news I feared.

"Reverend and Mrs. Birdsong, your son will not be attending Ellerhorst anymore. The district has made changes. He is going to attend Nystrom, since you reside in the community."

I am not going to speak negative about this position. If you were raised in Richmond during that era, Nystrom had a reputation. The school was known for fights and suspensions. The community became aware of Nystrom's status. Activities of gangs, drug dealers and shootings escalated in our community, by the early nineties.

We had neighborhood watch meetings in the eighties, where my parents and our neighbors came together to discuss solutions for the community to be more secure. Officers from the Richmond Police Department attended these meetings as advisors. In the highlight of Daddy's popularity, he became an advocate for the neighborhood watch meetings. I am going to resume this story. My friends were happy about me attending school with them. If they are reading this book, I became unhappy about the decision of the school district. These friends of mine were correct in one position. No classmates of mine at Ellerhorst came to visit me, except for Ian.

The clear majority resided in Pinole and Hercules. Some lived in San Pablo, El Sobrante, Hilltop, North Richmond, Central Richmond and El Cerrito. I did not have any that resided in Point Richmond. Ian and his parents lived in Kensington. Pinole and Hercules had a majority Caucasian population. Both cities also had African-Americans, Asians and Hispanics. I remembered a handful of families who were of Middle Eastern and Indian descent. Ellerhorst is not the only elementary school in Pinole. You have Collins, Shannon and Tara Hills.

On the first day of school, Mama hugged me as always. Standing next to the front door, she laid hands and prayed for me. Mama knew how I felt about Nystrom. I missed Ellerhorst and the school remained in my thoughts, for this pattern.

Daddy sat on his chair in our living room as usual. Mama kissed me on the cheek and said, "It's going to be alright. I am praying for you."

I said goodbye to my parents as usual, and walked across the street to begin the fifth grade at Nystrom. Upon arrival on campus, I went to the office. The secretary told me where to go for class.

James, your teacher is upstairs in Room 29," she said.

The first day of school was always productive. I immediately proceeded to class and there I met Douglass Castro. He was my fifth-grade teacher, for the 1990-1991 school year. Prior to teaching at Nystrom, Mr. Castro worked in the Oakland Unified School District.   Nystrom had a handful of new teachers that year. He was one of them.

The remaining teachers and staff were pleased about me being a student. They knew Daddy and his work as an activist in Richmond. Mrs. Raff transferred to Nystrom from Ellerhorst. I certainly was not alone in this situation. Mr. Castro had a teacher's assistant named Wanda Calloway. She knew Mama from many years ago. Mrs. Calloway attended Bethel Temple Pentecostal Church on Cutting Boulevard.

You read about Mrs. Dunn, the woman that was my baby

sitter through Jody and Friends, and a longtime family friend of ours. Guess what, everybody? Mrs. Dunn worked at Nystrom as a yard supervisor. I never knew that until the first day of school. Once I walked into Mr. Castro's class, he began with introductions from the students. Sitting at the desk, I listened to each of the classmates. Mr. Castro then glanced at me and said, "It is your turn now." Feeling nervous and not sure what to do, I went ahead and proceeded to introduce myself as the teacher suggested.

"My name is James, and I am new at Nystrom. Last year, I went to Ellerhorst Elementary School. I live across the street from here."

There were some boys in the class that literary made fun of me. I never had gone through this phase before. The first thought that came to me, "I do not like this school. I want to go back to Ellerhorst."

This 10-year-old boy did his best to adjust throughout the day. Another young man said to me, "You talk like a white boy." The comments were cruel and hurtful. I felt insulted and sad on the inside. Mr. Castro made observations of my interaction with my classmates and other students. I became a victim of bullying on the first day of school. Mr. Castro did tell the young men in our class to demonstrate respect for me and one another. The bell rang as classes concluded. I said goodbye to Mr. Castro and Mrs. Calloway. I just wanted to go home.

Once I walked in the house, Mama asked me, "How was your first day of school?" From that moment, she knew something was wrong.

"Mama, I do not want to go back to Nystrom. Those boys bullied and teased me. I want to go back to Ellerhorst."

Daddy was sitting in the living room on his chair. He heard the anger and unhappiness from their son. "Come here, Junior,"

Daddy said. At our house on Maine Avenue, the living room and dining room was to your left and the stairs to the second story was located right.

"Son, tell me what happened across the street at school." I told them about the young men and what happened. My father may have been blind and disabled, but he did not appreciate people wanting to do harm to his son. I am being honest.

James and Belinda Birdsong may have had their marital crisis. When it came to the well-being of their son, they placed their differences to the side. Mama and Daddy were very overprotective of me. They knew God blessed them with a special child. I told them about the young men and what happened. My father may have been blind and disabled, but he did not appreciate people wanting to do harm to his son. I am being honest.

After we had this discussion, Daddy said, "Junior, you are not going back to Nystrom."

"Where is he going for school?" Mama said to her husband.

"Belinda, I am going to call the school district on tomorrow and speak to the superintendent."

As you can see, James Charles Birdsong, Sr. was not playing games. The school administrators at that time, on Bissell Avenue, knew about Daddy's caliber in Richmond among the elite.

Mama said, "Is this phone call for our son to return back to Ellerhorst?"

"Yes, it is, Belinda," Daddy said. "I do not want Junior going to school and he is being bullied."

Uncle Roosevelt died a year earlier. He would not have been pleased on how his nephew was being treated. You must remember this is the early nineties, for this story. The next day, I stayed home from school after our family discussion. Daddy called the superintendent at the district office on Bissell Avenue.

I cannot remember who served in that capacity at the time.

However, Daddy did speak to Sylvester Greenwood, the assistant superintendent of the Richmond Unified School District. Many of us raised in Richmond remembered Mr. Greenwood and his contributions to the community. He once played professional football for the New Orleans Saints. He dedicated his life as an educator for the students throughout Richmond. Mr. Greenwood was well loved and respected. He knew my father. I considered him among the legends and icons in Richmond. Mr. Greenwood understood Daddy's concerns. He died in the late 2000s. There is an academy in Richmond named after him. I am referring to the Sylvester Greenwood Academy on Chanslor Avenue.

A man of compassion, Mr. Greenwood told Daddy, "Reverend Birdsong, I know you want your son back at Ellerhorst. We had to make budget cuts for the buses in our special education program."

My father wanted things as they were before.

"Your son had to go to Nystrom since he lives in the area," Mr. Greenwood said. "The district had to make those changes for all of our students."

To be honest, Mama and Daddy really did not want me back at Ellerhorst. I am not sure to this day. They advocated for Tara Hills. Ian was already there. Ms. Tripp transferred to Tara Hills as a Teacher's Assistant, upon Ms. Mahrt's retirement from Ellerhorst.

"Mr. Greenwood, how am I going to get Junior to Ellerhorst, and I really do not have anyone to drive him there every day?"

He tried to reason with Daddy and told him the truth. He said, "Reverend Birdsong, there is no more room at Ellerhorst and we had to cut the budget for the buses. The district is going through some hard times right now."

"What about Tara Hills Elementary School?" Daddy asked Mr. Greenwood.

Mama picked up the phone and joined the conversation, after she walked in the house. The conversation lasted for about twenty-five to thirty minutes. Mr. Greenwood told my parents, "I am going to call the principal at Tara Hills, to see if there is any room for your son to attend school. You will be responsible for his transportation."

Before he called the district office, Daddy had already spoken to Mr. Castro explaining the situation. Daddy still wanted the bus service for me. Arrangements for someone to take me to either Ellerhorst or Tara Hills was the last thought on his mind.

The eighties had departed, and fresh faces of leadership were in office during the early nineties. For the first two weeks of school, Mr. Castro, Mrs. Calloway and classmates did not see me on campus. My friends in the neighborhood knew something was wrong. I already told them about what happened. Sometimes in life, you cannot please everybody. I will forever be grateful for their concerns. They wanted me to be at school alongside them.

Parents, it is important to be active in your children's school activities and do observations of their teachers and principals. You have the lawful right and obligation to protect them and invest in their future.

James, did you resume your attendance at Ellerhorst? The answer is no. My season at Ellerhorst was officially over after fourth grade. Tara Hills did not have any more room. The school district informed my parents for me to return to Nystrom, immediately.

The principal at the time was Darlene Jones. She reminded me of the female Joe Clark from the motion picture, *Lean on Me*, starring Morgan Freeman. Mrs. Jones did not play any games and, yes, she believed in discipline. Aware of the situation, Mrs. Jones made a promise to my parents.

"I will watch out for your son," Mrs. Jones said. She was very fond of me. Mrs. Jones had one young man expelled from the school for bullying me.

After many years as a principal and, later, a special education specialist, Mrs. Jones retired. She is doing well. One cousin of mine that is very special to me, Seyyida Westbrook, attended Nystrom together with me. The two of us have been close since childhood. Her best friend and a young woman that I consider my cousin, Joyce, was there with us at Nystrom.

Seyyida was in the fourth grade. Her sister, Lula, attended Nystrom in the eighties. Lula and I share the same birthday. We have a five-year age difference between us. Seyyida did not appreciate the young men bullying me on campus. She knew how to fight. Lula told me years later about this incident.

Mrs. Jones suspended Seyyida for fighting. She lived three blocks from me, with Lula and their mother, Jackie, on Sixth Street. My cousin came home from Nystrom one afternoon.

Jackie asked her daughter, "Sadie, why did you get suspended?"

"Mama, I am tired of those boys at school messing with Cousin James," Seyyida said. "They always making fun and want to fight him. I had to fight this one boy for messing with him." I am laughing as this chapter is being written. Jackie could not believe this was happening. Many years later, I told this story to a church mother in a telephone conversation before her death.

Her words reflected on me. "Baby, those boys were jealous of you. They knew you were different, and the girls had admiration for you."

Other people also gave me confirmation. I did not begin to

like girls until the fifth grade. I had my first kiss, at 8-years-old, from a girl that lived two houses from me. The kiss was very real. It's hard to believe. We kissed more than once. I am not going to lie about this experience. She was about a year younger than me. Her sister and I were close friends. They lived in the neighborhood for four years, before moving to be close to Peres Elementary School. This girl and her sisters were students at Nystrom.

The awards continued to be bestowed upon me at the school. Mr. Castro presented me with honors, such as, Best Scholar, Outstanding Citizenship, High Test Scores and others. If you attended Nystrom, the Blue-Ribbon Program began in 1990 by Dorothy Reeves, a kindergarten teacher. She is now retired. I was one of the original Blue-Ribbon students that received twelve certificates of awards. I still have them to this date.

If you had an outstanding performance in class among your classmates, and academics, the teacher selected you to be a Blue-Ribbon Student. We would go downstairs to the multi-purpose room and watch movies on a large screen television. Popularity among the teachers and fellow students occurred in the fifth grade.

The establishment of friendships were made among peers of mine. They began to visit me at the house on Maine Avenue, and came to my defense if I was being targeted. A week before my eleventh birthday, Mr. Castro and Mrs. Raff accompanied their students to the popular California Academy of Sciences, for a field trip.

Located in the renowned Golden Gate Park of San Francisco, the California Academy of Sciences consisted of an aquarium and planetarium. I had visited the aquarium on three prior occasions. Earlier field trips for me were the San Francisco and Oakland Zoos, Tilden Regional Park in Berkeley, California,

Point Pinole Regional Shoreline near Pinole, the Lawrence Hall of Science at the University of California Berkeley, and further Bay Area attractions.

Mr. Castro knew I had a birthday. He had something planned for me and decided to move this into action. On the morning of May 16, 1991, he brought a cake on campus. Mama was in the kitchen washing dishes and looked out the window. She witnessed Mr. Castro giving the cake, sodas, napkins and plates to Audre Henry and another teacher.

He told them, "Today is James birthday and we are going to give him a surprise birthday party."

Mrs. Henry worked closely with Mr. Castro and Mrs. Raff, in the special education program. She was a teacher and a specialist. Mama already knew what they were doing. I had already arrived on campus. Later that afternoon, Mr. Castro told me, "James, I need you to take this to Mrs. Raff."

He sent me to her class as they prepared for the party. Remember now, I did not know about this plan. There were plans for a birthday party at the house on Saturday.

Mrs. Raff and her students greeted me. She asked me to do a lecture on astronomy. He must have told Mrs. Raff about the surprise birthday party. Her class became impressed with my knowledge of astronomy and the written correspondences with NASA. I had known Mrs. Raff since the first grade at Ellerhorst. She then turned around and said, "Class, do you have any questions for James?"

They asked me questions, and I did the best of my ability to answer them. I departed to make my way back to Mr. Castro's class. You are not going to believe what happened next.

Mr. Castro and the class yelled, "Surprise."

I took my hand and placed it upon my chest in shock. They began to sing Happy Birthday to me. Before I blew out the candles on the cake, I said, "Don't you ever do this me again."

They laughed as the party began. This was my first and only surprise birthday party. I am not a fan of surprise parties.

Mrs. Henry and her assistant came to the room. I told Mama about the party. She already knew about this from her witnessed account. In other words, she saw Mr. Castro giving the cake to Mrs. Henry and another teacher. On that Saturday, I had a second birthday party at the house. There were more than 100 people invited to attend. Only fifteen were presented. Ian and his parents came. The Teenage Mutant Ninja Turtles became one of the favorite animated cartoons of mine. The birthday cake had candles of the four turtles and Shredder. The cake had two different fillings. They were strawberry and lemon. A few of my friends in Mr. Castro's class attended the party.

On June 14, 1991, after a challenging year, I successfully completed the fifth grade at Nystrom. Ellerhorst became a memory for me. I did not desire to return there, at all. God knew what He was doing.

A few weeks later, Daddy called me into the room and told me about our upcoming trip to Disneyland. Since the age of eight, I constantly requested Mama and Daddy to take me there. If you go back and read Chapter Thirteen, I provided further details about the Disneyland adventure. The summer of 1991 became the longest time for me. Did I attend summer school anywhere in the school district? I decided not to go this route after completing fifth grade.

My mind reflects to this time. It's been twenty-seven years since I first stepped foot on Nystrom soil. Times does go by fast. All I ever wanted was for Mama and Daddy to reconcile their differences. I desired to be happy during the storm. I looked forward to the sixth grade, as the final stages of elementary school became the center focus in pre-adolescence stages. God had his hands upon me from birth. The story still needs to be told. I am not done speaking about the redemption.

JAMES C. BIRDSONG, JR.

CHAPTER FIFTEEN

When God Has His Hands on You

The scripture declares, "For I the LORD thy God will hold thy right hand, saying unto thee, Fear not; I will help thee" (Isaiah 41:13). Patience requires humbleness in the redemption. During the midst of trials and tribulations, God has His hands upon us. Our testimonies in victory comes from the test.

Eventually, I had to give myself reminders the Lord is going to bring me through the storm and rain.

I resumed the final stages of elementary school in September 1991, for the sixth grade, at Nystrom. Mr. Castro decided to transfer back to the Oakland Unified School District. On the first day of school, I inquired about him. Mr. Castro was a great teacher.

I had seen Mrs. Calloway on campus. "Where is Mr. Castro?" I asked.

She looked at me and said, "James, he will not be returning to Nystrom anymore. He's in Oakland teaching now."

Shocked and speechless, I made the decision to locate him. In those days, we had telephone directories. They had the white pages of residents. This was before the internet and online search engines. Daddy had around four telephone directories. I searched for Mr. Castro in the Oakland edition.

I located a listing for him. I made the pursuit to call Mr. Castro that week. We stayed in communication for the next several years. I had a new teacher. Her name was Donna Grove. She first arrived at Nystrom, at the same time as Mr. Castro. I had been blessed to be among wonderful teachers. She became my favorite teacher, and we became very close in later years. This woman knew I had potential, and gave me encouragement to move forth.

Everywhere I go, I always bring Mrs. Grove's name to the forefront. She and her husband, Ronald, have been very supportive to me since the sixth grade. The Groves lived in Hercules, at the time. They had a daughter named Justine. She once worked for NASA, at the Ames Research Center located at Moffett Field near San Jose.

Mr. Grove worked as a manager in the hotel industry. If any of the students disrespected Mrs. Grove, she knew I would come to her defense. The girls continued to approach me. In the fifth grade, they started to defend me from the boys that bullied me. Did the bullying and teasing continue toward me in the sixth grade? I made many friends. To be honest with you, I had more friends at Nystrom than Ellerhorst. They continued to watch out for me. During the final year of elementary school, I had a girlfriend. We really liked each other.

Out of respect for her, I am not going to mention this young lady's name. She still lives in Richmond. Daddy was very fond of her. We began to call each other and, yes, this young lady came over to visit me. By this time, Seyyida was in the fifth grade and had one more year to go.

The neighborhood began to escalade with violence. I am going to give a testimony of survival. Normally, I rode my bicycle every day after school. The tires became low on air. I stopped riding and said, "I need to add air to my bicycle tires."

Ben Marshall's Exxon Station was located on Harbour Way South and Cutting Boulevard near the Interstate 580 West entrance for the Richmond-San Rafael Bridge toll plaza.

Mr. Marshall and his brother, Morris, were highly respected in the community. They knew Daddy for many years. As a matter of fact, Morris worked as a mechanic. The Marshall Brothers lived to be into their eighties. I walked over to the gasoline station and greeted Mr. Marshall. Who can remember his smile and sense of humor? I am speaking to those that were raised in Richmond. He loved talking to customers.

"I need some air in the tires of my bicycle, Mr. Marshall."

He looked at me and said, "Go ahead, young man." This man truly loved his family and had compassion for others. I will always remember the elders in Richmond that made significant contributions to the community. Most are deceased. The Marshall Brothers died in the mid-late 2000s.

Once the tires were filled with air, I said goodbye to Mr. Marshall. I planned to resume riding the bicycle. Within seconds, my life flashed right before me. A shooting took place. Richmond had more murders than other cities of the Bay Area. The highest murder rate occurred in North Richmond.

Scared and not sure what to do, I had to be very cautious. I was praying and asking the Lord for His protection.

I walked on the left sidewalk of Harbour Way South alongside the bicycle. An elderly African-American married couple had a front yard. To this day, I cannot remember their names. I hid behind the bushes of their property. An elderly woman came to the screen of her door. Concerned for my safety, she said, "Hurry up and come in the house, baby."

Mama and Daddy were at home on Maine Avenue around the corner facing north. "May I use the phone to call my mother?" I asked the couple. "I live around the corner on Maine Avenue. Mr. and Mrs. Birdsong are my parents." They were familiar with my father's activism and work in the community.

I called Mama and she answered on the second ring. The only thing on my mind, "Lord, I just want to get home safe." Mama answered the phone. "Where are you right now, James?"

I know her and Daddy were paranoid. "I am at the house of an elderly couple on Harbour Way South near Virginia Avenue," I told her. "May I use the phone to call my mother?" "Let me speak to them," Mama said.

I passed the phone to the elderly lady as her husband listened. Afterwards, she made her way from the house and prayed. Mama had to be careful. Gun shots continued to roar. Richmond had a reputation of crime and violence, at the time.

Less than two minutes, Mama arrived safely at the elderly couple's house. She told the couple, "Thank you so much for your help."

"Please be careful going home," the elderly man said to us.

"We will," Mama said to the couple.

I retrieved my bicycle and walked behind Mama. The hands of God existed upon her, just as if she became Harriett Tubman. Cautious the whole time, Mama told me, "James, stay right behind me. We are going to walk quietly."

The shooting suddenly stopped. We walked to the corner of the house on Maine Avenue. Mama looked to see if the coast was clear.

"It's clear now. We are going to go inside the house very quickly."

We did not see anyone at that moment. The both of us walked to the stairs, and opened the door. We were now safe inside of our home. Someone in the neighborhood notified the police moments later.

The Lord delivered me. I reflect to this day and came to one conclusion. Ladies and gentlemen, James Charles Birdsong, Jr. could have been dead and named among the list of young people in Richmond that were victims of gang violence and shootings. More shootings happened in Richmond and reported on the news throughout the Bay Area.

Devastation came upon the thoughts of the community. It seemed like the shootings would never stop. They had their fears and worries. God's protection is upon us as His children traveling through this barren land. The Biblical writer quotes, "Be strong and of a good courage, fear not, nor be afraid of them: for the LORD thy God, he it is that doth go with three, he will not fail thee, nor forsake thee" (Deuteronomy 31:6).

When God has His hands on you, the enemy is defeated. No matter how much he tries to attack, the Lord always dispatches His angels of protection. Growing up in this era, I surrounded myself with anointed Men and Women of God that had a Divine connection through intercessory prayer.

In the early nineties, the Richmond Police Department developed a plan to build substations in different regions of the city. This became approved by the Richmond City Council as crime escalated. I want you to know despite how society views Richmond, there are those individuals that are a positive influence in the community. It would take me an entire year to name these men and women.

I remember being upstairs and looking out of our bathroom window on some evenings as fire and police officials were on duty. Sometimes they had calls from residents as far as Maine Avenue and 2nd Street. I will never forget the prayer warriors in our community. They prayed and cried out to God for a change in Richmond. Victims of gang violence were transported by helicopter to John Muir Hospital in Concord, California. This hospital was recognized in the Bay Area for treatment of trauma victims. As of today, John Muir Hospital is a primary medical facility.

Do I remember Cal Star helicopters landing at the Martin Luther King, Jr. Park? Yes, I do. In the evenings, the California Highway Patrol had their air patrol unit to perform from a helicopter. I remember that Bell Jet Ranger very well. I had the opportunity to view this aircraft up close on two separate occasions. Why the violence escalated in my hometown? People began to address these questions on strategies for peace in the community. Again, I must remind you, James Charles Birdsong, Jr. was a child of the inner-city that had a purpose in life ordained by God. Determination to beat the odds and pursue life success, primarily set the tone for my journey as a dreamer and achiever. I reflect to my life and transcend today on the well-being for today's youth.

The violence became worse in North Richmond. This section of my hometown, of that era, was majority African-American and a few Hispanics. My parents and I knew families that resided in North Richmond. I remember the bus drivers driving through North Richmond transporting classmates that attended Ellerhorst with me. They were residents, and attended church services with their parents and siblings.

Sometime in the early 2000s, one of the teachers from elementary school informed me about a classmate of mine at Nystrom. He was murdered as he sat in his car. The police found him the next day. You should have seen my facial expression upon hearing the news. I began to pray for my hometown, as well as inner-city communities throughout the United States.

The sad part of this young man's murder was based upon the fact he was only 21-years-old. I am not sure if he was mixed up with the wrong association of people. Some of the young men in Richmond, of my generation, at that time, did not live to witness their eighteenth or twenty first birthday due to the violence of the streets. Some were innocent bystanders, while others joined gangs. I am going to be honest. Please take a moment to reflect on the decision factor. Yes, the hands of the Lord are upon us in situations. He gives us free Will to become committed solely to Him alone.

The scripture reads, "If any man will do his Will, he shall know of the doctrine, whether it be of God, or whether I speak of myself" (John 7:17). The decisions become testing grounds of common sense. This is where the testing ground in decision factors presents opportunities for us to remain on the positive or negative direction. During the nineties, the community wore T-shirts that displayed the names of young men and women in Richmond and other cities that were murdered by drug dealers and gang members. The more names increased, the more T-shirts had to be made. My name could have been included on the T-shirt. By God's grace and His protection upon my life, I am a survivor of the storm.

I could have easily allowed the influence of the streets to capture my attention, to engage in this lifestyle. James and Belinda Birdsong raised me to make positive decisions. Our decisions can beco God had his hands upon me as I reflect to December 25, 1990. On Christmas Day, I received a new bicycle from Mama as one of my gifts. She knew I desired to have a bicycle.

On this morning, I woke up and ran downstairs to our living room, as usual. My mouth dropped as I saw this stunning blue bicycle with white tires. This bicycle was popular in the nineties. Our piano was decorated with Christmas cards from family and friends. There was one problem in this situation. This 10-year-old boy did not know how to ride a bicycle. me the maker or breaker moment in the pathway.

"We are going to go across the street so you can learn to ride it," Mama said.

I am grateful to the Lord for my mother. She has always pushed me to strive for excellence. It's the same bicycle I had when the tires were low on air, as I mentioned earlier in this chapter.

Later, in the morning of Christmas Day, Mama and I walked across the street to Nystrom. Once I sat on the bicycle, I began to ride and fell to the ground.

Mama smiled and said, "Get back on. You are going to try again." She was not going to give up on her son in this effort.

Nervous and not knowing what to expect, I said, "I cannot do this, Mama."

She was not going to accept that and gave me the words I will never forget. "You are a professor, James, and very smart," said Mama. "You can do this. Get back on the bicycle." I listened to her and proceeded with the second attempt. I fell off again and did a third attempt. Mama guided me as I rode the bicycle. She released me and I moved forward riding the bicycle.

"Mama, I got it now," I said with confidence.

She said goodbye and walked across the street to the house. I spent an hour riding on the grounds of Nystrom. God placed His hands upon my mother as a guide for me to learn this lesson in the inner-city south side of Richmond, California. This occurred twenty-seven years ago. It seemed like only yesterday. Times does transcend rapidly as the memories become a reflection.

An elevation in the making became God's favor upon my life. This scripture becomes a powerful statement, "Humble yourselves therefore under the mighty hand of God, that he may exalt you in due time: Casting all your care upon him; for he careth for you" (I Peter 5:6-7). I had to maintain joy and happiness despite living in the ghetto. I had been tremendously blessed to be in the presence of great men and women that motivated me.

They always told me, "James, the hand of God is upon your life." My self-esteem needed to be built from a solid foundation.

I am going to take a moment to express this position to our children. You need a coach as a guide to help build your self-esteem for a positive avenue. This is how the prayers of your parents and elders come to the forefront. They are going to intercede for God to move on their behalf.

James quotes, "Confess your faults one to another, and pray one for another, that ye may be healed. The effectual fervent prayer of a righteous man availeth much" (James 5:16).

They believed and positioned themselves on this scripture. I will forever be grateful to the parents and elders in the community that raised me. God ordained them to be our second set of families. They made themselves available in times of struggles and despair. My childhood friends that were raised with me on Maine Avenue and nearby streets can relate to this testament. Despite violence and gangs, the positive direction of our future as adults was implanted by the parents, teachers and elders.

I knew God had his hands on me as I struggled with mathematics in school. Yes, I said it. This was a subject I never discussed publicly till now. Mathematics was not my best friend as a child. The teachers noticed this problem in my academic studies. As a sixth grader at Nystrom, one teacher that worked as a special education specialist pulled me from class to tutor me in mathematics.

"James, we are going to go over 6x7 for this assignment," she said. This teacher was a woman named Audre' Henry. A native of Oklahoma, she died in 2003, after her retirement from the West Contra Costa United School District. Mrs. Henry served faithfully in her career as a teacher. Prior to her death, she was in the process of relocating to her home state.

We loved Mrs. Henry and she loved her students. Her colleagues respected her to the upmost.

If she was still alive today, I believe her words to me, "I am very proud of you," becomes a greater inspiration. Her contributions as an educator in Richmond should be recognized. I considered her among the icons in my hometown.

You are not going to believe this. She was one of the teachers that knew about my surprise birthday party in Mr. Castro's class. Her son, former Governor Brad Henry, a Democrat, served as the twenty-sixth Governor of Oklahoma from 2003 to 2011. Mrs. Henry was also very fond of me and believed in motivating her students to strive for greatness. I remained in touch with her, prior to her retirement.

Upon departing Nystrom, Mrs. Henry worked at the Transition Learning Center in San Pablo, where Mrs. Raff served as the principal. Mrs. Jones also worked there. I always called them. I looked at her and said, "Math is so hard."

She was determined for me to grasp multiplication as her assistant observed. I will never forget this moment I am about to share with you in this chapter.

"James, you can do this," Mrs. Henry said. "What is 6x7?'

The only student in her class, I looked at her and said, "The answer is forty-two."

Mrs. Henry smiled and said, "You got it now." She asked me again, "What is 6x7?"

I repeated forty-two. We continued to review other mathematical problems throughout the remainder of my sixth-grade year. Mrs. Henry worked closely alongside Mrs. Grove, for my academic progress in school. My parents were provided briefs of IEP reports through Mrs. Grove and Mrs. Henry.

Again, God does things for a reason. His hands were set upon me from the time Mama conceived me. No matter how much the devil tried to hinder me, the Lord rescued me from harm and danger. The preparation mode became a process for me to build strength for integrity. When I reflect on building a structure of integrity, the benefits of joy and happiness come full circle.

Again, I must apply the Word of God in this presentation as scripture declares, "Therefore my heart is glad, and my glory rejoiceth; my flesh also shall rest in hope" (Psalm 16:19). Writing this chapter has given me hope as God prepared me for the outcome. My childhood had concluded by transformation into adolescence. I am blessed to know God had his hands on me through the good and tough times.

Even today, I still believe and stand on this perspective of life. Mama always said, "Don't let anything take your joy away." This establishes the dialog for children as they soar their wings as an eagle. Parents, always be the guide and encourager for your children in their developmental stages. They will forever appreciate you for teaching them the lessons of life. Charity does begin at home. If I submit to God's Will and Purpose, His hands remain on me. We are forever being protected, if our hearts and minds are totally committed to Him alone.

The marriage of James and Belinda Birdsong continued to have cycles of non-improvement. I have taken you on a journey in fifteen chapters of this autobiography. A separation in my parent's marriage was already developing. I do not wish this on anyone. Pray my strength in the Lord, as this story continues to be told around the world.

JAMES C. BIRDSONG, JR.

CHAPTER SIXTEEN

Into the Separation

By this time, you should have already assembled a clear picture of my parent's marriage and situations I sustained in the process. There were still current events that made headlines. Michael Jackson continued to dominate the charts with the release of his 1991 album, *Dangerous*. When the King of Pop introduced this album, the New Jack Swing became popular in the nineties among R&B artists.

The music of the eighties and nineties are valuable. I can name every artist of that genre that had the New Jack Swing in their repertoire. One of those artists, Kenneth "Babyface" Edmonds helped change the game as a multi-platinum artist, songwriter, and producer. Even R&B legends, such as, Patti LaBelle, Aretha Franklin, Barry White and Gladys Knight, applied this style to their songs.

The Dangerous album was released on November 26, 1991, and became the fastest selling number one album, breaking the records, by entering the charts at #1 only three days after its release. It was also the first album released by Sony Music that had a Thursday release date, rather than the traditional Monday release (allmichaeljackson.com, 2002-2008).

His last three albums, *Off the Wall*, *Thriller* and *Bad*, were produced by Quincy Jones. Michael did not collaborate with Quincy Jones on the Dangerous album. The producer of this project was Teddy Riley, one of the most popular artists of the nineties. The famed gospel quartet, the Winans, collaborated with Teddy Riley on their hit song, *It's Time*, from their 1990 gold selling album, *Return*. He rapped on the song as Marvin Winans did the lead vocals. If you listen to Its Time, you will hear the New Jack Swing throughout the song.

The Dangerous album produced singles, such as *Black and White, Jam, Remember the Time, In the Closet* and *Who Is It*. The King of Pop went on his second world tour in 1992 and 1993, performing to sold-out concerts for the album.

I watched Michael on HBO one day on television, at Luzan and Kitara's house. The concert, *Live in Bucharest – The Dangerous Tour*, was filmed at the Bucharest National Stadium in Bucharest, Romania.

Racism continued to forefront the nineties. Who can ever forget about Rodney King, an African-American man that became a symbol of racial tension related to police brutality. On March 3, 1991, he was captured by the Los Angeles Police Department, following a high-speed chase. There were four Caucasian police officers that pulled Rodney King out of his car. They beat him brutally as George Holliday filmed it all on videotape. This happened before the Black Lives Matter Movement. The media reported this story nationwide. This made me upset on how Rodney King was treated.

The four L.A.P.D. officers involved were indicted on charges of assault with a deadly weapon and excessive use of force, by a police officer. However, after a three-month trial, a predominantly white jury acquitted the officers, inflaming citizens and sparking the violent 1992 Los Angeles riots (Biography.com, 2012).

On the third day of the Los Angeles Riots, he made a public appearance as journalists reported the story in the press. I will never forget his famous plea, "People, I just want to say, can't we all get along? Can't we all get along?" The United States Justice Department filed federal civil rights charges against the four officers and, in August of 1992, two of them were found guilty while the other two were acquitted (Biography.com, 2012). During the civil trial, Rodney King was awarded a settlement of $3.8 million dollars for injuries he sustained in the hands of the four police officers.

There have been more cases of police brutality against African-Americans since Rodney King. Let's take a moment to reflect on Michael Brown, Philando Castile, Eric Garner, Alton Sterling, Tamir Rice and many others in recent years. I cannot forget about Trayvon Martin and Sandra Bland. What do they all have in common? I am about to address this question.

They were all innocent victims that died in the hands of law enforcement officials based on the color of their skin. I am a person that believes all lives matter, regardless of a person's race or ethnicity. Two decades after Rodney King made national headlines, he was found dead by his fiancée, Cynthia Kelley, on June 7, 2012, in Rialto, California, at his swimming pool.

Governor Bill Clinton, a Democrat candidate in the 1992 Presidential Election, was elected as the forty-second President of the United States. As the Republican incumbent, President George H.W. Bush conceded to Governor Clinton. Prior to the election, Governor Clinton served as the Governor of Arkansas from 1983 to 1992. He took the oath of office for the presidency on January 20, 1993, at Capitol Hill, in Washington, D.C. President Clinton worked tirelessly to strengthen our nation's economy during his eight years in office. If you remember the Clinton Administration, he is indeed "the secretary of explaining stuff" as President Barack Obama said. Everyone, from the rich to the poor, in the United States, was blessed due to President Clinton's handling of the economy.

As the nineties became a decade of remembrance, in various genres, the problems at home on Maine Avenue did not improve for the better. Upon completing elementary school, I began a new chapter as a teenager. I attended Adams Middle School on Arlington Boulevard in Richmond. Nested in the hills near El Cerrito, this is where my seventh and eighth grade years were spent. Still in the special education program, middle school became a preparation for high school.

This became my first time having teachers that instructed in basic subjects. I am referring to English, Mathematics, History, Science and Physical Education. The classes were organized in five periods, with a one hour lunch break for the entire campus. Girls begin to approach me. This became a pattern that started at Nystrom Elementary School.

Most my friends and classmates at Nystrom attended Portola Middle School in El Cerrito. Three of my classmates in the sixth grade attended Helms Middle School in San Pablo, across the street from El Portal Shopping Center. Adams and Portola were in competition against each other. If you attended either school, this became the standard. When friends and classmates in the sixth-grade class found out one of their own was attending Adams, they were not pleased.

One of them approached me and said, "James, why are you going to Adams? You need to attend Portola."

With a serious expression on my face, I said, "I am not going to Portola. That school is rough, and I heard about the fights over there." They knew I told the truth. I guess their position was, "Oh, he is going to attend a middle school where white children attend."

From that time, at Knolls Language Center to Ellerhorst, the schools in the suburban areas became my camping ground. Adams was very diverse culturally among the facility and student body. My friends and cousins that lived on or near Maine Avenue always attended inner-city schools. They respected me for being in the church, and Daddy's role as a noted public figure in Richmond. Portola had a reputation of fights and suspensions. Both schools knew of each other's business among the students. I remember this very well as a seventh and eighth grader. Classmates at Adams would see me smiling and talking to people. They did not realize, once classes concluded, I had to return home among my parents arguing and Daddy's treatment of me, with personality changes. As a seventh grader, the bus would pick me and other students of special education up every morning and return us home in the afternoons. When I resumed the eighth grade, I began to ride AC Transit to the campus.

I realized the marriage of my parents was about to conclude in divorce. Mama had to attend a program for Battered Women due to the abuse she suffered. Something troubled her about me. I eventually stopped preaching the Word of God, for a while. Satan had already attacked the Birdsong household.

As a Michael Jackson fan, I began to do his dance moves on campus. The students began to refer to me as "Michael," and this hurt Mama. She knew God had a Calling on my life, before birth.

Daddy made me upset. I need the fathers to listen. If you have a son, the Lord gave you the obligation to teach and guide him into manhood. In March 1993, Daddy made the local headlines again. The West County Times learned he was an avid baseball fan. He never attended a major-league baseball game in his life. The Oakland Athletics had a game in Oakland. The West County Times interviewed and published a new story about Daddy's contribution to the community, and his knowledge of baseball. They offered him free tickets to the games.

I know you are asking me this question. Did you attend the game with your father? Unfortunately, he did not take his son with him to the Oakland Coliseum. Mama became upset and disappointed in her husband. Daddy only brought me an Oakland Athletics baseball cap as a souvenir item. He requested one of his longtime friends that lived in Richmond to accompany him for the West County Times story. This man knew my father from Greenwood, Louisiana. How could he do this to me? Most fathers took their sons to sporting events.

Did this person that knew Daddy since they were children tell him, "You need to take Junior to see the Oakland Athletes, in person." In my opinion, that never happened.

Fathers make the investment for their sons in their path of manhood. Eric Speir wrote an article published by Charisma Magazine, titled, *One Thing Sons Need from their Fathers*. He shares five practical insights for fathers to be the mentors in their son's lives. This advice captured my undivided attention. He needs one-on-one time with you. It might mean taking him to lunch or to get ice cream. He needs your undivided attention where you spend time with him engaging in a life-sharing activity (Charisma.com. 2015). Eric Speir is certainly on point in this article.

Allow me to explain wisdom and knowledge on this topic. A mother can love and nurture her son. Her prayers, sacrifices and dedication to the son becomes expressions of gratitude. He needs the leadership of his father to direct, guide and mentor him into manhood. God ordained the roles of mothers and fathers, as teachers, protectors and positive influences in the lives of their children. I need to set the record straight. Daddy did invest and spend the father-son relationship of my early childhood years.

Reflection of the eighties comes to mind. The changes did not occur until the early nineties. The dilemma had affected me mentality as a middle school student. This gave me doubts of failing the seventh grade. I am being truthful right now. My grades were impacted by the problems at home. Even though I was going through a dilemma, this allowed me to pray and seek God's direction. I did not know what to expect for the outcome.

God had to prepare me for what became in store for me. Our tests eventually become the testimony of victory. The lessons of redemption establish integrity of evaluation and respect.Prior to the seventh grade, Daddy and I attended the Ed and Ida Birdsong Family Reunion in Greenwood, Louisiana. This family gathering was held in July 1992. It became the first reunion in the Birdsong family, after years of discussions. Uncle Sidney first came with this idea before his death.

Aunt Ruby died on January 15, 1991, at 83-years-old, of a heart attack, in Shreveport. She, along with Grandpa Jim and their siblings that are deceased, prayed and desired for the family to reunite together. A member of our family told me the story. Aunt Myria and Aunt Gladys were the last two surviving children of Ed and Ida Birdsong, of that time. Aunt Myria battled initial stages of Alzheimer's disease. She still lived in Denver.

Neither she nor Aunt Gladys attended the family reunion. I did see Aunt Ola Mae for the first time since her son's funeral in Los Angeles. Aunt Ola Mae was confined to a wheelchair, by the time she reached her seventies. The family reunion was well attended. During the summer months in Louisiana the weather conditions feel as though a person is riding a camel in an African desert. Following the Disneyland trip, Daddy was discussing about us going to Disneyworld in Orlando, Florida. I wanted to attend the family reunion. For those of you that know me, family is dearest in my life.

Daddy made two visits to his hometown since migrating to California in 1967. Mama did not travel with us to Shreveport for the family reunion. I truly believe she would have attended if the marriage was on positive terms. Mama and Daddy continued to have their marital differences. Daddy requested a friend of his to drive us from Richmond to Shreveport in the blue Lincoln Town Car. I had the opportunity to visit family members among the Birdsongs and Durdens. It is a memory cherished for a lifetime.

Henry and Dorothy Jean opened their home in Shreveport, to me and Daddy, for the family reunion. After our attendance at the family reunion we returned home to Richmond, after three days on the road. In 1993, Mama joined Gloryland Apostolic Cathedral on 11th Street in Richmond, where my cousin-in-law, Bishop Tom Watson, is the pastor. He is married to Mother Hazel Fields-Watson. She is my cousin. They both watched me grow up from a baby. Despite the marital crisis, Mama continued to attend church and work in public relations of outreach. Daddy and I retained our church membership at Holy Mission. Gloryland has since changed locations. The church is now located on Barrett Avenue and 19th Street near the Richmond BART Station.

I finally crossed over to the path of adolescence of life on May 16, 1993. I decided to have a thirteenth birthday party, at home, on a Saturday afternoon. Ian and a few of my friends in the neighborhood attended the party. Kitara served as a chaperone for the party. She was in her early twenties at the time. She was in the final stages of completing her undergraduate studies in college. I thank God for my God sister.

Mama had a test on that day at Contra Costa College. I understand her position in obtaining a college education. However, this made Daddy upset. I remember the expression on his face. The problems never stopped. The community became aware of my parent's marital crisis.

When a book is written, the story is being analyzed by

readers. The marriage of James and Belinda Birdsong began to slowly approach a sad ending. The first three years of adolescence became difficult for me, in the tales of crisis. Redemption comes to mind.

I successfully completed the seventh grade at Adams, after a challenging school year, due to problems at home. The following summer, I attended two field trips with the youth of our city, in the Richmond Police Activities League, a popular non-profit organization founded by the Richmond Police Department. This is one of the organizations I admired and respected. The Richmond Police Activities League continues their mission today. While at Adams, I did encounter teasing and jealousy by some young men. I already mentioned earlier my classmates were not aware of what I had to endure at home.

The girls admired me. I became very popular at Adams. If you noticed, on photos in this book, my eyes are hazel. They are not contact lenses. Once I returned to Adams for my eighth-grade year, in September 1993, those same girls and their friends would still approach me. I begin to ride AC Transit for the eighth grade at Adams, from my neighborhood to the campus via the El Cerrito Del Norte BART Station in El Cerrito. Mrs. Grove gave me her telephone number on the day of my sixth-grade graduation.

On the last day of school in sixth grade, Mrs. Grove told me, "James, please keep in touch with me."

Mrs. Grove would always share updates with the teachers and students about the progress in middle school. I visited her and the teachers on campus after completing the sixth grade.

There is a feeling that God places inside of us as it comes to trials and tests. By the eighth grade, I began to slow down dancing like Michael Jackson and doing his famous moves. I can attest to one thing. The prayers of a mother do work.

Mama remained on her knees praying for me in this situation. We knew so many people in Richmond, especially the pastors, first ladies, ministers, evangelists, deacons and church mothers. I have always been fond of the mothers in the church, since childhood. Some of them were praying and asking God to save my parent's marriage. Mama had another mindset. Women in abusive relationships and marriages have a choice. They can either remain in the abuse or have an exit strategy.

The verbal abuse is just as worse as physical violence. A real man will never abuse a woman, regardless of the circumstances. Mama decided not to continue in the marriage with Daddy. She prayed and fasted while advice became obtained for her. She also witnessed the effects on me.

Let it be written. I am a person that still believes that marriage should last for a lifetime. My mother tried her best, throughout the later years, to be a good wife. She did not have any male friends during the marriage. Daddy was not willing to meet her halfway, by ending his friendships with certain people. My parents began to appear before a judge at the Contra Costa County Superior Court, in Martinez, California, for divorce proceedings.

Daddy had full control of the Lincoln Town Car. Mama had to either ride Amtrak or the public bus to the courthouse. This is hard to believe. I remember going to Mira Vista Lincoln/Mercury, at Hilltop Auto Plaza, in 1986, with my parents, as the Lincoln Town Car was purchased. Their names had been recorded on the documents as owners. This is not fair treatment. She told me about her means of transportation to Martinez. The Lord ordained James and Belinda Birdsong to be my parents. I am reflecting on this scenario right at this moment. The Lord is allowing me to write this book for a purpose. The next chapter covers the demise of James and Belinda Birdsong's marriage to family apartness.

JAMES C. BIRDSONG, JR.

CHAPTER SEVENTEEN

We're No Longer Together As a Family

Writing this chapter is a challenge for me. Separation had become the compass in our household on Maine Avenue. Divorce brings sadness for couples in marriage. Children are innocent victims. They believe the parents should live together happily, forever. The hearts broken and scattered in pieces can be difficult to mend.

My perspective of Mama and Daddy's marriage, to divorce, becomes our teachable moment in redemption. Mama began her exit strategy from the house on Maine Avenue. I understood people had their faith and hope for the marriage to be saved. Earlier in the relationship, James and Belinda Birdsong encountered their redemption of love, marriage and family.

However, this redemption of separation transformed from unity to division of conqueror. Allow me to give more charity. This book is titled, *The Best is Yet to Come: A Testimony of One Young Man's Redemption*. Mama and Daddy were blessed by God to join in holy matrimony according to marital covenant. Chapters one and two explained the depths of that redemption. God honored the marriage of my parents and, now, Satan walked through the doors. The enemy wanted to steal, kill and destroy.

The marriages of the 21st century is different from our parents, grandparents and great grandparents. Their generation believed in God being the focus of marriage. Admiration of couples in marital covenant for more than 40 years is a blessing from God. Marriages of our elders becomes the pure love story.

If my generation would listen to the knowledge and wisdom of the elders, in everlasting marriages, we would not observe the crisis of divorce. I still believe in marriage and the sacred vows.

I desired that longevity for my parents as I became an adult. This became a test of endurance and strength for me as a teenager. Mama had a compassionate heart for Daddy in one situation. Prior to my thirteenth birthday, I walked into our house after the bus driver dropped me off from school. Mama had her classes at Contra Costa College. I always greeted my parents and shared about my day on campus. Cinnamon Toast Crunch was my favorite cereal. I had a box in the kitchen at the top of our refrigerator. As I proceeded to eat some of the cereal, Daddy was lying on the floor. I immediately ran to him. He had a diabetic emergency.

"Daddy, are you alright?" I asked him. He was vomiting at the mouth. I never witnessed him in this position. He said, "Junior, help me to the room."

I helped him up the stairs to his room where he laid down. Moments later, Mama walked in the house. I ran downstairs and said, "Daddy is not feeling well. I just came home from school and found him in the kitchen."

She said, "He was on the floor?" I looked at my mother, "Daddy was lying on the kitchen floor vomiting." Mama and I walked upstairs to his room. She called the paramedics. They immediately responded and rushed him to Brookside Hospital.

Mama found the keys to the Lincoln Town Car. This was her first time driving the car in about three years. "Get ready to go with me to the hospital," she said in a serious voice. Almost four years earlier, in 1989, Daddy had this situation that related to diabetes. My father was being treated in the emergency room, upon our arrival at Brookside. We were sitting in the waiting area before visiting him. Around an hour later, the nurse came to us. "You can now go visit Mr. Birdsong," she said, as we followed her to the emergency room. Since he had diabetes, the doctor said, "He needs to inform his primary physician about this incident."

Daddy had already begun using insulin once a day, for a long time. The insulin is designed to maintain a person's glucose. The three of us returned home on Maine Avenue. Later, that day, Mama said, "James, I need to speak to you."

My parents were still sleeping in separate rooms. "You need to stay home from school on tomorrow. You need to be observant of your father since this happened." He had two diabetic emergencies in a four-year period. If I did not act, Daddy would have been dead. I stayed home from my classes as my mother suggested.

The eighth grade became the concluding chapter of middle school. Albert and Barbara, along with their children and siblings, continued to visit us despite my parent's marital differences. Clim and JoEvelyn made plans to purchase a new house in Vallejo. He decided to rent his house to tenants. They established themselves as landlords.

In September 1993, Gloryland Apostolic Cathedral had a recreation activity for Labor Day, at the Chevron Ron and Gun Club. Located at the Chevron Richmond Refinery, this was my second time visiting the popular recreation facility. The sixth-grade class at Nystrom Elementary School went there for our field trip the week of our graduation. I spent the entire day, with Mama, Bishop and Mother Watson, my family, and the congregation, at the Chevron Ron and Gun Club.

I remember the bowling alley, picnic tables and tennis court. A minister at Gloryland named Eric Grant worked at the Martin Luther King Jr. Community Center through the City of Richmond. I began to visit the King Center after school to play basketball, games and tutoring. He had been a faithful member at the church for years. Eric still attends the church to this day. I met him as a 10-year-old boy in the summer of 1990. It has been twenty-three years since the visit to the Ron and Gun Club.

The tenure of eighth grade became a time of private professional counseling sessions for me. Once a week, a licensed certified psychologist came to Adams. The sessions were recommended by Dr. Jenkins. Due to the nature of the sessions, I cannot publicly comment on this matter. The rules and regulations of counseling services are certified by laws. My father was not aware of this. I had to keep the sessions from him. I believed if he knew about the sessions, vengeance would have become a factor in the household.

Devastation came upon me mentally. In the eyes of a child, they feel trapped and insecure in situations as their parents are on verge of divorce. The verbal abuse Mama endured had a mental toll on her. She desired to further her studies at Contra Costa College, for an Associate's degree, in her field of study.

In September 1994, my mother resumed the fall semester. This should have been her final year at Contra Costa College before the graduation. Due to the circumstances of the marriage, she had to withdraw from her classes in the upcoming spring semester. God touched her heart to attend church services at Church of Deliverance on MacDonald Avenue, where the late Apostle Samuel Vann was the pastor. He and his wife, the late Mother Bobbi Vann, believed in the Pentecostal doctrine. She eventually joined the church and served as the public relations and outreach coordinator. One morning, Mama went to Pinole for business affairs of the church. Mama had documents to be mailed. Her only means of transportation was AC Transit. Daddy made me very disappointed in him.

Questions were already escalating in my mind. I wished I could have asked him, "Why are you treating Mama this way?" I need to make another confession. There were times I wanted to punch my father for the way he was treating his wife and son. Mama told me, "James, your father is blind, disabled and has diabetes. If you do that, the police will come and arrest you."

I have never mentioned this before until now. This becomes difficult to believe. My redemption was only beginning. Honesty speaks our episodes of stages in life. I had my own problems in this crisis. Thoughts of suicide at 10-years-old, the sleepless nights and mental distress in initial stages of adolescence, had me crying on the inside. Mama had to be strong for me, despite her circumstances. Demetrius and Alonzo were adults and not around when this happened.

Once she departed from the post office, my mother was planning to board the bus for Berkeley. Anticipating boarding the bus, she fell into a ditch on the sidewalk. Resulting in a knee injury, Mama made her decision to withdraw from Contra Costa College, alongside marital differences. I did not attend the court hearings in Martinez, while Mama and Daddy had to stand before a judge. Daddy requested to have custody of me. The judge granted this to Mama in divorce proceedings. How could a blind man take care of a child? I am sure the judge figured this out.

Mama made sure I had a monthly allowance. She would give me $25.00 to $50.00 a month. Did your father give you any money, James? The answer is only one dollar. He became selfish as it related to finances.

Once a month on a Saturday, I rode the bus to Hilltop Mall to purchase VHS cassettes to record popular television sitcoms of the nineties, such as, *Martin, In Living Color, Living Single, Roc, Hangin' with Mr. Cooper* and *The Sinbad Show*. I also purchased cassettes of Michael and Janet Jackson's album releases, Bruce Lee movies, See's candies, Hot Wheels and Matchbox cars, and visited the different stores. I remember when McDonald's first opened at Hilltop Mall. I would always come into contact among childhood friends and classmates. They were shopping with their parents and siblings, watching movies at the theater or spending time together as young people do today. This was the Hilltop Mall of the eighties and nineties. I eventually began to slow down going there as high school became the focus. I decided to celebrate my fourteenth birthday on May 16, 1994, during the lunch period at Adams. Mama made a cake for me. I brought the cake, two liter bottles of soda and two bags of Lay's Potato Chips. My classmates came to the cafeteria and sang happy birthday.

One of the students found out I had a birthday. He saw me walking in the school yard. I will never forget what this young man said.

"James, did you know Janet Jackson shares the same birthday with you?"

You should have seen my facial expression. "I never knew Janet Jackson was born on May 16th," I said to this young man.

So many of us boys had a crush on Janet Jackson. I was one of those boys. She was born on May 16, 1966, in Gary, Indiana. She is 14 years older than me. Janet just released her 1993 album, *Janet*, and did her second world tour to promote the project. The album produced the chart-topping singles, such as, *That's the Way Loves Go*, *If*, *Again* and *Anytime, Any Place*. Janet even did a concert at the Oakland Coliseum during her world tour. This became major for the entire Bay Area. I did not attend the concert.

Friends and classmates of mine, throughout Adams, were talking about this concert. A few days before my eighth-grade graduation in June 1994, the school hosted their annual awards ceremony at the multi-purpose room.

One of my teachers, Bonnie Glover, told me, "James, you are being recognized with an award in my class." She was one of the special education teachers at Adams. Mrs. Glover taught the Curriculum Assistance course. During the seventh grade, I did not receive any awards. God already knew this day was coming for me. Mrs. Glover had a smile on her face as she announced the news to me. I remember walking home from the bus stop on Cutting Boulevard after school.

With a smile on my face, I approached Mama. I said, "Adams is going to have an award ceremony. I was chosen by Mrs. Glover to be honored."

My mother was not surprised about the news. Mama had already seen all my awards and certificates throughout school, from kindergarten. She always told me, "You are a professor and very smart."

We boarded a bus to Adams for the award ceremony one evening. Due to the circumstances of mental stress in my parent's marriage and how Daddy changed towards us, I did not want him there. I know this sounds selfish. The first thought came to mind, "If my father attends, he will embarrass me."

The vice principal of Adams, Richard Avalos, called Mrs. Glover to the podium on stage. She shared with the audience a short profile about me. I walked on stage to accept the award in her class. I exited the stage and walked to Mama. I kissed her on the check. The attendees in the audience had smiles on their faces. There were other students and classmates who were honored with awards. One person in the audience recognized me. It was Ms. Mahrt's former teacher's assistant, Emma Tripp.

Her grandson Jeffrey was my classmate in Mrs. Glover's class. He also received an award. After the ceremony ended, I received many congratulations. Mrs. Glover learned about our transportation to the school. She told us, "Mrs. Birdsong, I am going to give you and James a ride home. I will never forget about Mrs. Glover.

I graduated the eighth grade a few days later. I did not attend the graduation. The situation at home became a toll on me mentally. There were times I would go to bed at night. I prayed and said, "Lord, I want to leave this house and Richmond all together." The murders in Richmond continued to get worse. By the early-mid nineties, childhood friends and their families began to move away from the community. I did not blame them one bit. They began to migrate to Pinole, Hercules and other suburban areas.

The next day, I knew it was the final journey for me at Adams. The eighth-grade class had a graduation party. Held in the multi-purpose room, I came in an all-white suit. You should have seen the reaction of the girls. A few weeks before, we learned about a popular Bay Area radio personality hosting the party. I am referring to Renel Brooks-Moon, formerly of KMEL 106 FM.

If you were raised in the Bay Area during that time, I know you remember her. KMEL 106 FM is the R&B/Hip Hop radio station in the Bay Area. Located in San Francisco, we would listen to this station. I could not believe Renel thought about us to make the appearance at Adams Middle School. She hosted our eighth-grade graduation party.

We voted for the students in our class that were popular and had status on campus. They voted me as the prettiest eyes among the students in the Adams Middle School Class of 1994. Despite problems at home, I did not allow this to hinder me from enjoying the final day of eighth grade. Everything from the dancing to music became a time of remembrance. The party ended. I boarded the bus to return home. I never visited Adams Middle School after graduation. I decided to close that chapter completely.

Mrs. Glover transferred to Tara Hills Elementary School. She eventually became the principal of the school. In the early 2000s, she returned to Adams as the principal. As of today, Adams Middle School is no longer in operation. The board of education for the West Contra Costa Unified School District decided to close the campus in 2009. One of the reasons was budget cuts. Another decision made to close Adams was based upon a structural engineering report, raised seismic safety concerns of the three-story building. There were also concerns of significant and irreparable earthquake damage.

Adams Middle School existed for 50 years. When I was a baby, Demetrius was a student at the school. At that time, it was known as Adams Junior High School. I had to attend summer school for six weeks.

The State of California would administer a test for students in public schools every other grade year. Mathematics became a struggle for me as a child. I made the decision to take the summer courses at DeAnza High School, in El Sobrante. I remember this one girl that liked me. She would always kiss me on the cheek. I am smiling right now as this becomes a reflection of memories. I successfully passed the test and six weeks of summer classes at DeAnza.

The chapter of high school had begun for me. Before completing the eighth grade, we had to sign an application requesting what high school to attend. There were five high schools in the West Contra Costa Unified School District, at the time. The five schools were DeAnza, El Cerrito, John F. Kennedy, Pinole Valley and Richmond High School.

My determination was El Cerrito or Pinole Valley. I did not

want to attend Kennedy nor Richmond. Those schools were known for fights and violence on campus. The rising of gangs was happening in Richmond. I did not want a repeat of the fifth grade at Nystrom Elementary School. I am not here to talk negative about the situation of my childhood in our community. Times have changed since the nineties.

Are you ready to hear the news? The school district informed me to attend Kennedy High School as a freshman.

I said, "Lord, here we go again. This is a repeat of me being bullied and teased."

Mama and Daddy were in divorce proceedings, the hurts and scars had me crying on the inside and more problems building on problems. I feared going to Kennedy High School. This became more preparation of redemption. I knew some students at Kennedy High School. There was one girl in our neighborhood that was preparing for her senior year. The both of us grew up together. Her brother and I are about a year apart in age. She knew about me being bullied.

The status of a 14-year-old teenage boy in the innercity became one simple question. What can I do to make a difference in the lives of children in broken homes, divorces among parents, victims of bullying, and those that are different from their peers?

I remember going to Safeway, a popular grocery store, one morning with Luzan. She would pay me for doing chores around the house, such as, vacuuming the carpet, watering the lawn, empting the garbage and washing her car. This happened for me when I was 13-years-old.

"James, what do you see yourself in life," my Godmother asked me as we were in route to Safeway on MacDonald Avenue. I had the answer for her. "I want to help the children around the world," I said. "My dream is to build a foundation for them."

Luzan smiled and said, "If that's what you want to do, James, then go for it."

She had always encouraged me to pursue my dreams. Since I had my share of trials as a young person under the age of eighteen, I prayed for the children around the world. I can honestly relate to our children of today. They are the innocent victims as their parents transcend from a marriage to divorce. I will always say this, until the Lord calls me home. The children did not cause the demise of their parent's divorce. Sometimes, they blamed themselves. I want to tell the young people, it is not your fault. Always remain focused on God, and you will never go wrong in life. Your parents may be in the process of divorce. Love, honor and respect them, regardless of the nature of their relationship.

By this time, I began to slowly prepare for my transition away from the ghetto. God gave me the strength to endure the trails and tests for my redemption. A 14-year-old boy desired for a change in his life. Life in the inner-city had challenges, from the treatment by peers to innocent people being murdered for no reason. The elders were on their knees praying and crying out to God for deliverance.

People were asking this one question. Why are our children being murdered and the young men being recruited into gangs? The parents wanted a better life for their children. They invested in us for advancement. I can honestly say Mama and Daddy invested into my education, despite their marital crisis. The situation did not change for the better in the Birdsong household.

One day, I decided to obtain boxes and pack my belongings. I did this for a year. When you know in your spirit a change is about to come, provisions are going to be made. God wants us to trust him in the process. I had no one else but the Lord to depend, lean and trust on. I had many questions in the redemption, and still needed answers. Why is this happening? How will I make the exit strategy from the place I once considered home on Maine Avenue? Where do I go from here? These questions were resting heavy on my mind. Stay tuned for more of the story.

CHAPTER EIGHTEEN
Leaving Richmond for Fairfield

For those of you raised in the inner-city neighborhoods, there is the motto, "You can leave the hood, but the hood won't leave you." This profound statement attests among the African-American community. There are agreements for children like myself, invested and spent their childhood in urban neighborhoods such as mine.

There are people that spent their childhood memories in the ghetto and departed to suburban neighborhoods for a better life.

In September 1994, I began a new chapter as a ninth-grade freshman at John F. Kennedy High School. While there were friends and classmates from previous schools in attendance at Kennedy, I stayed unhappy at the campus. I felt more alone at Kennedy. I may have experienced bullying at Nystrom. I had Seyyida, childhood friends, teachers, and Mrs. Jones to watch my back.

"Why I am going through this episode again?" I asked myself. I knew there were going to be problems. The girls began to approach me. History repeated itself like Nystrom and Adams. Some of these girls that liked me lived in the neighborhood, while others resided minutes away. Mama knew these young men wanted to fight me, for no reason.

She was constantly praying for me. "Lord, please watch over my son," Mama said in her prayer. "Those boys do not care for him. I need to get him out of Richmond." Multiple murders continued to increase among young people, under 18 years of age. The Bay Area knew about Richmond's reputation of murders. My hometown was once named the most dangerous city in the State of California. Drugs, gangs, and violence were rapid in Richmond. You also had the same activity in Los Angeles. During that time, it became major in Compton and South Central Los Angeles.

The birth of gangsta rap music came from the streets of Los Angeles. I have family that lived in those areas of Los Angeles.

I did not belong to Kennedy High School. By the grace of God, those young men never placed their hands on me for a fight. However, there were some students stealing from their fellow classmates. One incident happened on campus that I remember well.

Before I share the story, I was still a student in the special education program. I had already spent the first twelve years of public school in special education. One afternoon, I had to go downstairs to the Dean's Office. My teacher, John Knox, became the substitute Dean for a few weeks. He was my English and Mathematics teacher in the special education program.

Mr. Knox said, "James, how can I help you?"

You may think, "Why are you in the dean's office?" I lost my monthly bus pass and needed a replacement. Mr. Knox knew how I felt about the school.

I told him, "I lost my bus pass and I need help to get home."

"Go and sit in the waiting area," he said, with a smile on his face.

Moments later, two students walked into the office. I will never forget this girl crying. She and this young man were scared and worried. One of them said, "There was a shooting in the yard during P.E. class. Two boys were shot." The shooting made the local news throughout the Bay Area on television and newspapers. The two boys were Hispanic, and thankfully, they were not killed. Fear came upon me as the news spread throughout the campus. There were some young men at Kennedy High School that were affiliated with gangs. I knew this, and during my ninth-grade year I proceeded cautiously and remained prayerful. We had to walk through metal detectors on campus, following the shooting. Mr. Knox gave me some bus tickets for the entire week. I walked to the bus stop across the street, after school.

I returned home and told Mama, "There was a shooting today on campus." Daddy also heard about the incident. I reflect this day. I am grateful to the Lord for dispatching his angels of protection around me. I could have been one of those young men that was shot.

Mama said, "James, you are not going back to Kennedy. I am going to call the school district on tomorrow." I looked at Mama, "I want to attend El Cerrito High."

Before I graduated the eighth grade from Adams, they told me Kennedy was close to my house. I felt those the administrators at that time did not care. Breanna was a tenth-grade sophomore at El Cerrito High School. Several of my classmates from Adams were attending El Cerrito. Mercedes attended Pinole Valley High School. She and her sister, Jessica, lived in North Richmond. I knew a handful of students at Pinole Valley High School.

"This is not fair to me," I said to myself. "How can friends and classmates of mine that live not too far from me can attend the better schools while I am at Kennedy." I could never figure that out.

Mama tried her best to convince the school district, for me to transfer from Kennedy to El Cerrito. I remembered going to independent home study. I was not qualified for the program. A few weeks later, from being absent, the school district wrote a letter to Mama. They told her these exact words.

"Mrs. Birdsong, we understand your concern for James' safety and the problems at Kennedy. You need to express this to the principal and his teachers. He has been absent and needs to report back to Kennedy, immediately. He needs to remain there until the school year ends in June. If you want him to transfer at El Cerrito, he would have to wait until the next school year, which is the fall semester." Mama was upset about the decision. My father was very upset. They even had an argument about this, while divorce proceedings were in motion.

Daddy said, "Belinda, Junior has been out of school and needs to go back."

He did not even try to reach out and get this situation resolved. My father stayed active and remained in conversation with the school administrators on Bissell Avenue, at the office, my teachers and the principals I had as a child.

"James, I am worried about our son's safety. They had a shooting at Kennedy. He could have been dead." My father had so much weight in Richmond, in the seventies and eighties, among high profile people. It was not the same anymore, in that area, with him. If you have been reading this book, then you would have figured this puzzle by now.

I returned to Kennedy a few weeks later. My classmates were asking me, "James, where have you been?"

I did not share too many details with them. I experienced so much hardship and strife at Maine Avenue, with my parent's failing marriage, how Daddy changed towards his wife and son, being teased and bullied, of being different, jealousy among certain boys that decided to choose the street life and nightmares of the dilemma. I had to be humble, steadfast and strong.

I continued to obtain boxes and began to pack my belongings. Within my spirit, a change was about to come.

Mama did the same thing as well. By the last four months of 1994, my parents were still sleeping in separate rooms. I did not have too many friends and classmates that came over to visit me. They were moving out of the ghetto with their parents and siblings. I would call them. The girls liked me at Kennedy High School. There was one girl. I am not going to mention her name. She was an eleventh grader in her junior year. This young woman was Caucasian. She also had a crush on me. Kennedy did not have too many Caucasian students and teachers. The school was predominately African-American. We had Hispanics and Asians at Kennedy. I am going to tell you how I and this girl met.

I was introduced to her by one of my friends that graduated the eighth grade with me from Adams. She was also Caucasian.

"James, I have someone that I want you to meet."

For the record, I did not have a girlfriend at the time. My friend introduced me to this girl, and from there we connected. We had plans to go to Hilltop Mall one Saturday to attend the movies. This never happened. This girl and I called each other every day and wrote letters. Growing up as a child, I had always been attracted to girls of my race and especially the brown and dark-skinned African-American girls. I am being honest. I am a man that sees women of all complexions beautiful. I am a person that does not have an issue with interracial relationships and marriages. I don't see color. My parents taught me to see a person's character. We cannot forget the words of Martin Luther King, Jr., in his I *Have a Dream* speech.

She lived in Central Richmond. Central Richmond had always been multi-cultural and diverse. There were family and friends of mine that resided in this section of Richmond. The racial makeup of Central Richmond was majority Caucasian. I have been blessed to have friends and acquaintances of all ethnicities, throughout the years.

I have mentioned there were certain students stealing on campus. I remembered being in my third period, Arts & Basics class, at Kennedy. My mother purchased me a new backpack for Christmas. I asked my teacher, "Can I put my backpack in your office?"

He said, "Sure James, you can."

My teacher knew what I had encountered by some of the young men on campus. A few minutes after I placed the backpack in his office, the teacher began the class session. One of the students went into the room and took the backpack, while our teacher and my classmates witnessed this. "Please give me my backpack," I said feeling upset.

The teacher tried to stop this young man. He threw it to a girl in the class, and another young man in the hallway came to the classroom. The girl threw my backpack to the young man in the hallway and ran away. I had my gymnasium clothes, binder, and other items inside of the backpack.

I reported what happened on that day. Unfortunately, I never saw my backpack ever again. I returned home and told Mama. She said, "James when you complete the ninth grade, I am not going to have you going back to Kennedy High again." This was a brand-new backpack, and now it had been stolen in front of me.

We returned to class following the Christmas holiday break. I remember 1995, in many perspectives, from my personal life to current events in the media. First, I had a feeling that I would be transferring to El Cerrito High School for the tenth grade. Second, the final proceedings of my parent's divorce were being granted by the Contra Costa County Superior Court and, third, Sony Records just released another hit-making album by Michael Jackson.

The album is titled, *HIStory: Past, Present, and Future, Book. I*. Released on June 18, 1995, the project produced hits, such as *Scream, They Don't Care about Us, Earth Song, Childhood* and *You Are Not Alone*. I was very excited about this album due to the fact Michael and Janet collaborated on Scream. I remember watching the music video television premiere of Scream.

The King of Pop made history, as Guinness World Book of Records listed Scream as the most expensive music video made, estimated at $7,000,000 million dollars. He proceeded with the History World Tour in 1996 and 1997. It was Michael's last tour before his sudden death on June 25, 2009, at 50-years-old. Three months prior, he had announced his This Is It concerts in London, England.

After five years of praying and wondering, the divorce of James and Belinda Birdsong was in the final months of being finalized. The judge that presided over the divorce hearings gave his decision.

"Mrs. Birdsong, you and your son have until March 28th to vacate the premises. The court has already granted you full custody of your son. He will have visitation rights with Mr. Birdsong."

Daddy wanted us to leave. I cannot believe he said this. The mental status overpowered him. For the record, I did not attend the hearings since I was a minor under the age of 18. I continued to pack my belongings. Before that time, I began to give away some of my toys to friends in the neighborhood.

When a child begins to approach their adolescent years, puberty comes into effect. A child outgrows their toys, dolls, stuff animals and action figures. They engage more with computers, music, and video games. In high school, they participate in clubs, student government, rallies, sports, and proms. The position of dating and sex becomes a serious topic between parents and their teenage children.

The divorce of parents affects their children. The family love that was once shared in the home is damaged. Family love is the connection in a family that God only ordains. He only gives this love, not man. I have learned in this experience family love sustains you in unity. This bond allows families to be each other's support system in the good and tough times. The family love will last and strive for life if Jesus Christ is the first and foremost focus.

If the family love becomes separated due to specific differences, there is no unity in the bond. It reminds me of a vase being dropped on the floor and breaks. Mama began to search for houses and apartments in El Cerrito and Berkeley. She knew I wanted to attend El Cerrito High School for the following school year. On March 27, 1995, I attended Sunday morning services at Holy Mission. Daddy decided to stay home. The National Basketball Association just started their season. I already told you my father loved sports. One of my favorite teams in the National Football League, at the time, the San Francisco 49ers, just won their fifth Superbowl Championship on January 29, 1995. It was held during Super Bowl XXIX, at the Joe Robbie Stadium in Miami, Florida. The Superbowl is the final game of football season.

The 49ers were playing against their rival team, the San Diego Chargers. I remember watching the game. Daddy invited Albert to watch the game downstairs. I was upstairs in my room as the television was playing. A week before the game, everybody throughout Kennedy was talking about the Superbowl. We were desiring for our home team to win that year. I decided to do a petition and collected signatures of fellow classmates, asking them, "Who will win the Superbowl this year?"

Guess what they wrote? The 49ers. One young man even

wrote, "I will bet you $100.00."

Let it be written, I have never or ever will participate in bets. The 49ers won the game, at 49 points to the Chargers at 26. The Bay Area celebrated our team. I went to school the next day. We were celebrating as well. Our teachers were even smiling about the Superbowl win. It was our historical moment.

The 49ers had not won a Superbowl championship since 1995. I hope the current team is reading this book. The main players at the time were Stevie Young and Deion Sanders. In the eighties, Joe Montana was their quarterback.

I am going to resume my attendance at church services. I knew this became my farewell on Maine Avenue. Clim and JoEvelyn came to pick me up. They relocated to Vallejo in 1994. JoEvelyn told me one day, "Junior, I want to move out of Richmond." I did not blame her one bit. This became a time when families began to leave the city due to the increasing activity of drugs, gangs, and murders. The three of us arrived at the church. By this time, the choir was no longer in existence. A few days before, I called Jessica and Mercedes to come. I mentioned about how well they could sing. I walked up to the podium below the pulpit and made a statement.

"I have something to share with you."

The congregation gave me their undivided attention. So many things were going on in my mind. Mama words always reflected in me. "You have to be strong, James," she told me during this crisis.

I told the church, "Tomorrow will be my last day at the house on Maine Avenue. My parents are about to get a divorce, after fifteen years of marriage. My mother and I will be moving. The memories of good times will forever be in my heart," I said with courage. Clim and JoEvelyn were sitting in the pulpit along with the ministers. After speaking to the congregation, I turned and looked at Clim.

"Pastor, please watch out for Daddy." I made a plea with him.

He told me, "Junior, I will do that."

In Chapter Two, I told the story of Grandmother Charlene's request to him before she died. Clim had kept his promise to my grandmother.

"I made a promise to your grandmother many years ago. I have been close friends with your father for a long time," said Clim. I remember the reaction of Jessica, Mercedes and their mother, Cynthia. They will always be my home girls. As of today, they still reside in North Richmond near North Richmond Missionary Baptist Church, McGlothen Temple Church of God in Christ and the Chevron Richmond Refinery.

The next morning on March 28, 1995, I did not attend classes at Kennedy High. We gathered our belongings, with assistance, and departed the house on Maine Avenue. This is the home I was raised in and became a gathering place, from family to dignitaries. James and Belinda Birdsong were officially divorced. The marriage had ended on this day. I continued the remaining two and a half months of the ninth grade. I would go back and visit Daddy.

I believe he began to have a realization of what he once had, a good wife and a son. I reflect on the profound quote, "Yesterday they are here, but gone on tomorrow."

He had to figure out a plan for additional financial income. Daddy decided to rent out the rooms at the house. His tenants would pay him to rent once a month. I met some of the tenants during my visits. Mama continued to search for housing. I remember going with her to Santa Rosa, California one day. Santa Rosa is located one hour north of San Francisco, in Sonoma County. This is where I met the pastor that had a background in television and radio broadcasting. I am referring to Apostle Cecil Hale, Jr. and his wife, First Lady Anita Hale. He is the senior pastor of New Beginnings Ministry of Love in Santa Rosa.

He had a popular radio broadcast during the nineties on KDIA 1310 AM called, *Prayer on the Air*. Apostle Hale was a much sought-after evangelist and revivalist that traveled nationally throughout the years. A native of Shreveport, Louisiana, Apostle Hale had been the recipient of numerous awards for his leadership in ministry and the community. One of those awards was bestowed upon him by President George H.W. Bush during his term in office.

In the nineties, he was one of the most popular pastors in the Bay Area. Mama first met him and his wife in 1992, during a crusade he hosted in Oakland. She knew the Hales before I did. We were talking about moving to Santa Rosa. Mama wanted a different direction and change in her life. She witnessed the mental trauma I endured.

We visited two apartment complexes in Santa Rosa. Unfortunately, it did not work out in Santa Rosa, El Cerrito or Berkeley. Mama made a phone call to Adella. She and her husband lived in Fairfield, California. Adella knew what my mother had to endure during her marriage to Daddy.

"Adella, I really need to talk to you." She stopped and listened to her childhood friend. "What's on your mind, Belinda?"

"I need to get out of Richmond. James and I are divorced. My son has been through so much with those boys bullying him. I fear for his life. We need a change."

Adella tells Mama, "Please come to Fairfield, Belinda. It would be better for James. This is a military town where Travis Air Force Base is located. Fairfield High School will be good for him. These people don't play out there."

She told my mother about the apartment complex on Grande Circle. I am not going to mention the name. It is now a different name operated by a different management. "I will tell the manager you will be visiting the complex," Adella said. A few days later, Mama goes and visits Adella and David.

I did not learn about this until I completed the ninth grade at Kennedy High. I told a few of my friends, "I will not be back here next year. I am leaving Richmond." My prayers were answered. I did not return to Kennedy High School and, for the record, I never came back to visit. God delivered me. On June 14, 1995, I finally moved out of Richmond and made Fairfield my new home.

During the summer months, I continued to visit Daddy and call my friends. A pastor friend of ours, the late Bishop Arthur Eames, had a storage at the Ark of Jesus Holiness Church on MacDonald Avenue. He allowed us to place our belongings in the storage. We made multiple trips to retrieve our items. Mama and I were at peace. How will Fairfield High School accept me? Are you ready for another flight to the redemption? The show still goes on.

THE BEST IS YET TO COME

JAMES C. BIRDSONG, JR.

CHAPTER NINETEEN

The Pastor of Fairfield High School

Changes become the elevation stone in redemption. You evaluate the lessons and how to apply them in future goals. I spent the first fifteen years of my life in Richmond and attending public schools in two different environments. They were the inner-city and suburban communities. I had the opportunity to engage, experience and reflect in both worlds, in childhood and early adolescence.

Fairfield became a new adventure for me. I remember arriving at our apartment with my beloved parakeet, Sprite. I had him since the age of 13. Sprite was my baby. I had him until he died in 2002. The Lord blessed Mama with a gray 1994 Ford Tempo GL. In the duration of four years, she had to ride AC Transit or depend on friends and church members for transportation when we lived in Richmond.

The apartment was a two bedroom, one bath on the second floor. Travis Air Force Base was in our backyard. We would see Lockheed C-5 Galaxys and C-141 Starlifters and McDonnell Douglas KC-10 Extenders, in their takeoff and landings. These are the aircraft of the United States Air Force. During the first few weeks at our apartment, Mama and Adella would visit each other.

They were friends since childhood at Peres Elementary School. I remember traveling on Interstate 80 through Fairfield in 1990. We were in route to Sacramento, with Bishop Mobley and the congregation at Prayer House, where a church invited them for a service. Those summer months were challenging for us. Although I was happy to be residing in a pristine environment, the memories of my parent's marriage in good times came to mind. Daddy was still living on Maine Avenue, while we were across the Carquinez Strait in the North Bay of Solano County.

I became familiar with Fairfield as a child. My cousin, Carrie Fields-Ross and her husband Don, lived in Suisun City for many years. He worked at Mare Island Naval Shipyard in Vallejo, until his retirement. The military closed Mare Island in the mid-nineties, as they did Alameda Naval Air Station in Alameda, California near Oakland. I anticipated my tenth-grade year as a sophomore at Fairfield High School. I did not know anyone in my peers that already lived in Fairfield.

I did not have a phone at the time to call Daddy. My telephone calls to him were from a public pay phone. He asked me one time, "Son, how do you like Fairfield?"

"Daddy, I am new in this city and look forward to the tenth grade," I replied. "I will get adjusted here as time progresses." He never admitted the guilt and wrong of how his wife and son were mistreated. I even asked him, "Do you miss Mama instead of me?"

He avoided answering my question. Instead, Daddy asked, "Do your mother misses me?" I could not believe what I heard. This made me more disappointed in him. I said, "Daddy, I need to go now." I told Mama about our conversation. She did not respond that much. Belinda Birdsong knew her ex-husband's behavior.

To be honest with you, Daddy did miss the woman that was his wife for fifteen years. Before leaving Richmond, I made a vow to God, in prayer.

"Lord, I will never do this to my wife and children." This became a major attention grabber for me, at 15-years-old.

Years later, I still remind myself of the lesson. My father and grandfather might have made this mistake. The only person that can break this path is me. Mama even had a talk with me. The discovery of Fairfield became interesting. The people were friendly, pleasant and easy to engage in conversation. They were about families, education and planning the future.

"I love this engagement of conversation," I said to myself.

Before I began Fairfield High School, Mama said, "James, you are about to begin your sophomore year. This is going to be different. We are in a new community. You do not have to worry about being bullied. That is not going to happen."

In August 1995, something happened to me. God began to deal with me spiritually. He was preparing me to preach my first sermon. For this to occur, I stopped visiting Daddy for four months. He could not understand why his son suddenly stopped his visits. We did communicate. I was already disappointed in my father.

One day I said, "I am not going back home for a while. I need my space."

I began to pray and read the Bible even more. Sermon notes began to come. I wrote them on paper. Mama learned about this. She was so happy. I believe she may have said, "My son has been called and chosen by God before he was born." I had to leave Daddy, friends, classmates, and others in Richmond for my redemption journey.

I began my sophomore year at Fairfield High School on September 7, 1995. A few days before school began, Mama made a trip to Richmond at Kennedy High School. The Fairfield-Suisun Unified School District needed my transcripts from Kennedy. I did not go with her to Richmond. Mama told me, "James, you were asked about while I was in the office." A few of my friends from the ninth grade already knew I moved to Fairfield. The other students did not know.

I will always remember the first day of classes at Fairfield. A memory comes to me, for this day. As I walked on the campus, I prayed and said, "Lord, I am new here at Fairfield High School. I don't know anyone. I spent all my life in Richmond. I will be here for the next three years. Use me to be an example to the students, in Jesus' name." I met a few students and instantly became friends. I had a World Civilization class in the first period. On the morning of September 7, 1995, I walked in the classroom. The teacher at the time was Clarie Borge. She worked for many years at the Fairfield/Suisun Unified School District.

There was one young man that recognized me. He said, "I remember you last year at Kennedy."

I smiled and said, "You sure did go there. I remember you as well." His name was Fermin. We were classmates at Kennedy in our ninth-grade year. He was dating a girl I knew from Adams named Maria. Fermin and his family moved to Suisun City after our ninth-grade year.

Fermin and I became very close friends during our tenure at Fairfield High. While we were attending Kennedy, I would talk to him and Maria. I did not know him that well. God is good all the time. He came from a devoted Christian family. This young man could sing and perform. The two of us would talk about the gospel and Christian contemporary music industry, a lot.

Like me, Fermin had to leave Richmond. One class I had, Public Speaking, became my favorite course in the tenth grade. The teacher allowed us to introduce ourselves. I told the class about myself and my upbringing. I began to do public speaking at 12-years-old. I wrote my sixth-grade teacher, Mrs. Grove, a letter about my experience at Fairfield High. She was so proud and shared the news with the other teachers at Nystrom.

I began to give speeches on topics that were given to me. My classmates knew the preaching ability in me. They recognized that potential. The Lord began to use me in ministry at the campus. One student I remember very well decided to come up with a name for me. I happened to be known as Brother James on campus. My classmates and the students began to tell their parents about me. Guess what? The girls had approached me. I never had a girlfriend at Fairfield High School. There was one girl I had a crush on. She felt the same way about me. We were special education students.

One of my classmates told me during our telephone conversation, "Brother James, my mother wants to speak with you the next time." I began to pray and counsel my peers. Many of them were going through problems and situations. I never shared their personal conversations with me to anyone. They admired, respected and trusted me. I became the person they could depend on.

A few days before Halloween, I attended the public speaking class at Fairfield High School. I had a classmate that was a junior in his eleventh-grade year. I am not going to mention his name due to the nature of a situation. I was the new kid on the block at Fairfield High. I arrived on campus one morning. Upon departing World Civilization, I proceeded to the Public Speaking class for the second period. There were students crying.

"What in the world is going on, Jesus?" I asked myself. Not too long after that, I walked into the Public Speaking class. Some of my classmates were crying.

Moments later, I asked the teacher, "Can I go to the restroom?" She gave me the hall pass. Once I returned, she and my classmates were leaving for the library. It was a sad moment. Not knowing what had occurred, I approached a student named

Preston. He was in his final year of high school as a senior.

"What is going on, Preston?" I asked him.

He stopped and said, "One of our classmates committed suicide last night." You should have seen my facial expression. I said, "Lord, have mercy." The first month of my sophomore year was filled with tragedies. There were three other students at Fairfield High School that committed suicide. This young man in my class had one more year to pursue before his graduation.

I told Preston, "I saw our classmate yesterday and he seemed fine. Now, we come to school and he is gone." The news of this tragedy spread throughout the community. The administrators at the school contacted grief counselors through Solano County to provide counseling services for us. I remember them in the library. The pastors and area churches did prayer vigils.

Leaders are tested in situations for their strengths and weaknesses. As my teacher and classmates were in the library comforting each other, I went to the phone booth. Located in front of the office, I called Mama and told her what happened.

"I want to come home, Mama."

Being the Woman of God, of her character, she knew I was still adjusting to Fairfield High School.

"James, you need to be there today, she told me. "You need to be strong for the entire campus. Your classmates are depending on you." Reflecting many years later, I am glad she encouraged me to stay.

After I finished talking to Mama, I made a collect call to Daddy as he was at home on Maine Avenue. I told him about the situation. He was speechless. I had never encountered a situation like this before. Classes continued throughout the day. I made myself available to the students and classmates. They began to invite me to the churches they attended in cities of Solano County.

For my senior year, at Fairfield High School, the students acknowledged me later as "the pastor." I am still known as this today. You can even ask the city's local newspaper, the Daily Republic, on Texas Street. They have written and published several stories on me, since 1998. Apostle Hale had three churches he served as the overseer. God was preparing him to be consecrated as bishop. One of the churches was located on Webster Street near Travis Boulevard. Pastor Hale recommended us there. The Fairfield Church of New Beginnings was under the leadership of Pastor Claudia.

It was a transitional house for people that desired to turn their lives around for the better. Pastor Claudia owned the property and Apostle Hale designated it as New Beginnings Spiritual Hospital. The third church was in San Bernardino, California, east of Los Angeles. During the last four months of 1995, we were active and participants in Apostle Hale's ministry. Pastor Claudia became aware of the tragedy at Fairfield High School. Several churches in the area began to pray for the school, the students, and their families. A few days later, my classmate's funeral arrangements were announced.

The funeral was going to be held on October 31, 1995, at Holy Spirit Church on North Texas Street. This is a well-known Catholic Church in Fairfield. I have never attended a funeral or mass at a Catholic Church in my life. While having a conversation with Mama, at the apartment, I said to her, "I need to attend the funeral."

She smiled at me. "James, the teachers and students need to see you there."

I approached Pastor Claudia and asked her and a woman named Shelia to attend the funeral with me. They were glad to do this. Shelia and her daughter, Amanda, were members of New Beginnings. The four of us arrived at the church. My classmate was well loved and popular. I never had the opportunity to know him. I was still a new student at the campus.

The funeral was about three hours. The Catholic Church does their funerals different from Christian denominations. This is what I see. I was raised in the Pentecostal Church as Apostolic and Church of God in Christ. The Birdsong family's heritage is Baptist. I could have declined to attend the funeral. I went to support my classmate's family, Fairfield High School, and the community.

That is the characteristics of effective leadership. My pastoral journey began at Fairfield High School, as a 15-year-old teenage boy. Once the funeral ended, Mrs. Borge greeted me. I introduced her to Mama, Pastor Claudia, and Shelia. My classmates were smiling. They were expecting me to attend the funeral. As my classmate's family prepared for his interment at a nearby cemetery, Mrs. Borge and the others returned to the school. She and the students wanted to know if I coming to the campus for classes.

Mama said, "James will not be there until tomorrow."

It was Halloween when the funeral was held. I returned home with Mama. I needed time off from classes. I resumed my classes the following day. The students would not stop talking about this young man. My sermon preparation became the focus for me. Daddy continued to ask me about visiting him.

While attending Fairfield High School, my name continued to spread throughout the community. The area pastors even became aware of me. I began to receive invitations to attend their churches from my classmates. Another high school in the city, Armijo High School, on Washington Street, even knew about me. My classmates had friends that attended Armijo.

I also met the first African-American mayor of Fairfield that served one term in office. His name was Chuck Hammond. He operated an independently owned insurance agency in Fairfield. I remember meeting a group of Armijo students, while they were volunteering at New Beginnings Spiritual Hospital. They wanted me to leave Fairfield High School and attend their institution.

When my classmates at Fairfield learned about what the students at Armijo were suggesting, one of them said, "Brother James, if you leave us, then we are going to protest. We see what they are trying to do." I was not going to leave Fairfield High School, until my graduation in 1998. Two weeks before our Christmas break, Mama and I made a visit to New Beginnings Spiritual Hospital. I greeted Pastor Claudia in her office. She knew about my sermon preparation.

"Pastor Claudia, I need to make a phone call to the pastor of my home church in Richmond."

She smiled and said, "Sure, you can."

The person I was referring to was Clim. I called him at his home in Vallejo. He answered the phone and said, "Hello, Junior. How are you doing?"

I am doing fine, Pastor," I said. "I need to share something with you."

Clim stopped and listened. "What is going on, Junior?"

I broke the news to him. "Pastor, I know Daddy has been asking about when I will come and visit him. It has been four months since I last came home to Richmond. The Lord has finally brought me back into the ministry."

Clim was so happy to hear this. "I have been knowing you all of your life, Junior."

"I know that, pastor. Our families go way back. I have been preparing to preach my first sermon. I need to know if I can come home and do this at the church." He said, "I will give you fifteen minutes before I come forth." I was smiling and rejoicing during the conversation. I had one more thing to tell Clim.

"Please don't tell Daddy I am coming home to visit him. I want to surprise him."

We ended our conservation and I called Daddy. He did not know about the plan. Clim promised me he would not share the news with my father. This was going to be a reunion with him, in four months. On December 1, 1995, I attended classes at Fairfield High School. My classmates already became aware of my preaching engagement in Richmond. Once school ended, Mama and I proceeded on Interstate 80 towards Richmond. Daddy continued to rent out rooms at the house on Maine Avenue. We pulled up in front of the house. My father was upstairs in his bedroom. I rang the doorbell and one of his tenants, named Susan, answered the door.

I said very softly, "Susan, don't mention my name. I am about to surprise Daddy. It's been four months." She was very glad to see me. Susan would inform me what was going on with my father during the visits. This woman had a disability. However, she was very smart and wise.

While Mama was outside in her Ford Tempo GL, I began to tiptoe slowly upstairs. Daddy said, "Who is at the door? I didn't say a word and neither did Susan. He walked out of his room and walked downstairs.

"Who is at the door?" Daddy asked. He stopped and said, "Junior, is that you, son?"

I said, "Yes, it's me, Daddy."

My father was overcome with emotion. We hugged right there in the middle of the stairs. Susan was smiling. With a smile on his face, Daddy said, "How have you been, Junior?" I looked at him and replied, "I am doing fine, Daddy. I will be here until Monday."

He returned to his room as I walked outside to retrieve my clothes and items from Mama's car. I said goodbye to her. She went to visit a friend of hers before going back to Fairfield. A few minutes later, I walked into Daddy's room and we began to talk.

I told him, "I am preaching my first sermon this Sunday at the church."

"Does Clim know about this, son?" I said, "Yes, he does, Daddy. I called him two weeks ago. This has already been discussed."

Daddy told the story of his son receiving the Holy Ghost in our living room when God healed me from my speech impediment. He said, "Son, I was holding you by your feet when they placed you on the coffee table. Something told me to let you go." You know what I believe, everybody? My father knew the hands of the Lord were upon me. He knew about my preaching and singing abilities. I made a visit to Luzan and Kitara later that day. Kitara had graduated college two years earlier, in 1993, from the University of California of East Bay, in Hayward, California. She obtained her Bachelor's degree in Communications.

My Godmother and God sister were shocked about what I told them on this visit to Richmond. They were wondering where I had been for the last four months. I returned home on a mission from God. I preached the sermon on December 3rd, 1995, at Holy Mission Christian Center. The opening text scripture came from Ephesians 6:4, "And, ye fathers, provoke not your children to wrath: but bring them up in the nurture and admonition of the Lord." The sermon became a message to the fathers, for their God-given responsibility to their children.

I returned home that Sunday afternoon to Fairfield. The

Lord blessed me to successfully complete the last three years of high school. Between late 1996 and early 1998, I began to record sermon tapes on audio cassettes on my mother's tape recorder. I considered them "preaching albums" and presented them to my classmates. They began to play them in their cars and homes. I did a total of five. They would consist of speeches, gospel stories, testimonies and mini-sermons on one cassette. The recordings become so popular that they were on demand.

My classmates would ask me, "Brother James, when are you going to do another one? You can really get down in your preaching." The responses were heart touching to me. I even had classmates to tell me, "My family loves you." I did one more recording. It was my first live effort. I returned home to Richmond, at Holy Mission Christian Center, for the recording, after completing high school.

The most memorable time was the twelfth grade. I am referring to my senior year. This is where the highlight became for me. I began to meet noted figures that were respected in Solano County, from pastors to educators. My journey in community service and business administration began at 17-years-old. One of those individuals was Seretha Jefferson. She worked as a special projects coordinator for the Solano County Office of Education, and later, the California Department of Education. She became one of my mentors. We are still close to this day. I was introduced to her by my home economics teacher, Alice Claiborne. I graduated with honors from Fairfield High School on June 12, 1998.

While the memories of Fairfield High School will forever remain in my heart, I had a tragic loss in my family before I completed high school. No child ever wants to experience this in their lives. This is not easy for me to write. I am going to be strong.

A day I will never forget, my graduation at Fairfield High School in Fairfield, California

JAMES C. BIRDSONG, JR.

CHAPTER TWENTY

Losing Daddy

June 10, 1997, will be a day I will never forget. The day I learned Daddy had died is still unbelievable many years later. Ian's birthday is on this same day. Albert also shared the same birthday. Occasionally, I still have my moments of grief. Young people, I really need you to listen right now. Losing a parent is one of the hardest feelings to adjust to. No matter how much you try, the tears still come.

Right now, I am reflecting on a song by one of my favorite gospel artists, Bishop Paul S. Morton. He recorded a song in 1993, titled, *Your Tears*, written by Bishop Richard "Mr. Clean" White.

This song became a national hit for Bishop Morton. The song says, "Your tears are just temporary relief. Your tears are just a release of the pain, sorrow, grief. Your tears are expressions that can't control. A little crying is alright, but after a while, you won't cry no more." The part of the song that encourages my heart, when Bishop Morton sings, "Don't you worry, God's gonna wipe every tear away." One of these days, there will be no more sadness.

I am going to explain exactly what happened regarding my father. A year before his sudden death, I continued to visit him once a month in Richmond. Our family experienced another tragedy in the summer of 1996. I was about to complete the final weeks of the tenth grade at Fairfield High School. Mama and I began to attend Sunday morning services at New Beginnings Ministry of Love in Santa Rosa. Apostle Hale was on demand in his preaching, television and radio broadcasting and traveling nationwide as an evangelist.

Albert had retired from Sunset Books four years earlier. One day as he was at home in Benicia with Barbara, he picked up the phone and called Daddy.

"James Charles, guess what, boy?" Daddy stopped and listened to his cousin. They had been close since they were children in Greenwood, Louisiana.

"What is going on, man?" my father asked.

Albert said, "I am going home to visit Mama."

I am referring to Aunt Ola Mae. She was in her early eighties. Albert flew to Shreveport and spent time with his mother. He lost two of his brothers, Robert James and Huey "Woo" Birdsong. Albert was the sibling among Uncle George and Aunt Ola Mae's children they could depend on.

After spending time with Aunt Ola Mae, he returned home to the Bay Area. Albert suffered a stroke. This was his third and it was very severe. He was rushed to Kaiser Hospital in Vallejo. Albert slipped into a coma. Daddy learned the news from Barbara. He immediately called Clim.

"Clim, if Junior calls you, please tell him to come home. Albert suffered a stroke. He's in a coma." Devastated by the news, I knew Daddy had endured so much when it came to family members and close friends that were special to him. The news about Albert's stroke spread among our family, his friends, former co-workers, the community, and especially, Friendship Missionary Baptist Church.

Once school concluded for the day, Mama picked me up. "I need to call Daddy," I said to her. We arrived at a phone booth, at the Shell gas station, at the corner of North Texas Street and East Tabor Avenue. I could not reach Daddy.

I proceeded to call Clim. He said, "Junior, I am so glad

you called me. Your father told me to share this with you about Albert."

"What is going on with my cousin?"

Clim gave me the devastating news. "You need to call your father again. Albert went to Shreveport to visit his mother. He just returned home not too long ago. Albert had another stroke." I said, "Oh my God. Is Albert alright, pastor?"

The news was not good. "He lapsed into a coma. Albert is at Kaiser here in Vallejo. His brothers and sisters are on their way."

"Thank you, pastor. I am going to call Daddy again and come home to Richmond."

Mama knew something was wrong. "Did you get ahold of your father?" she asked me.

I looked at Mama and said, "No, I didn't. I just finished talking to the pastor. Albert had another stroke. He is now in a coma. I need to go home and see Daddy."

Mama said, "Lord have mercy."

Right after Albert lapsed into a coma, Aunt Ola Mae died. All of Albert's surviving siblings attended their mother's funeral in Shreveport, Louisiana.

Aunt Ola Mae's health was failing. Albert went to Shreveport for the last time to visit her. She dies and he lapsed into a coma at Kaiser Hospital. Mama took me to Richmond the next day. I walked in the house and talked to Daddy. I said, "I want to see Albert."

He asked a friend of his to drive us to the hospital. The two of us walked in Albert's room. I will never forget to see him lying there connected to a life support machine. I had never witnessed this in person. Daddy began to talk to his cousin.

"Albert, we love you. I have Junior with me. We are praying for you." Daddy was crying during this time. I had to be strong for him and myself. I thought about Barbara, Albert Jr., Orland

and his grandchildren. For the next two years, I prayed, trusted and believed in God for a Divine Healing regarding Albert. I wanted God to heal Albert completely so he could go home and be with his wife and family. He did eventually come out of the coma. However, my cousin never fully recovered. Albert had to be transferred to a care facility in Vallejo.

The Lord called Albert home on February 5, 1999, at 56-years-old. He died almost two years later, after Daddy. Albert's funeral was well attended at Friendship. I miss Albert. He was a good man that was well loved and respected. I was 18-years-old when Albert passed away. Barbara, I want you to know Albert's legacy will continue to live on. I am going to proceed further with the story of my father's sudden death. The last time I visited Daddy was on March 29, 1997. I had engaged in professional vocal lessons to help me sing more effectively.

By now, you already know about the musical roots of the Birdsong family. I was in my junior year as an eleventh grader at Fairfield High School. I am going to proceed further with the story of my father's sudden death. The last time I visited Daddy was on March 29, 1997. I had engaged in professional vocal lessons to help me sing more effectively. By now, you already know about the musical roots of the Birdsong family. I was in my junior year as an eleventh grader at Fairfield High School.

Two months earlier, Mama and I began to attend services at Emmanuel Temple Apostolic Church on Fifth Street in Vallejo, where the late District Elder Jerry Hubbard was the pastor. The church is now pastored by Suffragan Bishop Bryan Harris, a veteran of the United States Marine Corps. Mother Johnnie Hubbard is the associate pastor of the church. She was Elder Hubbard's wife.

I will never forget Mother Lillian Chitmon. She died in 2015. Mother Chitmon supported the young people. She loved me and my mother. Bishop Harris served as the youth pastor during Elder Hubbard's tenure. Mama joined the church not too long after our second visit. Since my arrival at Fairfield High School, I was invited to Emmanuel by one of my classmates that graduated in 1997, named Kimberlee. She was like a sister to me during our tenure at Fairfield High School. She was dating Preston. They have been married for more than 10 years and have two wonderful children. Kimberlee, along with her parents, brother, and sister, were longtime members at Emmanuel.

I met many people at the church. Not too long after I met Mrs. Claiborne, she told me about a popular college and career conference for African-American youth, in Northern California, named after Booker T. Washington. It was held once a year at the campus of Solano Community College in Fairfield. Seretha Jefferson was the visionary of this conference.

Mrs. Claiborne said, "James, we are going to have the conference again. I would like for you to be a workshop facilitator." I was her teacher's assistant during my eleventh-grade year.

"I am going to visit my father for the weekend, Mrs. Claiborne," I said.

The conference was held on March 27th. During this time, my goal was to rebuild the father-son relationship with Daddy. There were times I wanted to come out and express my opinion on how he treated me, and why he mistreated Mama. I still had questions for him after the divorce.

"What am I going to do? How should I approach my father and tell him things he never knew during the five-year dilemma I experienced?" I also asked myself, "Should I tell him his son wanted to commit suicide?" I wanted to confront Daddy. I think he knew I wanted to have a serious talk with him. So many thoughts went in my mind. I was thinking, "I love my father very much. I also know he will explode on me about this."

I went to Richmond and visited Daddy that weekend. There were three more months until the completion of the 1996-1997 school year at Fairfield High. I was already popular on campus and throughout the community. When I made the visit to Daddy, he was no longer a member at Holy Mission Christian Center. Solano Community College in Fairfield. Seretha Jefferson was the visionary of this conference. I would visit Daddy once a month and attend services with Clim and JoEvelyn. My childhood friends that sang in the choir were focusing on completing high school and preparing for college. I was in the same position.

Daddy joined Peniel Missionary Baptist Church on San Pablo Dam Road in El Sobrante, where Reverend J.L. Porter was the pastor. Reverend Porter knew Daddy, Grandmother Charlene, and Uncle Roosevelt when they were members at Elisabeth Missionary Baptist Church in the 1970s. He and a few members that came out of Elisabeth wanted Daddy to join. This occurred in late 1996.

A longtime member of Peniel, named Dorothy Yopp, was a longtime family friend of Daddy, Grandmother Charlene and Uncle Roosevelt. She began to do bookings for my father to perform in local gospel concerts throughout Richmond. Daddy even performed in Vallejo. I never attended the concerts, since I lived in Fairfield. The people loved his singing.

"Son, I am about to go record in the studio," he told me weeks before I came home to visit him. I called Mama and shared this with her. She said, "James, I tried to have your father to record and perform in gospel music. He had those opportunities many years ago."

She was telling the truth. I really believed my father was

going to move forward and record. He was 58-years-old, by this time. I also learned that he was making plans to attend the Durden family reunion in Greenwood. My father was going to sing and preach at the family church for the service. I am referring to Greenwood No. 1 Baptist Church. This would have been his fourth visit in his hometown. The last time Daddy went to Greenwood was in July 1992, for the Ed and Ida Birdsong Family Reunion. The family wanted to see him again. He wanted me to accompany him to Shreveport.

"Daddy, I am going to summer school for six weeks at Armijo High School. I am graduating next year, in 1998." He knew I was determined to finish high school. "I look forward to that day, son," Daddy said proudly.

I said, "Before you go to Shreveport, I will come home and spend Father's Day with you." This was a few weeks prior to June 10th. My last Father's Day with him was in June 1996. He was still a member of Holy Mission Christian Center. Jessica, Mercedes and their cousin, Jocelyn along with myself, did a reunion performance of a song we sang in the choir. It was our first time singing together in four years. This was the Father's Day service in 1996. The congregation was blessed. My father was impressed.

Daddy asked his home care provider to go with him to the family reunion. He already had his flight reservations. Henry and Dorothy Jean told him he could stay with them during the Durden Family Reunion.

After I visited him, I decided to focus on completing the eleventh grade. We continued to remain in contact. My father appeared to be in good spirits during our final talks. I called him one day and he told me, "I look forward to being a grandfather one day."

"Thank you, Daddy, for the compliment," I said, with a

smile.

The week before Father's Day, I purchased a card and mailed it to Daddy. I was going to give it to him in person. My father loved Lincoln Town Cars. He was in the process of purchasing a new 1997 Lincoln Town Car sedan, once the family reunion ended. Daddy wanted to give me the 1984 Lincoln Town Car he and Mama purchased, once I graduated from high school. That was the plan according to what Clim told me.

I called Daddy on June 7, 1997. It was a Saturday morning. I no longer had to call him from a payphone. He answered the phone after the first ring. "Hi, Daddy. How are you doing?" "I am doing fine, son. I received your Father's Day card. Thank you so much."

Our conversation lasted approximately 15 to 20 minutes. He was excited about me completing the eleventh grade, the family reunion and his son graduating high school in 1998. I was about to visit him for the first time in almost three months. I had already packed a few of my clothes. Moments later, Daddy said, "Junior, I have to answer this call. Call me back on Monday."

I said, "Okay Daddy. I love you."

This is very hard for me to share. I did not realize June 7, 1997, would be our last time we ever spoke. The following day, on Sunday, Mama and I attended services at Emmanuel Temple Apostolic Church.

Mother Hubbard would give the young people $20.00 for their birthday. On June 9, 1997, I went to Serendipity Bible House on Madison Street in Fairfield, after school, to purchase the cassette of Dorothy Norwood's new album at the time, *Hattie B's Daughter*. As you know, she is a living legend and icon in gospel music. Ms. Norwood is known as "the World's Greatest Gospel Storyteller."

Fermin gave me the cassette of her previous album, *Shake the Devil Off*. I gave him BeBe and CeCe Winans *Different Lifestyles*. This is my favorite album by the brother and sister duo.

I played the cassette of Hattie B's Daughter, in Mama's car, as we were on our way home on Grande Circle. This was also the final week of my eleventh-grade year in high school. I had to submit my final assignments and tests. I was determined to return in September as a high school senior. The Fairfield High School Class of 1997 was graduating that week.

I forgot to call Daddy back as he requested. My mind was focused on finals and summer school for six weeks. I returned to school on June 10th of that week. Everything was fine on this day. Mama picked me up after school. We lived about five to seven minutes away from Fairfield High School. Once we approached the apartment complex on Grande Circle, a sudden thought came to mind.

"Mama, I need to call Daddy. I forgot to call him on yesterday." She said, "Okay James." We lived on the second story of the complex. Once Mama and I walked inside of our apartment, I immediately walked into my room and greeted my parakeet, Sprite. I picked up the phone and called Daddy. The first attempt was no answer. I made several more calls.

"James, did you get ahold of your father?" Mama asked.

Something was wrong. "This is not like Daddy at all." I had a feeling inside of me. Mama stopped and said, "Call Clim."

I called him and he answered the phone. "Pastor, I have been trying to reach Daddy since I came home from school. Have you heard from him?"

"Yes, I did, Junior," he said. "Let me speak to your mother."

I passed the phone to Mama. Clim broke the news to her. Standing there by my door, Mama passed me the phone. I am going to be strong, ladies and gentlemen. Clim breaks the news to me no child ever wants to hear. I am going to tell you exactly what he said.

"What is going on with Daddy?" I asked.

"Junior, I am sorry to tell you. Your father died early this morning." Mama witnessed my reaction. The only thing I could say was, "What?"

I needed answers. Clim told me Daddy had a heart attack. I was like, "Daddy never had any heart condition." After the phone call ended, I needed time for myself. While I was in my room trying to digest the news, so many things were going through my mind. First, I was planning to visit him for Father's Day, before I began summer school. Second, he looked forward to attending the Durden Family Reunion in Greenwood, Louisiana. Third, we talked Saturday and now he is gone forever.

From what I was told, Daddy was found in his room at Maine Avenue unresponsive. Mama and I made several phone calls to family and friends about Daddy's sudden death. I could have stayed home from school on June 11. Daddy knew his son was about to embark in his final year of high school. He also heard me talking about singing gospel music and attending a Bible college. About an hour later, I felt his presence in my room. This had never happened to me before.

I am not sure what was going on during his final days. I prayed that night and said, "Lord, Daddy is gone. I know there are more members of the Birdsong family out there. I never met them. Help me, in the Name of Jesus, to find them."

Years later, the Lord answered my prayer in that area.

I want the world to know, I had already forgiven my father for what he had done, prior to his death. I am going to share these lessons in the concluding chapter of this book.

I went to school on June 11th and told my teachers and

classmates, "I will not be attending the graduation. I just lost my father."

Condolences were coming for me on campus. My family learned about Daddy's death. Before he died, I reflected on his words, "Son, you are going to be a famous man someday." People tell me, "Your father knew that before he died."

Mama wanted to attend the funeral. She decided not to go. I cannot share too many details of Mama's decision, the funeral arrangements, and burial. Daddy's funeral was held on June 13, 1997, at Peniel Missionary Baptist Church in El Sobrante.

I rode with Clim and JoEvelyn in their 1993 Lincoln Town Car, for the funeral. Mama dropped me off at McDonald's on North Texas Street in Fairfield, where Clim and JoEvelyn could meet me. On our way to the church, we stopped by to pick up Mercedes. JoEvelyn asked Mercedes to attend the funeral as a support to me. The four of us arrived at Peniel. I walked into the sanctuary to view Daddy. He was wearing a black suit, with a burgundy dress shirt, and his gray tie with burgundy and white pinstripes. The casket was a medium burgundy. Rose Manor Funeral Service handled the arrangements. I placed a photo of me taken at Fairfield High School in the casket on his chest. I wanted to cry. The tears just did not come out. Since Albert was still in a coma, Barbara and Albert Jr. attended the service with Mary Lou and Myria. The directors at Rose Manor closed the casket as the family did the procession. Reverend Porter delivered the eulogy. Two of my father's tenants attended the funeral.

Prior to the eulogy, I walked to the pulpit where he and Clim were sitting.

Clim was about to say something to me. When Reverend Porter saw what happened, he said to him softly, "Let Birdsong's son speak. That was his father. It's alright."

I cannot remember what I said. However, I do remember saying, "I will be graduating high school next year and Daddy will not be here." You should have seen the facial expressions.

The casket was reopened for the last time. I looked at Daddy and said, "I will see you again in heaven." I took two of my fingers and kissed them. I touched his forehead. I gave the notice for the directors to close the casket. After the funeral ended, we proceeded to Rolling Hills Memorial Park for Daddy's interment. He is not too far from Grandmother Charlene and Uncle Roosevelt. Once the burial was completed, I hugged Barbara, Mary Lou, and Myria.

The Birdsong family legacy had been inherited to me on that day. Daddy was 58-years-old when he died. He had a birthday coming up in one month. He attended services at Peniel that Sunday and died two days later. I still have questions to this very day. I was 17-years-old and did not know what to do next in this situation.

I wanted my father to be around for a long time, despite the marital dilemma between him and Mama. I returned home to Fairfield that afternoon, with one parent left. This became another process in the redemption. From time to time, I still have my moments when the tears come. I did learn a lot from my father as a child. He made sure I knew about the Birdsong family legacy. I may resemble James Charles Birdsong, Sr. Daddy was his own person. For the next few years, I needed to evaluate my life on what God had in store for me and be a man. This occurred after high school, with the new millennium. The storm is still passing over.

THE BEST IS YET TO COME

JAMES C. BIRDSONG, JR.

CHAPTER TWENTY-ONE

A New Century and Millennium

The stage of adulthood can be a challenge. I have my share of this process. The death of my father and completion of high school had sanctioned me to take a journey on finding myself. "What do you mean, James, finding yourself?" Allow me to give clarification. A new century and millennium were on the horizon, and I needed to take that time to develop into manhood. By the laws of the United States, you are considered an adult at 18-years-old.

After I graduated with fellow classmates, at Fairfield High School, on June 12, 1998, I had taken the time to move forth with the next chapter of my life. Some of my classmates were going to attend Solano Community College, while others were making their plans to join the United States Armed Services or move away to cities, such as Los Angeles and outside the State of California.

I wanted to attend a Christian college and major in Theology. I continued to research and learn the gospel music industry. A few days after Albert's funeral, I attended three classes on Saturdays at the Allen Temple Leadership Institute in Oakland on International Boulevard. This is the two-year Bible College of Allen Temple Baptist Church where the Reverend J. Alfred Smith, Sr. was the pastor. He is now the pastor emeritus.

The church is now pastored by his son, the Reverend J. Alfred Smith, Jr. When Reverend Smith was the pastor, he was my professor in Theology at Allen Temple Leadership Institute. He is a nationally known professor, scholar and theologian that has authored books and lectured at noted universities throughout the United States.

The Allen Temple Leadership Institute is a partnership between the church, Patten College in Oakland and the American Baptist Seminary of the West, in Berkeley. I successfully completed the three courses. I was planning to return there for the fall 1999 semester. However, I was unable to complete their Certificate in Theology program due to transportation arrangements between Fairfield and Oakland. I planned to graduate there in 2000 and transfer to Patten for my Bachelor of Arts in Theology.

God had another plan for me in academics. Two weeks after my high school graduation, I went to Wal-Mart in Suisun City to purchase my first desktop computer. It was an Acer Aspire with Windows 95. Microsoft just introduced Windows 98. They were encouraging the users of Windows 95 to upgrade. I never upgraded my computer to Windows 98. I also purchased a Hewlett-Packard inkjet printer.

A few months before my graduation, I told my mother, "Mama, I am going to convert my room into an office." That is exactly what I did. I began to display my awards throughout the years and what I received prior to high school, on the wall, in frames. My high school diploma was also on display.

I got rid of the twin bed that was given to me in Richmond and purchased a sofa bed. You should have seen my home office by the time it was completed. It remained my office for the next seven years. In the summer of 1998, Mrs. Claiborne called me about the planning committee meeting for the upcoming Booker T. Washington Revisited Student Conference. It was going to be held on March 26, 1999, at Solano Community College.

I decided to join the planning committee. This is where

I learned how to do administrative duties and preside over meetings. I always acknowledged Seretha in this effort. She is the one who taught me about the organizational administration. I was 18-years-old, at the time. Seretha announced this would be the tenth anniversary and the final conference. With Seretha's approval, I wrote a letter to General Colin Powell inviting him to deliver our keynote address at the conference. He had another prior engagement.

I still needed to find out the definition of redemption in my life. I lost my father and needed answers in many areas. By the final months of 1998, my name was still well known throughout the community. My classmates that graduated, either with or after me, remained in touch. They knew "the pastor" was still available. I still read the many messages in my high school yearbook.

Many of them told me, "Fairfield High School will never be the same after you leave us." I am still touched from their compliments and encouragement to this present day. The new millennium was on the minds of millions around the world. President Clinton had two more years until his term ended on January 20, 2001. He and his wife, First Lady Hillary Rodham Clinton, worked tirelessly for the American people during his eight years in the White House. He was reelected for a second term in the 1996 Presidential Election, after defeating his Republican opponent, Senator Bob Dole.

I will never forget when Fairfield High School allowed the students to do an activity to vote for either President Clinton or Senator Dole. Since we could not vote until the age of 18, our principal at the time was preparing us on voting in a political election as adults. They had boxes and we cast our votes. The school newspaper made an announcement prior to the election.

The Lord was still dealing with me about the pastoral

ministry, after high school.

In August 1998, I called Clim and said, "Pastor, I have not been back at Holy Mission Christian Center since last year. I am ready to come home."

I took time away from Emmanuel Temple Apostolic Church. I would do mini-sermons and speeches on Sundays at Holy Mission. I began to travel with Clim and JoEvelyn to district meetings in Sacramento and Stockton since they were Church of God in Christ. I remained at the church until early 1999.

After eight years of being a member, the Lord allowed me to be released. By this time, I was 19-years-old and needed a change in my life. JoEvelyn's granddaughters and the young people I knew from our choir days were now adults, like me. We were focusing on college and career opportunities. I could not stop thinking about Daddy. Sometimes, I would find myself viewing old family photos.

The memories of the good times continued to reflect on me. Sometimes, I would cry and say, "I miss Daddy. I wish things were like it was in my childhood." Mama and Daddy had a beautiful marriage in the eighties. I did not allow friends and former classmates to see me in this way. They always looked up to me for strength and guidance. Pastors and ministers are human.

They have their good and bad days. Society views them as action heroes to save the day. Only Jesus Christ saves, delivers and sets free. As the new millennium was approaching, I had to pick up the pieces where Daddy left off as it came to the Birdsong family legacy. The older members of my family were sharing different things with me.

They began to say, "James Jr., you look exactly like your father." This is still being told to me today. I had to tell them, "I want you to see me for me. There is no way I can ever replace my father." He knew all the birthdays and the history very well. If he was still alive today, I would have told him, "You are the historian of the Birdsong family."

Once I departed as a member of Holy Mission Christian Center, I limited my visits in Richmond. There were still murders occurring in the city. This is the city where I was born and raised. Richmond remained in my thoughts and prayers. I loved Fairfield and the community loved me. The trials and tests of this season had me to say one thing, "Through the trials, tests, and shedding of tears, my best is yet to come."

I knew from a child God had a great future in store for me. Will this finally happen in the new millennium? There were many decisions to be made in my life, spiritually and naturally. I needed a change in my life.

I asked myself one day, "Should I moved out of Fairfield?"

Friends and former classmates of mine from Fairfield High School were also in the same position as me. They began to transition out of the area. I remember this very well. All of us began to feel a change and wanted better. Even to this day, I still have former classmates that live in the Fairfield/Suisun City area. There is only a handful of them, to my knowledge. The public would not stop talking about 2000.

It became the discussion, from the pulpits on Sunday mornings to the media outlets. Before 2000, I went to Food 4 Less, a popular grocery store on West Texas Street in Fairfield, with Mama. As we proceeded to the checkout counter with our groceries, I saw a tabloid magazine on the shelf. Young people, do not believe what they write and publish. Those magazines publish stories of famous celebrities, events, and politicians that are not the truth.

This magazine reported Jesus Christ will return on Y2K. I said, "The devil is a liar. These people need to stop."

The scripture declares, "Heaven and earth shall pass away, but my words shall not pass away. But of that day and hour no one knows, not even the angels of heaven, not the Son, but the Father alone" (Matthew 24:35-36). Only the Lord Himself knows of his Second Coming. Even to this day, there are still predictions of the Second Coming of Jesus Christ. We cannot predict this in our lifetime.

For the first six months of 1999, Mama and I became members of Macedonia Church of God in Christ, in Suisun City, where Elder Kenneth Martin, Sr. is the pastor. The church was in the Marina Center Shopping Plaza next to State 12. They moved to their current location on Walters Boulevard once their new sanctuary was completed.

Prior to Macedonia, Mama moved her church membership from Emmanuel Temple Apostolic Church and joined Flame of Fire Outreach Ministries, in Fairfield, where Reverend Mark Johnson was the pastor. I attended Fairfield High School with his daughter, Natasha. She can really sing. I hope she records in the gospel music industry, someday.

I had some other classmates that were members at Flame of Fire. This is another church in the area I was invited to during my high school years. While I never joined Flames of Fire, I had visited the church on a few occasions. We were members of Macedonia for five months. Before I met Elder Martin, he was already familiar with me. One of my classmates was a member of Macedonia. He and his wife, First Lady Cheryl Martin, supported the young people in their church and the community. He even gave me a ride to the Allen Temple Leadership Institute in Oakland, for my classes, one Saturday afternoon, and returned home to Fairfield.

Not too many pastors will do this for their congregation. During my time of living in Fairfield, all the area pastors knew each other. They heard about me being "the pastor" at Fairfield High School. I made several visits to the administration, teachers, and students at my alma mater, after graduation.

I was truly being missed on campus. This tells me, "James, you are still loved and not forgotten."

After many discussions and what the media had reported, the moment had finally come. We said farewell to the nineties and entered the year of 2000. The 21st century came our way. We are now in the new millennium.

We also opened a new chapter of my life as I now became an adult. I was about to turn 20-years-old and embark into the twenties. The stage of redemption was not officially completed, for me. I still needed more growth and development to do. In other words, I had entered into manhood. Fatherless and not knowing what to do, my faith was being tested.

The Lord did bring older men into my life that became father figures. One of them was Apostle Hale. He eventually became a mentor to me, in my pastoral ministry journey. I wanted to go back at New Beginnings Ministry of Love. We returned there. Apostle and First Lady Hale welcomed us back, with opened arms.

Daddy has already been decreased almost two years when 2000 came. I began to miss my family and wanted to see them. I was planning to visit them in Shreveport, Louisiana during the summer of 1998. The Lord was not ready for me to do this then.

Earlier in this chapter, I said, "The best is yet to come." I am being very open and honest with the world. In our lives, there are happy times in the journey. On January 13, 2000, the Daily Republic published a story on me. This was not the first time I had been featured in this popular daily newspaper.

However, this story became very special for me. It became my first ever interview in the media. The article, titled, *The Pastor: Teen Authors Books, Sets Sights on Ministry*, gave me the opportunity for the public in Fairfield, Suisun City, and surrounding areas to know the real James Charles Birdsong, Jr. and my story, of an inner-city African-American boy on how he had to overcome obstacles. The newspaper had learned about the release of my first book, *One Marriage, Many Tales, And a Separation: A Message of Hope*. It was published by AuthorHouse in Bloomington, Indiana.

I first began to write the book in 1994, at 14-years-old, when the marital crisis of my parents was on the verge of divorce. I was still living in Richmond, at the time. The manuscript was completed three years later. I had submitted it to some major book publishing companies and smaller presses.

You are listening to a young man who knows the book publishing industry very well. The writer of the article, Amy Maginnis-Honey, came to my apartment on Grande Circle to do the interview. Her photographer, Judith Sagami, took a photo of me sitting at the piano Daddy purchased for me when I was 7-years-old. The photo was published in the article.

Once the story was published, it became the major talk throughout the community and surrounding areas. My family even heard about the story. I decided not to visit Fairfield High School that day. I already knew I would be treated like a celebrity.

The community knew who James Charles Birdsong, Jr. was all about. My mother decided to call Fairfield High School and spoke to the receptionist.

"Do you know James is featured in today's issue of the Daily Republic?" Mama told the receptionist. The receptionist asked, "Our very own James Birdsong is in the newspaper?"

"Yes, he is," Mama told the receptionist.

"Ms. Birdsong, I am about to go and read the article."

For the next few weeks, I became the conversation at churches, family dinners, schools, the buses, businesses, organizations and more. A pastor that even lived in Fairfield called me one evening. He wanted me to speak at his church in Richmond. I was unable to do the engagement.

There was one girl that graduated with me that heard about the story. We graduated Fairfield High School in 1998. I called her one day. Her stepfather answered the phone. I will never forget what he said.

"Brother James, you are about to go national."

They were members of Mt. Calvary Baptist Church, in Fairfield, where Dr. Claybon Lea, Jr. is the pastor. Dr. Lea even mentioned my name during a Sunday morning service. The book was eventually in stock at Serependity Bible House and available online through Barnes and Noble, Amazon and other major retailers.

The Lord blessed me to be featured in other print media, outside of my area and the State of California. I focused on promoting the book for the next three years. I had opportunities to be interviewed on local television and a few radio stations outside the State of California. When God gives you a revelation of His Will and Purpose for your life, it does become a reality.

In 2001, the Lord began to deal with me about leaving California. I wanted a new direction and purpose in life. Sometimes, we must leave our comfort zone and take the step of faith. I had always wanted to live in the south.

There was one city in mind. I am referring to Atlanta, Georgia. The only place to the south I experienced was Shreveport, Louisiana, for family visits. Atlanta was becoming the city of opportunities for African-Americans throughout the

United States. I wanted to go further in gospel music and attend a Christian-based university as a Theology major in pastoral ministry. California began to change in the late nineties. I did not begin to feel those changes until 2000.

I was not alone in this situation. There were friends and classmates of mine that wanted to relocate out of California to the south, as well. I wanted to do a visit in Atlanta and experience what had been written and reported in the media, for myself. This is the birthplace of Martin Luther King, Jr. and the home of noted African-Americans in the Civil Rights Movement.

Atlanta is also the home to famous African-Americans in entertainment, music, sports, business, media, pastors and politicians, such as, Tyler Perry, Keisha Knight-Pulliam, Usher, TLC, Jermaine Dupri, T.I., Monica, Dorothy Norwood, William Murphy, III, Dottie Peoples, James Bignon, Keke Wyatt, Angie Stone, baseball legend Hank Aaron of the Atlanta Braves, radio personality Frank Ski of V-103, Congressman John Lewis and many others.

The popular television reality shows, *The Real Housewives of Atlanta* and *Love & Hip Hop of Atlanta* are filmed there. Bobby Brown and Whitney Houston lived in Atlanta when they were married.

One morning, I was feeling frustrated. "What's wrong, James?" Mama asked.

With a sad look on my face, I said, "I am tired of California. I want to leave and go to Atlanta. I want to break into the gospel music industry. I want to go to Bible College."

Mama knew my heart's desire. She wanted a change in her life, as well.

"James, God is going to make a way for us to go to Atlanta," Mama said, smiling. "We have to be patient and have faith."

My mother has always been a woman that had so much faith.

When your mother speaks words of wisdom and knowledge, you better listen to her. God is speaking through our mothers. I reflected on her words of encouragement. The new millennium prepared me for my moment, while the redemption became lessons in class. I may have graduated from high school three years earlier, and attended college courses for one semester at Allen Temple Leadership Institute, I was still a student in learning.

I am referring to the lessons of redemption in my initial stages of adulthood. I was in my early twenties. "When I was a child, I spake as a child, I understood as a child, I thought as a child: but when I became a man, I put away childish things" (I Corinthians 13:11). This scripture gives me the reflection of transition from childhood to adulthood.

During the storms, my faith began to build stronger. Our testimonies are birthed out of tests. The experience becomes our story of life essentials. This begins when we are born. Applications of these essentials became the central focus for the next four years. God's blessings continued to come for me.

In March 2002, I received a letter from the editors of Marquis Who's Who Publications, in New Providence, New Jersey. The letter stated I had been considered for inclusion in the biographical reference book, Who's Who in America. It was for their 2003 57th Edition. I was not listed in the reference book. The consideration alone was an honor itself. The Daily Republic made the announcement in a small article. Even during awards and proclamations being bestowed upon me locally and nationally, the dream of moving to Atlanta rested heavily on my mind. During my twenties, I was not dating a young woman due to the focus in ministry, the gospel music industry, college and relocation to Atlanta.

After almost 10 years of living in Fairfield and spending

twenty-five years of my life in California, the time had finally arrived for me. Mama and I made the huge step of faith and began our journey to Atlanta. We placed our belongings at a storage facility in Fairfield. Prior to the transition, I had two farewell parties in the Bay Area. On August 1, 2005, we boarded a Greyhound bus from Vallejo and went to Dallas, Texas. Mama told me one day during our brief time in Dallas, "James, I don't know how God is going to do this. We are going to step out on faith and go to Atlanta."

My faith was being tested again. We boarded the Greyhound Bus and departed Dallas on November 2, 2005. Mama and I arrived in Atlanta the next day. For two weeks, we were homeless and sleeping at a shelter in Forest Park, Georgia. The Lord brought us through the storm. Before we departed California, the nation was in shock about September 11, 2001. I had promised family and friends about the status of this book and what to expect. I am going to talk about the day that forever changed the course of history.

Being recognized by Reverend Rosa Mills-Arnold, the founder of the Albert T. Mills Enrichment Center in Atlanta, Georgia at their graduation ceremony. I gave a speech.

A reunion with a few of my friends and classmates at Beulah Heights University in Atlanta, Georgia following a gospel concert on campus to raise money for the homeless

JAMES C. BIRDSONG, JR.

CHAPTER TWENTY-TWO

9/11

Our nation will never forget the tragedy of September 11, 2001. Sixteen years later, people still remember what they were doing when the World Trade Center towers in New York were hit by two commercial passenger airplanes. I can remember this as if it happened only yesterday. Nine months prior, President George W. Bush took the oath of office as the forty-third President of the United States on January 20, 2001.

He served as the forty-sixth Governor of Texas, from 1995 to 2000. A Republican candidate in the 2000 Presidential Election, he defeated his Democrat opponent, Vice-President Al Gore. The nation observed the results of this election.

I was still living in Fairfield when this occurred and three years out of high school. Subsequently, Mama and I joined Faith Tabernacle Church of God in Christ on Parker Road, in Fairfield, near the Travis Air Force Base entry. Elder James Bellamy was the pastor of this church. I already knew one of his daughters, Sophia, and a few of my former classmates were members of Faith Tabernacle.

As of 2002, Faith Tabernacle Church of God in Christ is no longer in existence to my knowledge.. Elder Bellamy made the choice to restart his ministry in evangelism.

Elder Bellamy had four ministers serving with him. I served as one of them. Two of them were in their twenties, like me. The third minister was an older gentleman. God truly used me during ministry at Faith Tabernacle. The church was located inside of a shopping center complex. I attended Bible study on Wednesday nights and participated in the Friday evening services. Faith Tabernacle became another church in the area I had been invited during high school. As soon as former classmates that were members noticed me for the first visit, they were very delighted. Elder Bellamy recognized I existed as a minister. The ministers labored together as a team. I remember a time when Elder Bellamy and his family were on vacation in Taiwan. He gave us instructions on what to do in his absence. A few weeks before 9/11, I arranged plans for a speaking engagement at Booker T. Washington High School, in Shreveport.

The principal at the time and my friend, Dr. Curley White, extended the invitation. I had an on the air interview for the Stellar Award winning gospel radio station, KOKA 980 AM, with Reverend Eddie Giles, and a forthcoming printed story in the Shreveport Sun, the city only African-American owned newspaper.

A preaching engagement arranged for me at New Greenwood Baptist Church, in Greenwood, was additional for the itinerary. Reverend Charles Gardner was the pastor at the time. After his departure, Reverend Bertnard Bailey was selected to succeed him. Reverend Bailey is now the pastor of New Greenwood Baptist Church.

It was going to be my first time in Shreveport, since 1992. A thought came to mind. "This is going to be the first time going to Shreveport without Daddy." Deep inside my heart, he would've wanted me to go visit our family. I intended to fly from San Francisco to Shreveport. Plans were about to transform in what you are about to read in this chapter.

On the morning of September 11, 2001, I happened to be at home in Fairfield. The moment I awakened from my sleep, Mama said, "James, the first World Trade Center tower just been hit by a plane. The news is reporting it now." I turned on the television. American Airlines Flight 11 departed Logan International Airport, in Boston, Massachusetts, at 7:59 AM EST. The flight destination was bound for Los Angeles. There were seventy-six passengers on this flight, with eleven crew members on board.

At 8:45 AM EST, the Boeing 767 aircraft flew into the North Tower of the World Trade Center. All the passengers and crew members on board were killed.

Media reports stated the aircraft was controlled by hijackers. United Airlines Flight 175 departed Logan International Airport. The departure time was 8:14 AM EST. For this flight, bounded for Los Angeles, there were fifty-one passengers, with a crew of nine. At 9:03 AM EST, the hijackers flew the aircraft into the South Tower of the World Trade Center. Everyone on this flight was killed. Various media outlets around the world showed actual footage of both airplanes flying into the World Trade Center towers.

"I cannot believe what is happening," I said. Both towers had collapsed. The World Trade Center towers were 110 stories.

There were two more commercial airline flights. American Airlines Flight 77, a Boeing 757, departed Washington-Dulles International Airport, at 8:20 AM EST, bounded for Los Angeles. There was a crew of six and fifty-three passengers on board. It flew into the Pentagon in Arlington County, Virginia. This happened at 9:37 AM EST.

The United States had been attacked. People were speculating, "What is President Bush going to do?" The world observed this tragedy on television, and they were testing President Bush's leadership.

Minutes later, Lula calls me. "Cousin James, are you watching the news?"

"Yes, I am, Lula," I told her. "This is a sad day in our nation."

She was at home in Fairfield, with her 4-year-old daughter, Ilexia. Her husband, Louis, had worked the day before. I am not sure if he had just arrived home from work. We had our televisions on discussing this state of emergency. Journalists described the fourth flight, United Airlines Flight 93. With its destination for San Francisco, the Boeing 757 departed Newark International Airport, in Newark, New Jersey, at 8:42 AM EST. The four hijackers breached the aircraft's cockpit.

They overpowered the onboard crew of seven and thirty-three passengers approximately 46 minutes after takeoff. As passengers attempted to subdue the hijackers, the aircraft crashed into a field in Stonycreek Township, at 10:03 AM EST. Stonycreek Township is near Shanksville, Pennsylvania. Over 3,000 people were killed during the attacks in New York City and Washington, D.C., including more than 400 police officers and firefighters (History.com, 2016).

Based on a federal investigation, the attacks on September 11th were caused by 19 militants associated with the Islamic extremist group called al-Qaeda, as suicide attacks. The attackers were from Saudi Arabia and several other Arab nations, according to media reports. In my lifetime, I have never witnessed a tragedy such as 9/11. The nation went into mourning. At our apartment in Fairfield, the televisions remained on throughout the day as media reports continued discussing what happened in America.

Over 3,000 people were killed during the attacks in New York City and Washington, D.C., including more than 400 police officers and firefighters (History.com, 2016).

Based on a federal investigation, the attacks on September 11th were caused by 19 militants associated with the Islamic extremist group called al-Qaeda, as suicide attacks. The attackers were from Saudi Arabia and several other Arab nations, according to media reports. In my lifetime, I have never witnessed a tragedy such as 9/11. The nation went into mourning. At our apartment in Fairfield, the televisions remained on throughout the day as media reports continued discussing what happened in America.

Lula and I called each other at various times. Weeks prior to 9/11, the plans to make a speech at Booker T. Washington High School were still being finalized. On the morning of September 11, President Bush made a visit to Emma F. Booker Elementary School, in Sarasota, Florida. The press displayed a video of President Bush reading *The Pet Goat*, a children's book published in 1995. The authors were Siegfried Engelmann and Elaine C. Bruner.

The students, a group of second graders, in their class, recited the story. The Pet Goat attained nationwide awareness. At about 9:10 AM EST, White House Chief of Staff, Andrew Card walked over to President Bush. He notified him about a second airplane that struck the World Trade Center. President Bush was scheduled to deliver a short press conference, at about 9:30 AM EST.

Accompanied by the United States Secret Service agents, President Bush made a speech about the attacks before departing for the White House that evening. Since America was attacked, I made the decision to reschedule my itinerary for Shreveport in November. Commercial airline flights all over the country remained grounded due to this condition. Only military, police and medical flights were permitted.

Civilian air traffic resumed on September 13, 2001. Stricter airport security checks took place, disallowing box cutting knives. The hijackers used them during the 9/11 attacks.

I immediately approached Mama and said, "I am going to

ride Greyhound instead of the airlines, for Shreveport." She stated the right decision had been made. I saved three hundred dollars intended for flight reservations.

Thereafter, I called Dr. White, and requested, "Can I come there in November?" He said, "Sure you can, Mr. Birdsong."

Reverend Gardner was notified for the rescheduling of my preaching engagement at New Greenwood Baptist Church.

Pastors of numerous denominations held prayer vigils and revival services, for God's intervention in the United States. Elder Bellamy telephoned the ministers to attend services on Friday night. Faith Tabernacle had services on Friday evenings. This is common in the Church of God in Christ.

One of the ministers picked me up for the service on September 14. Faith Tabernacle was a small church at a shopping center. Elder Bellamy preached an anointed sermon. We united together to pray for the nation. Some of the members were crying. The ministers assisted Elder Bellamy through the altar call.

The country had one emphasis on their minds, the victims of 9/11 and why this appeared. I pointed out to President Bush's leadership is tested. Sorrow came for the victim's families. They expressed grief over their mothers, fathers, sons, daughters, uncles, aunts, cousins, grandchildren and friends. Subsequently, I prayed for the nation, the victim's families and political figures in office.

9/11 had shaken the entertainment world as postponement of concerts was made after the terrorist attacks. The Latin Grammys and Emily Awards had to be canceled based on reports by journalists. Michael Jackson joined forces alongside various artists for United We Stand, a benefit concert on October 21, 2001, at the Robert F. Kennedy Memorial Stadium in Washington, D.C.

They performed *What More Can I Give* and *Man in the Mirror* as a tribute to the victims of the attacks. Artists of different genres of music had to change their plans. Madonna had a performance scheduled in Los Angeles. The concert had to be postponed. When Janet Jackson released her *All for You* album, she canceled a concert in Tampa, Florida as well as the entire European leg of her world tour. Numerous theme parks, landmarks, film productions, public transportation systems and parks had an important impact, in prompting cancellations and closures. Every individual, from the homeless to billionaires, felt the effects of 9/11. Personally, emotions came upon me. I may not have been in New York or Washington, D.C. on September 11, 2001. Mama and Daddy nurtured me to have compassion for others in their period of mourning. When a tragedy happens, it affects everybody. President Bush had much on his plate, regarding the attacks. The country looked to him for answers. He realized as commander-in-chief, a president's job is heavy labor.

Let me give you a reminder of leadership principles. We are going to be tested in our strengths and weaknesses. How was President Bush going to handle this situation in his presidency? This became the question for millions of Americas, including myself. I was only 21-years old when 9/11 happened. Will the American people present their judgment of his leadership?

Later that evening on September 11th, President Bush delivered an address to the nation, at 8:30 PM EST, from the White House Oval Office. Airing live, throughout the country, on television, his address took six minutes. I recall him expressing sorrow as he quoted these exact words.

"Today, our fellow citizens, our way of life, our very freedom came under attack in a series of deliberate and deadly terrorist attacks. The victims were in airplanes, or in their offices:

secretaries, businessmen and women, military and federal workers, moms and dads, friends and neighbors. Thousands of lives were suddenly ended by evil, despicable acts of terror."

He acknowledged emergency teams in New York and Washington, D.C. and members of Congress. President Bush quoted Psalm 23:4, "Yea, though I walk through the valley of the shadow of death, I will fear no evil: for thou art with me; thy rod and thy staff they comfort me." The nation continued to grieve, and people still needed answers.

None of my family members or friends traveled on September 11, 2001. Memorial services were held for the victims. I did not stop praying for their families. The country and the world listened to President Bush's reaction. The question on people's minds, "What is going to happen next?" He addressed a joint session of Congress on September 20, 2001, at Capitol Hill, in Washington. D.C. Held on a Thursday evening, he announced his plans for action about the attacks on 9/11. The American people were waiting for President Bush's response to their questions.

"The evidence we have gathered all points to a collection of loosely affiliated terrorist organizations known as al Qaeda. They are some of the murderers indicted for bombing American embassies in Tanzania and Kenya and responsible for bombing the USS Cole," he said to the joint session of Congress. From that point on, the American people figured this out.

"Oh Lord, have mercy, Jesus. The Saints need to start praying."

One month later, U.S. forces (with UK and coalition allies) invaded Afghanistan to oust the Taliban regime. Operation Enduring Freedom began on October 7, 2001, as British and U.S. conducted airstrike campaigns over enemy targets. The capital city of Afghanistan, Kabul, fell by mid-November. Prior to the war, President Bush made remarks on the White House lawn as journalists listened.

"This crusade, this war on terrorism is going to take a while," he said. People still raised questions about 9/11, the deaths of their loved ones, and parents had sons to fight in combat. As soon as President Bush's term ended, after serving eight years in the presidency, this operation continued as President Obama succeeded him. It broke my heart to hear the press announce the deaths of 2,356 U.S. services members in the line of duty. My heart went out to their families, and especially, mothers and fathers.

President Obama made the decision to officially end Operation Enduring Freedom on December 28, 2014, after a 13-year war in Afghanistan. Military officials did a ceremony in Kabul. I had former classmates that joined the armed services, after completing high school. They had to sacrifice their lives on the battlefield and leave their families behind. Thankfully, these former classmates survived. As the months went on, journalists announced a federal investigation into the 9/11 attacks. Millions of Americans still demanded answers about their loved ones and the victims whose lives were cut short.

In response to the investigation, a legislation by Congress and the signature of President Bush created the 9/11 Commission on November 27, 2002. This became an independent, bi-partisan commission chartered to prepare a detailed account of the circumstances surrounding the terrorist attacks on September 11, 2001.

Chaired by former New Jersey Governor Thomas H. Kean, the ten-member commission called government officials that served under the Clinton and Bush administrations to testify. Former President Clinton and former Vice President Gore gave private testimonies, whereas President Bush and Vice President

Dick Cheney insisted on testifying together and not under oath.

The Commission issued their final report on July 22, 2004, as a publication, before being closed almost a month later. The report is now available to the public as a book and archived item.

Prayers for healing, reconciliation, and trust began to escalate in the hearts and minds of our country. Trust is a topic of dependence. At that time, the American people felt all hope was gone after 9/11. Sometimes in life, a situation places us in the position where thoughts of giving up come to mind. After the sacrifices made, upon our best abilities, we question God on why the situation happens. This is part of life in daily challenges and routines.

Older people often say, "Never question God." Yes, I understand the elders' position. The scripture reads, "My God, my God, why hast thou forsaken me? why art thou so far from helping me, and from the words of my roaring?" (Psalm 22:1). 9/11 placed people in a position where they felt the Lord had forgotten about them. I am here to say God observes our tears and sorrow. A perfect example is Job. The Bible describes him as a man who lived righteously to the Lord.

If you are aware of the story, Satan prompted to challenge Job's integrity. He only served God as the protection was upon his life. Suddenly, the protection became removed, allowing Satan to take his wealth, his children, and his physical health. Job's character had to be tested. One day, his wife tells him, "Curse God and die."

Did Job listen and proceed? No, he did not. Instead of doing that, Job cursed the day of his birth. His anguished over his plight and stops short of accusing God of injustice. At the end of his dilemma, Job received ten times more of blessings. The point of this scenario is due to our situations, and we feel alone in despair. God is there during tragedies, whatever, of personal and public life.

Fifteen years later, the hurts do not disappear. Those lives affected are still mourning over loved ones. Memorial services are held once a year as the anniversary of 9/11 is observed throughout the country. Accounts of this tragedy gave people different perspectives. I remember the time airports did not have security checkpoints before boarding a flight.

Formed in 2002, the United States Department of Homeland Security is responsible for public safety, from antiterrorism to disaster prevention. This federal government cabinet was created in response to the 9/11 attacks. Before you board a flight at airports, TSA agents employed by the United States Department of Homeland Security conduct passenger screenings.

A year before 9/11, I flew Southwest Airlines from Oakland to Los Angeles, to visit family for a week during my twentieth birthday. There were no security checkpoints for passengers at airports, at that time. Now, you must produce your airline boarding pass and ID to a TSA agent, before the screening process. I experienced this first hand in November 2009, for a Delta Airlines flight from Atlanta to Oakland, with a layover in Salt Lake City, Utah, to speak at my high school class reunion, for the Fairfield High School Class of 1998. Times have changed since that tragic day on September 11, 2001.

A word of encouragement to the families of 9/11 victims. I may not have any family or friends that were in New York or Washington, D.C. Through life, I learned the memories of those that transition to eternity will forever remain in our hearts. The deaths of Daddy, Uncle Roosevelt, Albert, Uncle Paul and others had their effects on me. There is not going to be a day the thought will disappear. On that day, the nation and millions worldwide mourned with you. Every man, woman, boy and girl of all ages, cultures, and races felt your pain. Your labor for justice and truth is not in vain. I am also reflecting the families of our armed services members that lost their lives in combat during Operation Enduring Freedom.

Prayers for the families of the 9/11 victims and Operating Enduring Freedom are with you. I cannot forget about the survivors and veterans. They suffered so much, and regaining the happiness they once had is not the same.

The older saints always said, "We need the love and peace of God." Can I get a witness, somebody? Individuals that thought enough of the 9/11 families and survivors became good Samaritans. God bless those men and women that lend their helping hand. Random acts of kindness demonstrate compassion. This is the lesson instilled in me from birth. We expect the Lord's blessings, and our works have not been performed. In other words, God does his part if we take the time to abide by His Word. Millions of Americans were doing different activities, from school to work, as to September 11, 2001, changed the course of history.

While there are more questions to be raised, we still have more work to do on this journey. I do know one thing for sure, things are going to get better one day. I believe this with all my heart. I am asking for the readers around the world to never stop praying for the 9/11 families and the veterans that placed their lives on the battlefield.

The most important prayer for this request is the children that lost their mothers, fathers, grandparents, brothers and sisters, aunts, uncles, and cousins. They must grow up without their loved ones to witness their accomplishments, such as high school and college graduations. 9/11 happened during my lifetime, and I had to share my thoughts in this book. Now,

I will share the story of how gospel music became my second Calling. Family and friends have been waiting for this to be told. Choir rehearsal is about to begin.

Me with Bishop William Murphy, III

Me with Dorothy Norwood

Being honored again at Nystrom Elementary School in my hometown

Me with Harvey Watkins, Jr. of the Canton Spirituals

Kendal Richardson of the Grapevine HIV/AIDS Foundation, former gospel radio personality Sandi Sam, mom and myself at the 6th Annual Agape Gospel Awards show

Leah Curry-Williams of the Mississippi Mass Choir, myself and mom

THE BEST IS YET TO COME

CHAPTER TWENTY-THREE

Journey in the Gospel Music Industry

Since I was a child, the desire of singing became a dream for me in life. The Lord had called and chosen me to preach the Gospel of Jesus Christ, at 3-years-old, after being miraculously healed from a speech impediment. I would be singing by making up songs. God blessed the Birdsong family with the gift of singing.

I listened to Daddy singing around the house and in the church. He had 45 LP albums of gospel artists from the Golden Era, such as, Sam Cooke and the Soul Sitters, the Harmonizing Four, Mahalia Jackson, Madame Edna Gallmon Cooke, the Swan Silvertones, the Caravans, Brother Joe May, the Clara Ward Singers, the Highway Q'Cs, the Five Blind Boys of Alabama and his favorite singer, the Reverend Cleophus Robinson.

People continuously question me, to this day. "James, how did you encounter all these professionals in the gospel music industry?" I made a promise about this journey of gospel music, and it will be revealed.

For me to pursue a career as a recording artist and songwriter, I had to be educated about the business of gospel music. This all began in September 1996, as an eleventh-grade student, at Fairfield High School. We had internet access for our library computers. Before this happened, a determination came upon me about being a gospel artist, in life. One afternoon during the lunch period, Fermin and I walked into the library. At the computers, we browsed websites of the national gospel and Christian contemporary artists. They were signed to major record labels, had songs that made the Billboard Gospel and

Christian Top 10 charts and winning Grammy, Stellar and Dove Awards. These artists also had sold out concerts.

I was raised on the music of Edwin, Walter and Tramaine Hawkins. Natives of Oakland, the Hawkins Family are legends and trailblazers of contemporary gospel music. KDIA 1310 AM played songs by the Hawkins Family. Alongside them, there was Shirley Caesar, Reverend James Cleveland, Vanessa Bell Armstrong, Reverend Timothy Wright, Myrna Summers, Andrae Crouch, Keith Pringle, Reverend F.C. Barnes and Reverend Janice Brown, Minister Thomas Whitfield, the Clark Sisters, Reverend Milton Brunson and the Thompson Community Singers, and the Winans.

Vickie Winans came onto the scene through the highlight of the Winans popularity. Her first hit, *We Shall Behold Him*, made the gospel charts. Douglas Miller made his signature song, *My Soul Has Been Anchored* famous throughout the United States. The Richard Smallwood Singers recorded *Center of My Soul* that is now considered one of gospel music's greatest songs.

Quartets, such as the Mighty Clouds of Joy, the Jackson Southernaires, the Rance Allen Group, and the Williams Brothers, were popular in my childhood. These gospel artists had concerts at the Paramount and Calvin Simmons Theaters in Oakland. The concerts would be sold out and on demand. As the nineties came, the young people started to focus on Kirk Franklin, Yolanda Adams, Fred Hammond, John P. Kee, BeBe and CeCe Winans, Trin-I-Tee 5:7 and Hezekiah Walker. They were the new generation of gospel artists.

I visited the websites every day at school, reading their success stories in the industry. My eleventh-grade English teacher instructed the class to write a report about career opportunities of our interest. Gospel music became the passion for this assignment. She gave me a passing grade. For the remainder of high school, I continued to study and research the gospel music industry. A month before Daddy's demise, Mrs. Claiborne and the students of her Foods and Fashion Merchandising classes went on a field trip to San Francisco. She took her students every year for a fashion tour of businesses that specialized in the fashion industry.

As a child, I would go to San Francisco for field trips at popular attractions. I was not a student of Mrs. Claiborne as an eleventh grader. I served as her assistant where I received grades. Before her students arrived for class, she asked me, "James, would you like to go with us on the field trip?"

"Sure, Mrs. Claiborne, I would love to go with you and the class," I said.

The last field trip for me was during the eighth grade in Mrs. Glover's class, at Adams Middle School. We went to Stinson Beach north of San Francisco in Marin County. The beach is very beautiful where the Pacific Ocean exists. I have not returned there since the eighth grade. That's been a long time of ago for me.

A few days after the conversation with Mrs. Claiborne, I accompanied her as the teacher's assistant on their field trip to San Francisco. Her daughter, Kinya, came along. She graduated Fairfield High School, with me and our classmates, in 1998. Mrs. Claiborne had numerous connections in the fashion industry. She wanted her students to learn about the business for a potential career.

While I am not involved in fashion, it developed the learning experience for me. Through the lunch hour, I walked to the Virgin Records Store in downtown San Francisco. Mrs. Claiborne and her students were nearby. I had about $25 dollars in my wallet. Once I stepped inside the store, I proceeded to the gospel music section. You can imagine my facial expression.

Something else captured the attention of this 17-year-old boy. Reading has been a foundation for me.

Moments later, I walked over to the magazine shelf. There was a magazine on the shelf. It was the April/May 1997 issue of Gospel Today, a national African-American gospel music and ministry magazine. Robert Townsend and Suzaune Douglass were featured on the cover. They were the leading actor and actress of the television sitcom, The Parent Hood. This was one of the sitcoms in the nineties.

"I never heard of this magazine," I said to myself.

I picked up the magazine and began to scroll through it. About three minutes, I placed the magazine back on the shelf. Then suddenly, I walked away and found myself reading it again. I needed to learn more about the gospel music industry based on the national perspective.

Guess what, everybody? I decided to purchase the magazine. Five months earlier, I began vocal lessons in singing. My favorite male gospel artist at the time was Reverend James Moore. He was anointed by God and knew how to engage the audience during live recordings and concerts. Mama began to purchase VHS cassettes of Reverend Moore, Shirley Caesar, the Mississippi Mass Choir, Albertina Walker, the Canton Spirituals, Slim and the Supreme Angeles, the Williams Brothers, Douglas Miller and Helen Baylor.

We had a VCR in our living room. She played those VHS cassettes daily. Mama knew I was a fan of Reverend Moore. When Tramaine Hawkins recorded her Grammy Award winning album, *Tramaine Hawkins Live*, in 1990, at the Calvin Simmons Theater in Oakland, she did a video of the entire recording session. I was 9-years-old when Tramaine did the recording. We had the VHS cassette to her album.

For the next year, I began to read the issue of Gospel Today magazine every day. The more reading for me allowed the engagement to begin my plan of moving forward. Eventually, I became a monthly subscriber of Gospel Today for five years. I want to publicly acknowledge the visionary of Gospel Today, Teresa Hairston, for inspiring me to learn the business of gospel music. A month before leaving California, I attended Sunday morning services at Love Center Ministries on International Boulevard in Oakland. This is the church Walter Hawkins was the founder and senior pastor. I met him one time during my visit to the church. I will never forget what he said following services.

"James, I would love to talk to you. We have an engagement in San Francisco."

He, along with Edwin, Lynette and the Love Center Choir, had to perform at a special event for the United Nations. I remained in contact with his manager, James Edmond. Walter died on July 11, 2010, at 61-years-old. It became a major lost in gospel music. I never had the opportunity to know Walter Hawkins. The one time of meeting him became a blessing for me.

He wrote the songs Tramaine recorded, such as *Changed, He's That Kind of Friend, Going up Yonder, Holy One,* and *The Potter's House.* Walter knew how to write and composed songs.

When I was in Dallas for two months, I made a telephone call to Andre Gates. For those of you in the gospel music industry and entertainment arena, at large, he serves as the Manager to Dottie Peoples. He is actively involved in the Stellar Awards. Andre once worked for Atlanta International Records in Atlanta, where Dottie was their biggest selling artist. We became close friends.

Andre and I have been friends for almost twelve years. He always shared my testimony with our colleagues in the industry.

He can be in Los Angeles, Chicago, New York, Detroit, or in another country. My name is mentioned in the conversation. I met Dorothy Norwood and Dottie Peoples through him. Dorothy and Dottie were already aware of me. I began listening to their music in high school.

Once Mama and I moved to Atlanta, I began to put my plan into action. The Gospel Music Workshop of America is the most recognized organization in this genre of music. Founded by Reverend Cleveland in 1967, his vision was to bring together singers, choirs, quartet groups, songwriters, and musicians, to demonstrate their God-given gifts on the national platform. Many of our national gospel artists received their beginnings at the Gospel Music Workshop of America. The organization is still going strong, after Reverend Cleveland's death on February 5, 1991.

Before I moved from California, I had the opportunity to correspond with Evelyn White on several occasions. She serves as the Chapter Representative of the Gospel Music Workshop of America, Atlanta Chapter. We refer to her as "Auntie." I joined the Atlanta Chapter and they welcomed me with opened arms. The doors continued to open for me in gospel music.

I told Andre one day during my time in Dallas, "When I move to Atlanta, I am going to join the Gospel Music Workshop of America."

He was very excited. Ms. White and another friend of mine in the organization, named Ralph Davis, also knew this ahead of time, prior to the relocation from California. Ms. White's Assistant Chapter Representatives are Ted Jeans, Earnestine Gray, and of course, Ralph himself. I am still a member of the Gospel Music Workshop of America, to this day. I am affiliated with the Atlanta Chapter. God has allowed me to meet and network with many of our colleagues in the organization that is members of local chapters outside Atlanta.

One of the chapter representatives, Terry Williams, presides over the Shreveport Chapter. He knows my family in Shreveport, personally. I still desired to sing professionally in gospel music. I have also been blessed to meet Reverend Calvin Bernard Rhone, one of gospel music's greatest songwriters that have been recording nationally since my childhood. He is now the Chapter Representative of the Gospel Music Workshop of America, Los Angeles Chapter.

In the early nineties, Reverend Rhone wrote and recorded, *Live in Me Jesus* that became a national hit in gospel music. I remember hearing this song on the radio. His songwriting credits range from Reverend Cleveland to Tramaine Hawkins, the late Daryl Coley and the Gospel Music Workshop of America Mass Choir. Mama encouraged me to resume vocal lessons. One of my classmates I met in my freshman year of college at Beulah Heights University, Myra Franklin, told me about a friend of hers named Vivian Varner. "

James, I am going to tell Vivian about you." Myra said. "She is an excellent vocal instructor and choir director."

Vivian served as the director of the Shades of Pink Breast Cancer Survivor's Choir. I began the sessions with Vivian. Every Saturday afternoon, I would take Cobb Community Transit to Kennesaw, Georgia, to meet with her. I was 27-years-old, at the time. Myra died of complications of breast cancer in 2007. She was well loved and is missed, to this day.

I will never forget the first meeting with Vivian. She asked me to sing a song. I did a few verses of Amazing Grace. A serious expression on her face, she said, "James, you have it in you. Your range is high and like Walter Hawkins and Donnie McClurkin." She needed to hear me so I could sing more effectively. Vivian is a professional singer in this field.

Her encouragement gave me the confidence to pursue this industry. I knew this was my calling and desire as a child. As the months went by, I did everything Vivian told me to do. I recorded our sessions on my audio cassette recorder. There was an improvement. I prayed and asked the Lord to help me, in this process.

I remember when my favorite vocalist of the Mississippi Mass Choir, Lillian Lilly, recorded her solo album, *Gotta Have Faith*. She is best known for singing the choir's hit song, *It's Good to Know Jesus*. After Malaco Records released her solo project, I purchased the cassette at Serendipity Bible House.

One day, at home in Fairfield, I told Mama, "I want to meet Lillian Lilly." I began to listen to the Mississippi Mass Choir in high school, along with their collaborations with Reverend Moore. In 2007, Lillian was being honored by a friend of hers, at a gospel music awards ceremony in Mississippi. I called this person. She learned I was a fan of Lillian. The Lord knew what He was doing. Lillian's friend said, "Do you want to speak to her?"

The excitement came upon me. She connected me to her and the rest is history. Lillian is one of my closest friends in the gospel music industry. We remained in touch. I saw her at the 2009 31st Annual Mississippi Gospel Music Awards in Jackson, Mississippi. The ceremony is held at the Marriott Hotel, yearly.

I finally had the opportunity to meet three of the Canton Spirituals. They were Harvey Watkins, Jr., Cornelius Dwayne Watkins, and Merlin Lucious. I met several major artists that were nominated for awards. The honorees that evening was Dorothy Norwood, The Jackson Southernaires, and the Pilgrim Jubilees. After the ceremony ended, I greeted Dorothy and offered my congratulations. This was my second encounter with this living legend of gospel music.

I called Andre upon returning home to Atlanta. He said, "Ms. Norwood told me she saw you at the award ceremony in Jackson, Mississippi." I have been blessed to speak with Dorothy on the telephone more than once. I decided to attend the Mississippi Gospel Music Awards, again, in 2010.

I also believed in supporting the college gospel choirs in Atlanta. As a college student, I visited the gospel choirs at their campuses. They would host concerts throughout the year. The Lord blessed me to work with them. I made many connections with the students of their college gospel choirs. One of those choirs was G.I.F.T.E.D., at Georgia Institute of Technology. The acronym is God's Influence Flowing through Every Disciple. My friend and a talented actress, named Dréa Lewis, founded G.I.F.T.E.D. as an undergraduate student at Georgia Institute of Technology.

In 2008, they hosted their annual Gospel Explosion at the Ferst Center for the Arts. The choir requested me to collaborate with them in the event. Canton Jones was the national artist for this concert. We had choirs from Georgia State University, Emory University and a few colleges throughout the metro Atlanta area. It became a remarkable success. G.I.F.T.E.D. returned the favor when Beulah Heights University did our first ever concert in 2009. They were one of the featured artists.

The concert raised money for Hosea Feed the Hungry, a non-profit organization in Atlanta founded by Civil Rights legend, the late Reverend Hosea Williams. He was one of the soldiers in the Civil Rights Movement during the 1960s and marched with Martin Luther King, Jr. Hosea Feed the Hungry is respected and admired throughout the community. His daughter, Elisabeth Omilami, is now the CEO of the organization. I attended Beulah Heights University with her daughter, Juanita, during our undergraduate studies.

There was one person I wanted to meet. I am referring to none other than Dr. Bobby Jones. He hosted the popular television broadcast, *Bobby Jones Gospel* on Black Entertainment Television, for 35 years. Dr. Jones is a legend, icon, and trailblazer in gospel music. He provided the opportunity for artists to perform on national television. His background as a Grammy Award-winning national recording artist, author, educator, radio, and television personality has been recognized nationally and abroad.

In 2010, Mama and I attended the Agape Gospel Awards, at the Porter Stanford III Performing Arts Center, in Decatur, Georgia. We arrived there in a black Lincoln Town Car limousine. Vanessa Bell Armstrong and Vickie Winans were being honored. Several of my industry friends and sources in Atlanta, including, Kendal Richardson, of the Grapevine HIV/AIDS Foundation, and Sandi Sam, formerly of the Sandi Sam Show, attended the ceremony. Andre also attended.

A young woman I met during the planning process of the Agape Gospel Awards, named Talesa Harris, came from Alabama. She is a talented actress. She graduated high school two years prior. I am very proud of her accomplishments. Talesa and I remain in contact. In 2015, she made an appearance on the *Steve Harvey Show*, hosted by Steve Harvey.

When I learned Dr. Jones was going to host the awards, I proceeded with the opportunity. I remember being at the VIP Reception on the red carpet. One of my friends in the industry, Larry Young, of the syndicated Larry Young Morning Show on the Stellar Award winning WIGO 1570 AM "The Light", did his live radio broadcast. As I was talking to people and taking photos, Larry walked up to me, and said, "I have my friend, James Birdsong, here."

I looked at Larry not knowing what was going on. He

interviewed me on his broadcast in 2008.

"We are live on the air right now," Larry said. I went ahead and did the interview. My friend put me on the spot that day. He is one of the most respected radio personalities in the nation. I was already familiar with him in the Bay Area. Larry is married to Chandra Currelley-Young, a gifted singer, and actress, known for her work in some of Tyler Perry's stage plays.

Before the ceremony began, Mama and I approached Dr. Jones. As we were talking to him, for a few minutes, he said, "James Birdsong, that name sounds familiar."

"Dr. Jones, I am friends with Danyelle Haley." He looked at me, and said, "You know Danyelle?"

"Yes, I do. Every time I speak to her, I always gave her messages to give you." Dr. Jones is very familiar with the Birdsong family. Danyelle is a member of the Nashville Super Choir that performed with Dr. Jones on his broadcast. Danyelle was in town on that same day. I called her a few days later, at Dr. Jones's office in Nashville.

"Girl, where were you at? I didn't see you at the ceremony."

"James, I attended the Bronner Brothers International Hair show," she said. During our conversation, she asked me if I saw Dr. Jones. I told her, "Yes, I did and I wanted to see you, too."

Danyelle began to laugh. She is one of the sweetest and nicest persons to be around. She will have you laughing. I saw her at the 2014 29th Annual Stellar Awards in Nashville. She had to sing background for some major artists that evening. We spoke briefly. Andre had been encouraging me to attend the Stellar Awards, for about five years. I finally decided to go.

In 2016, I joined SAGMA, the membership alliance of the Stellar Awards. I am also a professional member of the Gospel Music Association. They are responsible for the GMA Dove Awards. It is a blessing and honor to participate in the submissions and voting for the nomination process.

I have another friend of mine in the Mississippi Mass Choir that the Lord blessed me to meet. Leah Curry-Williams is one of the founding members of the choir. On the Mississippi Mass Choir's self-titled debut album, she sings *Near the Cross,* with their founder, the late Frank Williams. Leah and Lillian have been members of the Mississippi Mass Choir since they were organized.

The Lord is still blessing me to meet and connect with more people in gospel music. For the last three years, I have been able to connect with gospel artists and industry professionals through Facebook and Twitter, via social media, reside outside the United States. They have been very supportive of me. I met Kirk Franklin once, at the 2014 29th Annual Stellar Awards. He is the "Michael Jackson of Gospel Music," in my opinion. Kirk is the biggest selling artist and won numerous Grammys, Stellars, Doves, platinum records and other awards.

People have inquired about my plans for the gospel music industry. For the last decade, I've desired to establish a record label in Atlanta. Andre is going to be the label executive as time comes. For the A&R director, Kendal will serve in this capacity for the record label. He is excellent in this field. For the last two decades, in a 21-year period, I have studied and researched the gospel music industry thoroughly, from contracts to marketing, media coverage, and promotions.

There is politics in the industry. I always tell those that desire to be in this field, "It is all about ministry and winning souls to Jesus Christ, in music." Albertina Walker once said, "It's the anointing that makes the difference." I want to give back and help those artists that need their opportunity to be exposed nationally.

I plan to record albums, write songs and tour as well. I can continue to speak and offer advice. An established entertainment attorney should review the contract presented to you, by a record label. They will explain the dos and don'ts. I am still learning and developing in the gospel music industry. God already knew, before the foundation of the world, this would happen in my life. The music changes daily. One thing that will never change is the message. This presentation is still not completed.

Me and the President of the Cobb County NAACP Deane Bonner following my preaching engagement in Marietta, Georgia

One of my mentors, Seretha Jefferson, and my high school economics teacher Claiborne

On the red carpet with Larry Young at 6th Annual Agape Gospel Awards show

Posing next to the Stellar Awards poster at the 29th Annual Stellar Awards show

Preparing for my radio interview with Tony Ki KMJJ 97.5 FM in Shreveport, Louisiana

CHAPTER TWENTY-FOUR

James Talks to the Youth

Times changed through the course of twenty-five to thirty years. Since you had the opportunity to know the real James Charles Birdsong, Jr., I did not want to complete this book without an in-depth conversation with our young people. I have been on a mission, since 14-years-old, to help the youth as a mentor and role model. This chapter is going to allow me to speak directly to them.

Young people, God has given you a purpose in life, in His Will, to become the dreamers and achievers of tomorrow. We turn on the news and hear media reports of children being abused, bullied in school, involved in gangs, murders, drugs, prostitution, raised in single parent homes, molestation, and the list goes on. It has become a growing trend in the United States. As a person that has a great-niece and numerous cousins, under the age of eighteen, this grieves my heart. There are many questions being asked, and there are still no answers.

During the eighties, Nancy Reagan introduced the Just Say No to Drugs campaign as First Lady of the United States. I remember this as a child. The campaign's intention teaches our youth to do the right thing, by not engaging in drugs. Mrs. Reagan visited numerous schools and spoke to students. I am longing that we can go back to that campaign. This is needed more today than three decades ago.

Growing up in the ghetto, Mrs. Reagan's message was proclaimed in the schools. As I attended Nystrom Elementary School, students became participants in the D.A.R.E. program.

Located in Los Angeles, the acronym for D.A.R.E. is Drug Abuse Resistance Education.

Launched in 1983, D.A.R.E. is a comprehensive K-12 education taught in thousands of schools in America and 52 other countries. D.A.R.E. curricula addressed drugs, violence, bullying, internet safety, and other elevated risk circumstances that today are too often a part of students' lives (dare.org, 2017).

As a participant in the D.A.R.E. program, you will sign a pledge not to use drugs or join gangs. The curriculum lasted for ten weeks. The students were informed by local police officers about the government's beliefs and position about the dangers of recreational drug use. My classmates that participated in the D.A.R.E. program was wearing the black T-shirts given to them by their mentors.

I remember some of the young men in my hometown. When the murders were rapid in the nineties, it became a war zone in certain neighborhoods. I want to tell the young people we make choices in life. You can either decide to engage in the gangs and have a criminal record, or remain on the straight and narrow path as my mother always tells me. The straight and narrow path is preparing for your future, in educational and career opportunities, for success.

My teachers told us, "Stay out of trouble and you will go far in life." Some of these young men made wrong decisions, caused them to engage in drugs and gang activity. Some of them are incarcerated in jail for crimes they have committed. There are those that tragically died in shootings. I could have made that choice. Thankfully, I had parents that raised me in the church and taught principles of positive direction.

Being a child of the eighties, we did not have iPhones, tablets, MP3 devices, DVD players, notebook computers, social media, and text messaging. The internet was not even introduced until the nineties. Our center of focus was the church, school, family, friends, recreational activities and pursuing our future. Our parents and teachers motivated us to climb the ladder of success.

They depended on my generation to carry their wings. If you were raised in the eighties, then the connection of this conversation transcends to our ability to mentor the children. Today, the young people are more focused on the influences of iPhones, text messaging and social media. Facebook, Instagram, Twitter and Snapchat has become the modern-day trend of communication. I do not condone social media. I am on Facebook and Twitter, among many followers. The young people that have college and careers in their plans should be applauded.

We are in a major crisis as the topic about our young people is discussed. First and foremost, our children are special in the eyesight of God. As adults, we may not approve of their decisions. Sometimes, we forget about the wrong decisions in our childhood years.

For instance, you may have been told by your parents not to associate around the wrong assembly of people in school and the neighborhood. We disobeyed their warnings and proceeded to our position.

Ephesians 6:1-2 reads, "Children, obey your parents in the Lord: for this is right. Honour thy father and mother; (which is the first commandment with promise)." This Biblical passage addresses God's plan for children to honor, obey and respect their parents. Once adulthood enters into us, the obligation of raising children becomes our kingdom assignment mandated by God Himself.

This generation carefully analyzed and made observations of our actions. I am also talking to the parents and grandparents in this chapter. It grieves my heart and spirit when some adults say, "You are a bad child." Never tell the children they are a bad person. Once they hear those words, it has a mental effect on them. Those words can carry them into adulthood. Young people must learn from their mistakes. This does not necessarily make them a bad person.

For the last decade, I have given speeches in school rallies and graduation ceremonies. The Lord has allowed me to share my story with the children, of my beginnings as a child in the inner-city born with a developmental disability, and how I became an overcomer. The parents would be addressed in the speeches. "Always love your children, encourage them and never discourage them," I tell the parents.

The Holy Spirit began to deal with me in the early 2000s about speaking directly to parents, in speaking engagements, whether they were in churches or the schools. God's blessed you with your children. They are your future as the legacy is being carried. Children are a gift from the Almighty God. It is your obligation to value the gift with integrity and respect. The purpose of redemption once again comes to mind in this chapter. Before I proceed further, the status of bullying has been a concern for both children and adults in America. For the last three to five years, cyberbullying on social media has become a national crisis. There was no propaganda, such as, cyberbullying, in my childhood. Again, the internet was not in existence.

Cyberbullying is based on insults and threats made about a person on the internet. Many of our young people today that has been victims by their peers are most likely to be bullied on social media. Our law enforcement agencies and school administrators across the United States are aware of this problem.

The question I propose, "Is there enough being done to resolve this crisis?" Parents, it is very important to have effective communication with your children daily. When I was growing up, the fights were held either during lunch or after school ended. The fights had a set time. For example, if the person says, "We are going to fight at 3:00 PM," then it proceeded as scheduled. Bullying is more serious now than the eighties and nineties.

There have been children victimized by cyberbullying among their peers. Sadly, the child as an innocent victim, was either murdered or committed suicide. I reflect on the time I became a victim of bullying. Our principals and teachers believed in conflict resolution. Ken Sande explains the purpose of conflict resolution in his book, *The Peacemaker: A Biblical Guide to Resolving Conflict*. God delights to make his children instruments of peace and reconciliation during conflict. We will carry out this challenging responsibility more effectively if we understand why peace is so important to our heavenly father (Sande, 2004).

The principals and teachers would have a conversation, between the child being bullied as a victim and their classmate that is making threats of violence towards them. The parents of both sides were requested to be in the meeting. I am sharing this on how things were in my childhood, in public schools. Sometimes, the child that was the victim of bullying eventually became friends with their classmate. Solutions help all involved parties to resolve issues. Only the Lord can do this.

A young person reading this book will ask this one question. "Why I am being bullied in school and harassed on social media?" I am going to address the question to our children of today.

God created you in His image. Before the foundation of the world, He had a purpose for your life. When you were born, children, it was not by accident. Your parents were given their assignment by the Lord as a mandate to raise, guide, protect and teach you, for preparation into adulthood. One of the reasons a child becomes the victim of bullying is based on being different from their peers. Allow me to express myself, young people.

Once I began to attend inner-city schools, some of the young men demonstrated jealousy and insecurity. They were not pleased when the girls began to like me and even wanted me to be a boyfriend. I was different from these boys. I remained to focus on my education and pursuing a future. The young men I am referring to were being suspended from school due to fights, being disrespectful in class and stealing.

Once gangsta rap was introduced in the nineties, our parents, teachers and other adults in the community did not approve it. They were against this genre of music since it promoted gang activity, murders, degrading women, sex and images of profanity. It became a national trend in the African-American community, at that time. The music was based on life in the ghetto. Some of the young men that did not particularly care for me eventually turned their lives around and are doing well. I praise God for that.

There is nothing wrong focusing on a positive direction, instead of engaging in a life of crime, violence, and gangs. Yes, you are going to be addressed names that are disrespectful to you. I know the feeling. What has kept me rooted and grounded in my journey is being faithful to the Lord, according to His Will and Purpose. The more I've been talked about the stronger I became, with determination. The people God placed in my life as a bridge knew of the potential to succeed. They have demonstrated unconditional love and support for me. Never forget about those who invested their time into your lifetime potential. Even when you are being teased and told about being different from your peers, the bridges encourage confidence to stay on the straight and narrow avenue.

Discrimination also becomes a factor of why a child is being bullied. From the ages of three to ten, I remained the only person out of my friends, in our neighborhood, attending schools in suburban areas. Diversity had always been embraced throughout my life. Discrimination is more than a person's ethnicity and culture. It includes a person's demeanor of character, in appearance, speech and a disability.

It really saddens me when a child goes to school, and they are being victimized by one of their classmates for being different. The school is supposed to be an institution of learning. I did not experience bullying from the students at the suburban area schools, where the high percentage was predominantly Caucasian. After I began to attend an inner-city school, the environment was different. I lived in the ghetto until the age of 15. This is when my parents divorced and I moved away to Fairfield. I remember talking to an 8-year-old boy in 2004. He and his mother were members of New Gethsemane Church of God in Christ on Roosevelt Avenue in Richmond, where Superintendent Archie Levias, Sr. is the pastor. I have known him and his wife, the late Mother Irwien Levias since I was 9-years-old. This young man was being bullied in school by his classmate. The classmate was another young man. They attended elementary school together.

This young man was being bullied in school by his classmate. The classmate was another young man. They attended elementary school together.

My mother and I were members of New Gethsemane during that time. After services ended, the congregation had dinner in the church's dining hall. I supported the young people at the church. I saw this young man and knew something was wrong. He opened to me about his situation at school. I told him my story as you are reading this book. I could relate to his situation. He wanted to know why bullies in school seem to always choose classmates to victimize that are innocent. I am going to continue this in-depth conversation.

People that turn around and establish themselves as bullies were victims of harassment themselves. Power structure comes to mind in this explanation. As this young man and I had our conversation, bullies want to "fit in" among their classmates that are honor roll students, have established friendships with one another and respect towards adults. Our children need to be educated, at some early age, this is not the avenue of gaining friendships.

I gave the young man advice on how to handle the situation, and to always inform his parents and teachers of his progress in school. He eventually shared with me about a meeting scheduled for him, the young man, their parents and the principal on how to resolve this situation. He thanked me for taking the time to speak with him. Conflict resolution again speaks volumes in this agenda. We are also witnessing the growing trend of sex among today's youth. Many of our young women, under the age of eighteen, are having babies before they graduate from high school. During a time of adolescence, in my generation that are eighties babies, this happened as well. Today, it is more on the horizon than the nineties. Society promotes the message of safe sex and protection from HIV/AIDS in advertisements.

According to the Center for Disease Control, teen pregnancy rate is still substantially higher than in other westernized industrialized nations. In 2014, a total of 249,078 babies were born to women aged 15-19 years, for a birth rate of 24.2 per 1,000 women in this age group (cdc.gov, 2017). Recently, there was a decline in birth rates.

The report also stated rates of teen pregnancy fell 11% among young women between the ages of 15 to 17, and 7% for 18 to 19 years old. This is based on recent years. Although reasons for the declines are not clear, more teens may be delaying or reducing sexual activity, and more of the teens who are sexually active may be using birth control than in previous years (cdc. gov, 2017).

Despite the statistics, our young women need to be loved by their parents and the adults in the community. As I mentioned earlier in this chapter, our children will do things we may not approve of. I am a strong believer in abstinence. I still value this teaching based on God's Word.

As a high school student in the nineties, HIV/AIDS and teen pregnancy prevention education became popular nationwide. If I did a comparison of my childhood and adolescence years to today's generation, there are some similarities. Honestly, I wish the young people of today were raised in my time, where our parents and teachers invested their time into our future.

There is some parents and teachers today that are more focused on themselves than the child. Just listen to media reports of the last decade. What is the church doing in this effort for the well-being of the children? I am going to give my observations of the relationship between the church and today's youth. Honestly, the children feel as though the church has failed them.

There are pastors that are doing their part of supporting our children to make the right decisions in life, raising money for scholarship funds and encouraging them to demonstrate their God-given gifts in ministry. I do applaud those pastors and their congregations. With the problems of today, in these last days, there is a great falling away from the church among our children. Their views are different from the time of my childhood. There is a generational gap between them and the elders.

In the gospel music industry, there have been artists introduced since the Kirk Franklins, the Yolanda Adams, the Fred Hammonds, the John P. Kees and the Hezekiah Walkers. The generation of today can relate to Mary Mary, Tye Tribbett, LeCrae, Tasha Cobbs, Kierra Sheard, Jekalyn Carr, Canton Jones and Deitrick Haddon. If you noticed, their music is more geared towards the young people, in urban contemporary, praise and worship and gospel hip-hop.

When this genre of gospel music was introduced in the nineties and the new millennium, some of the older generation thought it was too secular. I remember them saying, "This does not belong in the church." The young people observed their comments very clearly. I listen to all genres of gospel music, from the traditional style of Sunday morning to the urban flair made popular today.

This is the conclusion of the matter. I am a person that believes the young people need a genre they can relate to. Just as an older person from the old-school loves Thomas Dorsey and Mahalia Jackson, will not relate to a Kirk Franklin or Mary Mary. The same thing for a young person that enjoys modern day gospel music will not listen to the pioneers. Can you see my point?

There is one legend in gospel music that supports the young people. I am referring to Shirley Caesar. In recent years, she has collaborated with today's artists and producers the young people identify with musically. If you listen to *I Know the Truth*, she surprised the public by rapping. Shirley garnered our young people's attention on this song.

I am not discrediting the legends and pioneers. I have the utmost respect for them. Their music has ministered to me during a time of crisis. At the same time, we have the generation of today. They should not be condemned. Our children are hurting and lost respect for the church. I am very concerned about the young people and especially our African-American boys. They feel the church is nothing but a fake. Yes, I know there are pastors and elders that are hypocrites. Through the last decade, I heard numerous stories of our children being abused, assaulted sexually or victims of molestation by a pastor, teacher or an adult they trusted. This is not only a problem in the African-American community.

Ladies and gentlemen, it's a national problem that is uncontrollable. Satan has engaged in the homes and the churches. There was a time where respect and trust were among each other. The young people are finding the truth of matters. Before the new millennium, prophecies were going forth to our children. It has declared God is going to use the young people to lead and guide future generations. There is a Biblical passage that speaks on this concept.

The scripture declares, "And it shall come to pass in the last days, saith God, I will pour out of my Spirit upon all flesh: and your sons and your daughters shall prophesy, and your young men shall see visions, and your old men shall dream dreams: And on my servants and on my handmaidens I will pour out in those days of my Spirit; and they shall prophesy" (Acts 2:17-18).

I am a believer of this prophecy. There is a place for our young people in the Kingdom of God. The Word of God reads, "And he took them up in his arms, put his hands upon them, and blessed them" (Mark 10:16). This continues to be the reminder of loving children. Only the love of God can guide us on how to love our children, regardless of their decisions. In my concluding thoughts in this chapter, the young people are appreciated. The United Negro College Fund's motto, "A mind is a terrible thing to waste," is much needed today than before. I challenge today's youth to never allow obstacles from hindering your desires to pursue future opportunities. Someone had to encourage me as a child to focus on positive avenues.

I remember being asked, "James, what do you want to be when you grow up?" I smiled, and said, "I want to be rich and famous."

God knew my heart's desire of what he wanted me to do in life. If your dream is to be a doctor, attorney, athlete, teacher, entertainer, computer technician or the President of the United States, do the necessary steps of preparation.

Surround yourselves with people that love you enough to provide guidance and motivation. I am sharing this lesson from experience. I could have accepted the negative thoughts. Mama and Daddy raised me not to be a quitter. The most important lesson in life is being humble and steadfast in God's Will and Purpose. You will never go wrong if Jesus Christ is first and foremost. This has been the direction in my life.

Reflect on this passage, "But they that wait upon the LORD shall renew their strength; they shall mount up their wings as eagles; they shall run, and not be weary; and they shall walk, and not faint" (Isaiah 40:31). You are destined for greatness in life, children. The Lord has purposed you to mentor the next generation. You are the dreamers and achievers of tomorrow. Give yourselves a reminder of this every day, in school and the community. I am now going to move forth in the concluding chapter of this journey. The destination for this flight is now boarding.

Me and Belinda Munro

Deanna Ransom and myself at the 7th Annual Black Essence Awards show

and Doug Williams of the Williams Brothers

Me and Helen Baylor

Me and Lee King

Me and Lillian Lilly of the Mississippi Mass Choir

One of my closest friends in the gospel music industry and entertainment arena at large Andre Gates

Reverend Calvin Bernard Rhone and myself following church services in Los Angeles, California.

Being honored in my hometow Nystrom Elementary School as t cipient of their most prestigious

The late Councilman Richard Griffin and myself in Richmond, California.

An encounter with the Chairma of the Gospel Music Workshop America, the one and only Bishc Albert L. Jamison

Taking this photo with Dot tie Peoples at her CD releas signing in Atlanta, Georgia

CHAPTER TWENTY-FIVE

The Best is Yet to Come

We come to the final chapter of this book. There are lessons that become our story of redemption. You have taken this journey with me. The time has come on how this book has transformed for the outcome in my redemption. Lessons of redemption cultivate on transcending in this moment.

When I wrote, *One Marriage, Many Tales, And a Separation: A Message of Hope*, I remember sharing the importance about a message of hope. I remember writing this important statement, "It is a blessing from the Lord to have a message of hope because the world needs it." (Birdsong, 2000). After these years, the message of hope continues to impact millions of people, of all ages, cultures, and nationalities.

My message of hope provided me the opportunity to adapt lessons in the redemption status. Throughout my life, from a child raised in the inner-city south side neighborhood of Richmond, California on Maine Avenue, to the point of today, I can truly say God brought me through a mighty long way. I had my share of the good and tough times.

The redemption of forgiveness allowed me to demonstrate the perspective of forgiveness towards my father. I realize he was blind and had a disability. I still had to love Daddy, regardless of his mistakes. He never apologized to me and Mama for allowing the marriage to fail. I already came to the closure of forgiveness in this perspective after his death. I spent my entire life in the church, from Sunday school to Bible study, revival services and choir rehearsals. The elders taught us what the

Scripture declares, "For ye forgive men their trespasses, your heavenly Father will also forgive you; But if ye forgive not men their trespasses, neither will your Father forgive your trespasses" (Matthew 6:14-15).

I came to this conclusion as the redemption of forgiveness is being discussed. Not only had I to demonstrate forgiveness towards my father, the young men that bullied me in school, and others that had mistreated me needed to be forgiven.

When it comes to the conversation of forgiveness, we have a tough time adapting. For us to have our peace of mind, the first steps are to open ourselves for deliverance. Destiny became our journey for dreams and goals to be fulfilled. If I had not applied the redemption of forgiveness, opportunities would have been missed for me. How are we going to expect our elevation from the Lord, if the redemption of forgiveness has been surpassed? How can we teach our children about forgiveness, if the practice has not been applied in our lives as adults? Please take the time to reflect on this principle.

The redemption of love has allowed me to have the unconditional love of Jesus Christ in my heart. I am thankful for Mama and Daddy for teaching me about loving myself. It begins with us as an individual. Society has many misconceptions as the topic of love is discussed. Our children are told about love, and they still solicit questions.

If we allow the Holy Spirit to minister in our spirits, the process of love will flow through. Love is an action word. You are familiar with the quote, "Action speaks louder than words." The evidence must be presented for your point to be made across. Here is a good example of what I am about to share with you. When a case is being argued before a judge in court, the plaintiff and defendant present evidence to prove their testimony of truth. The decision can either be made in favor of the plaintiff or the defendant, or both parties lose the case based on substantial evidence. Again, the point needs to be made. The scripture points out clearly, "Beloved, let us love one another: for love is of God; and every one that loveth is born of God, and knoweth God" (1 John 4:7). Lessons about love are applied as soon as we are born. Love is more than romance and intimacy. The redemption of love teaches us how to give back to our families, friends, loved ones, and those that are less fortunate. Only God can do this in our lives.

The redemption of love had to teach me how to love my enemies as scripture says, "But I say unto you, Love your enemies, bless them that curse you, do good to them that hate you, and pray for them for them which despitefully use you, and persecute you" (Matthew 5:44).

While being bullied by the young men in school, I had to love them with the love of God in my heart. Hatred is not from God and causes us to miss our blessings. The example of my parents and elders during the early years taught me the lessons. Love guides, love heals, love hurts, love prepares and love teaches us for our common purpose.

The redemption of family and friends allowed me to appreciate the people God placed in my life as a support system. I remember the elders saying, "A family that prays together stays together." Throughout this journey of triumph, the adoption for family and friends has provided the wings of hope. The redemption of family and friends' values integrity. In the process, I had to accept those that received me compared to individuals that were against me.

I will now elaborate the concept about friendship. I am grateful to the friends God has placed in my life. Those friendships have been cherished. Maturity has created the tone on depth avenues. There are major differences between friendships and acquaintances. Friends are ordained by the Lord for a common purpose. They will love you unconditionally and take their position on the truth. In other words, friends will love you enough when you are right or wrong.

We should always value those friendships. Friends will become your family as your own lineage may disconnect themselves. I can relate to David when he says, "A man that hath friends must shew himself friendly: and there is a friend that sticketh closer than a brother" (Proverbs 18:24). This gives our example in the redemption of family and friends as brought forth.

Acquaintances are like co-workers at your job. They are your social settings of connections. God does things in seasons. I often say there are people in your life for a season, while there are those for a reason. Often, acquaintances are there to help for a specific area in your direction as guides. I had my share of this aspect. God had to give me His revelation of my loyal friends in this redemption. Not every person you come into encounter with is a friend.

I heard an older mother of the church say once, "Jesus and family are all you have." As a 37-year-old man, this made me grateful for a loving family and friends that truly love me.

The redemption of survival happens to be my conquest for victory. I remember reading this scripture, "But thanks [be] to God, which giveth us the victory through our Lord Jesus Christ" (I Corinthians 15:17). Satan knew about the Calling placed on my life from the Almighty God. Being born and diagnosed with a developmental disability, the speech impediment and one leg shorter than the other, divine intervention came through prayer.

Hezekiah Walker recorded a song, *I Need You to Survive* that encourages us to stand together for survival. It has a truthful message about love and prayer, for one another, as brothers and sisters in the Lord. Gospel radio stations across the nation continue to play this song as the ministry is brought forth. For me, I can relate to this song as the redemption of survival impacts trials and tribulations during bondage. There are times the episodes of situations I endured comes to one conclusion. This young man had to endure tears of sorrow for strength. Believe me, I had no other choice than to cry for God to intervene.

On June 14, 2002, Nystrom Elementary School invited me to deliver the commencement address to their sixth-grade class. The students were aware of me, after watching my appearances on *Gospel Search with Dr. Madalynn Peterson*, a Bay Area television show hosted by my friend, the late Dr. Madalynn Peterson. This opened the doors for me on television.

Ten years after graduating from Nystrom Elementary School, in the sixth grade, God opened the door for me to return there. It became a homecoming in the neighborhood where I first obtained my beginnings. The speech, titled, *A Testimony of a Dreamer and Achiever*, became my story of being an overcomer for survival.

During the ceremony, I encouraged the students to have God first and foremost in their lives, work hard, respect their elders and one another, and importantly, stay away from drugs and gangs. The Lord also allowed me to encourage the parents to never discourage their children from pursuing their fullest potential in life. The following year, I returned to Nystrom as they bestowed the Blue-Ribbon Honorees Award upon me. This is only awarded to current and retired teachers, school administrators, dignitaries, parents and supporters of the community. They have never honored a former student.

I became the first alumnus in the history of Nystrom Elementary School to receive their most prestigious award. I still cherish this award today. Congratulatory messages came from

Governor Gray Davis and several politicians, in proclamations. If you have not heard *I'm Still Here by* Albertina Walker, this song remained her testimony of how God kept her strong while she was alive.

The redemption of peace helps and guides us for happiness. Often in life, we always say, "I just want to have peace and be happy."

After the divorce of Mama and Daddy, I found peace once the transition to Fairfield had taken place. Changes of associations and environments must happen for God to elevate us higher. Only God can give us peace in our situations. Again, the Holy Spirit must intervene for deliverance. In his letter to the church at Philippi, Paul writes, "And the peace of God, which passeth all understanding, shall keep your hearts and minds through Christ Jesus." This is found in Philippians 4:7. Our deliverance brings forth peace. This happens through prayer, fasting, and giving our worship to the Lord. I found peace through love and forgiveness.

I shared about the redemptions of love and forgiveness earlier in this chapter. The Lord has placed me in a different position of life. There are times people have approached me and said, "James, you are always happy and smiling."

I also find peace as I enter God's presence to worship and praise Him, with thanksgiving. In the redemption of peace, this becomes a lesson of strength. The redemption of hope transcends to positive reflections as Jeremiah declares, "Blessed [is] the man that trusteth in the LORD, and whose hope the LORD is" (Jeremiah. 17:17).

Writing this book have given me hope for more goals in life. I know God is not through with me in His Kingdom assignment. The words of Mama always come to me. She told me from a child, "James, you are one of God's chosen." This continues to be the avenue of hope today. I could have given up a long time ago. Encouragement from family and friends inspired me to board the flight of dreams.

God places desires in our hearts, whenever it includes singing, preaching, speaking, writing or teaching. When a person is passionate about their gifts, a hunger develops. You will do the necessary steps to be dedicated and faithful, in the passion, as the Lord develops your gift. Another of my favorite scriptures speaks clarity. "A man's gift maketh room for him and bringeth him before great men" (Proverbs 18:16).

The encouragement of my parents, teachers and loving support by family and friends has inspired me to be motivated in the redemption of hope. Example setters provide our children the path for their destiny in life. I did not understand what the adults had seen in me. Now, I observe back and believe in the redemption of hope for my future. I need to address the redemption of leadership. Throughout my life, the observations have been made. The admiration of leaders that became role models and mentors gave me encouragement to be pushed. When it comes to the subject of leadership, this is very passionate to me in a personal way. These lessons were obtained after God's healing in my life, at 3-years-old. Surrounded by leaders, from parents to noted figures, I had to apply the foundational structure for myself.

Leaders are builders in the vision ordained by God. They create strategies to benefit a coalition. I remember sitting in classes of elementary, middle and high school as teachers lectured their subject matters from English to Social Studies.

The students were members of a team as our teachers became coaches. We developed a goal to create effective learning from the classroom. For us to win the game, our dedication for homework and study time, mid-terms, finals and SAT testing for college had to be enforced. Those strategies in effective learning prepare us for our adulthood in the real world. The redemption of leadership gives us the urgency as followers to guide and mentor others. At the same time, accountability remains on the agenda. Growing up in the inner-city, I had admiration for leaders that made significant contributions. Articulation inquires us for the in-depth engagement of foundation.

Often, you will hear a person say, "I want to be remembered in the legacy for future generations." Leaders should build their legacy in the present times. Sooner or later, the torch needs to be passed down to their successors. The elders always encourage the younger generation to carry the torch.

Now, I understand what the elders said. In the redemption of leadership, we cannot wait for others to do their assignment. All of us have an essential role in the process. John Borek, Danny Lovett, and Elmer Towns said it best in *The Good Book: Case Studies from the Bible*. Leadership is more than a child's toy. It is who you are and how you influence others to be accomplished more than they are or could do otherwise. I will forever be grateful to the Lord for the leaders that influenced my life as the redemption of leadership continues to produce results.

There are two more points to be discussed in this chapter. The redemption of achievement presents efforts of challenging work. Teachers give their students necessary direction to be goal achievers. This happened to me throughout childhood and adolescence.

Our works will produce good fruits in the labor. A tree is known by the fruit it bears as Matthew 7:17 speaks. The awards and accolades bestowed upon me, from kindergarten to present times, such as, proclamations, congressional recognitions by members of the United States House of Representatives, the Black Essence Award, in the gospel music industry, Marquis

Who's Who in America, the United Negro College Fund and the Wall of Tolerance induction at the Civil Rights Memorial Center in Montgomery, Alabama, came by having God first in my life and being faithful according to His Word.

There is a teacher I will never forget, Ceola Mayfield. We met on the day of my commencement address to the Nystrom Elementary School Class of 2002 sixth grade class graduation. She called me one evening. As the conversation went forth, Mrs. Mayfield asked me this important question.

"James, what is your ultimate dream in life?"

This had me smiling. The reply became simple, "My ultimate dream is to make it into heaven."

Once my assignment on this earth is completed, I will be in heaven living with Jesus Christ. This should be our focus in the redemption of achievement. Daddy told me before he died, "Tomorrow is not promised to us."

He was right. Now, I understand what my father said. The reminder of Daddy's words does come to mind. We can be here today and gone tomorrow. Life is too short and should be cherished. God is the giver of life. Every moment needs to be a gratitude of giving praise and thanksgiving to the Lord for blessing us. Never take this for granted. I say this due to the current state of society.

The greatest achievement a person can ever receive in life is the salvation of Jesus Christ, for Eternal Life. This is more valuable than material things. When we transition from this world into Eternity, our degrees, homes and financial salaries pass away. The Word of God becomes our standard as the redemption of achievement creates this agenda.

I am going to share the last position as the redemption of unity comes to fruition. This book has given direction for me to embrace humanity as one voice. Cultural diversity becomes the role in uniting together. I embrace this throughout ministry and outside the church walls. The words of Martin Luther King, Jr., in his I Have a Dream speech, still, grasps my attention. God ordained Dr. King to proclaim his dream of a better America not only just for minorities. He wanted all of us to unite together for principles to nonviolence. I grew up listening to Dr. King's speeches, reading books and watching documentaries about his life in the Civil Rights Movement.

Racism is still alive and well in America. As a child of God, I cannot demonstrate hatred towards a person when they may not embrace diversity. The redemption of unity becomes more than ethnicity. It brings communities together and joining forces to make a difference. Initiatives are presented to the table as solutions are suggested. The suggestions are who, what, when, why and how.

Memories of Maine Avenue comes to full circle. I remember the elders that were dedicated in the church. They knew how to pray and seek the Lord for wisdom in bringing our community. For me, I may have been raised in the inner-city and had to adjust with my disability as a child. Mama and Daddy made sure of this lesson. They taught me to love everybody, embrace diversity and have integrity. Respect comes along in the redemption of unity.

To gain respect, you must earn it first. The redemption of unity became a teachable moment for God's plan in life. I had embraced this lesson as a pastor, gospel artist, songwriter, motivational speaker, entrepreneur, and advocate for children. Unity demonstrates how to love one another. I believe, if this message is embraced, the world would be a much better place.

Each of us has our status as redemption outlines the production to our destination. It becomes the flight path from one point to another. Once the flight lands, this is where the exit comes as a new chapter is written. Plans are currently being written in the present. I had people to approach me. They inquire of the next phase for "the pastor."

Like every man that was raised around family, I truly desire to be a husband and father. The older generation of the Birdsong family always asks me the question about me being married. They believe in marriage and family. I have dated and been in relationships. Yes, I want to be in true love that proceeds to marriage.

Later, the school of hard knocks had to inform me, "She is not the one for you, James." God knows my heart's desire for the family structure. I rather not comment on the past relationships, out of respect. Currently, I plan to write an additional memoir in two to three years on reflections of Christmas at Maine Avenue. I believe this book will touch the hearts of millions worldwide. There is so much God has placed in me, from pastoral ministry to the gospel music industry as a singer, recording artist, songwriter and record label owner.

The children are my heart's desire in this journey. I want to help them to attend college and present scholarships. I told Mama many years ago about a goal to establish a foundation to help our children. I cannot neglect the minority youth of our inner cities throughout America. I was one of those minority children from the ghetto that have never forgotten where God brought me from. In three more years, I will be 40-years-old on May 16, 2020. Prior to my fortieth birthday, I will obtain a Master of Arts in Organizational Leadership, at Regent University, in Virginia Beach, Virginia. I may pursue another master's degree or do doctoral studies in either business or communications. Yes, I will be a married man. There are more adventures in the world for me to witness.

Maybe one day, James Charles Birdsong, Jr. will go to the

White House and meet the President of the United States. We never know what the Lord has in store for us. The truth has been declared during this journey. There is a hunger to have a closer relationship with Jesus Christ. Pieces of this puzzle have been placed together throughout the path. You have allowed me to share this testimony of redemption. This book is more than a typical autobiography.

It is the lesson of the redemptions as our stories are told daily. The road did not come easy overnight. Along with this cycle, God had to prepare me for something, before the foundation of the world. I want to leave a legacy for the future generations to carry this torch. Please take a moment and reflect on your life. Your children and grandchildren are depending on you to coach them along the way. The best is yet to come, in Jesus' name. Amen.

ACKNOWLEDGEMENTS

First and foremost, all of the honor, glory, and praise belongs to our Lord and Savior Jesus Christ. He has given me the integrity to move forth in my destiny and purpose in life. I am abundantly blessed in this journey. My parents always told me, "In everything you do, put God first." This has been the foundation of my life.

There is a woman that gave me encouragement since I was a child. I am referring to my mother, Belinda Germany-Birdsong. She and Daddy instilled lifetime lessons in me. The scripture says, "Train up a child in the way he should go: and when he is old, he will not depart from it" (Proverbs 22:6).

My mother has three sons. I am the youngest of my brothers: Demetrius and Alonzo Barb. I am requesting the public to uplift them, in your thoughts and prayers. They are certainly not forgotten in this effort. I am the uncle to four beautiful nieces: Giselle Merriweather, Geminese Barb, Demetria Barb and Rolonda Seinger. They are adults with a positive direction in life and, now, I have a great-niece named Tory Alexandra Hibbett. She is Demetria's daughter.

I appreciate the encouragement of Connie Brown. She is a wonderful sister-in-law, with a testimony. John and Teresa McCarroll have dedicated their lives of raising Demetria and Rolonda to be productive young women. I want the world to know they are appreciated very much.

The Birdsong family proclaimed lessons of family unity as one voice. Ed and Ida Birdsong had eleven children and their youngest daughter, Gladys Birdsong-Murray, is my last surviving great aunt. She is our matriarch of the family and a woman of grace, strength, wisdom, and knowledge. Seyyida Westbrook is one of the cousins closest and dearest to me. Our bond has always been like a brother and sister since we were children. Aaron, Destiny, and ShaVonce are grateful to have her as their mother.

Seyyida's mother is my cousin, Jackie Fields. She did an excellent job of raising her to be the woman of today. We lived close by each other in Richmond, California. I also appreciate my cousins, Catherine Fields-Tyler, Makeba and Princess Fields, Lamont Fields, Leela Tyler and Joyce Williams.

My mother has a niece that is another cousin dearest to me. I appreciate Breanna Ford and the support she has offered me. I am requesting the readers to remember her sons, Jeremiah and Joshua, in your prayers. They are my younger cousins. I want them to become productive young men in life. A family has become the practical foundation in my life and continues to establish volumes today.

Luzan Graham watched me grow up as a child. As you are aware, she is my Godmother. She has made observations of my accomplishments through the years. Her only daughter, Kitara Wilson, is my God sister that has been blessed to be a wonderful wife to her husband, Jahid, and mother to their children. I am anticipating the release of her book and tour soon. I want to publicly acknowledge Ian Spath, for our friendship, for more than thirty years. The memories of our childhood will have a special place in my heart. David and Linda Spath did an excellent job of raising their son.

Sandi Sam, for editing the manuscript of this book. She always tells me, "You are a mover and shaker." Her contributions to the gospel music industry as a radio broadcaster have become the inspiration for others to follow. Thank you for making a difference. The motivation of my sixth-grade teacher, Donna

Grove, and her husband, Ronald, inspired me to strive for excellence.

I remember being a student in Mrs. Grove's sixth-grade class. I am grateful to the support of Nystrom Elementary School, and their many sacrifices for the students today in Richmond, California. I reflect on the years of high school at my alma mater, Fairfield High School, in Fairfield, California.

The journey of pastoral ministry birthed preparation in leadership. Alongside teachers, administrators, former classmates and my fellow alumnus in the Fairfield High School Class of 1998, this cultivates the foundation for this present stage of today. Alice Claiborne was my home economics teacher at Fairfield High School. She has mentored many of her students throughout Solano County, California.

Seretha Jefferson, for being one of my mentors when I was a student at Fairfield High School. I have learned so much from you. The efforts of Timothy Flemming, Jr. and the staff of T&J Publishers in Atlanta, Georgia, for publishing this book. T&J Publishers is the answer for authors to share their stories with millions of readers. This has been a long effort for me to write this book.

Eight years after high school, I enrolled at Beulah Heights University in Atlanta, Georgia. I obtained a Bachelor of Arts degree in Biblical Education. I express my sincere gratitude to the entire Beulah Heights University family. Every pastor should have a dedicated Administrative Assistant on their church administration. I am truly grateful to God for Bronica Gray-Williams. As the founder and senior pastor of Gospel Outreach Tabernacle Church, she has been very supportive. I cannot forget about her 13-year-old daughter, Kolia, for being one of my fans.

My family in the gospel and Christian contemporary music

industry throughout the United States, Canada, Japan, the United Kingdom and abroad, you are colleagues, motivators, and supporters. There is a pastor that became my brother and close friend. I first met him as an undergraduate freshman in college. I am referring to Pastor Willie Ellis and First Lady Rachel Ellis, of Liberty Ministries Family Worship Center in Forest Park, Georgia. He believed in me and the entire congregation offered their love throughout the years.

I also would like to take this time to give acknowledgments to their daughter, Angel Ellis, for her compassion to our children as a teacher in the DeKalb County School District in Decatur, Georgia. Jesse and Deane Bonner have been a blessing to me. Mrs. Bonner is the longest serving President of the Cobb County NAACP in Marietta, Georgia, where I am a proud member. She always tells me, "My cup runneth over." I also appreciate the support of Mattie Small, Agatha Knight, Margaret Jones, Frances "Missy" Cook, Willie Davis, and the Executive Committee of the Cobb County NAACP. To the national leadership of the NAACP, and the members of the local branches nationwide, never lose focus on your assignment, ordained by God.

Jeriene Bonner-Grimes adopted me as her little brother. She has been there for me. Her compassion for the children in Marietta, Georgia as an elected member of the Marietta City Schools Board of Education continues to inspire the community. Jeriene has a daughter that is a talented young woman with a positive future on her shoulders. Her name is Sydnee and has served faithfully as the President of the Cobb County NAACP Youth Council.

The support of friend and colleagues in the gospel music industry, media and entertainment, such as Andre Gates,

Dorothy Norwood, Lillian Lilly and Leah Curry-Williams of the Mississippi Mass Choir, Eva Sabiniano, Eddie Sabiniano, Pastor Calvin Bernard Rhone, Larry Young, Jay Francis Springs, Jonathan Simmons, Vivian Varner, Kendal Richardson, Andre Carter, Cornelius Dwayne Watkins, Evelyn White, Ted Jeans, Ralph Davis, Earnestine Gray, LaVoria Resse, Prophetess Cherli Montgomery, Paula Martin, Dr. Mona Scott, Pastor Eddie Giles, Rhonda Sanders-Phillips, Melvin Jones, Johnny Sheppard, Terry Williams, Alice Tisdale, Sarita Smiley, Wendy Stoneberger, Dennis Cole, Tom DeKorne, Pastor Jerone Bell, Belinda Munro, LaDonna Ferguson, Lee King, Tommy Granville, Jr., Sean and Yolanda Dancy, Danyelle Haley, Juliet Lindsay, Talesa Harris, LaCora Stephens, and David Reid, have inspired me to move forward.

To Pastor Tracy Wells-White, you presented me the opportunity to be featured on your television broadcast, *Let's Talk with Pastor Tracy Wells-White*, for the Atlanta market on WATC Channel 57, in Norcross, Georgia. You have touched many lives in your ministry.

I am grateful to the Lord for Bishop Neil C. Ellis and our entire Global United Fellowship family. You have embraced me with loving arms. I will do my contribution for Bishop Ellis's vision.

To my friends at Marietta City Hall, Stephane Guy, Yvonne Williams and Shirley Thompson, you have been very supportive. Your dedication and service to the citizens in Marietta, Georgia is a blessing and inspiration. I cannot forget about Senior Assistant District Attorney Brendan Murphy, Associate Municipal Court Judge Nathan Wade, Chief Magistrate Court Judge Joyette Holmes, and Magistrate Judge Kellie Hill, for your prayers and encouragement. The citizens of Cobb County, Georgia have the right leaders in place.

The Lord has blessed me with a dedicated support system in Shreveport and Bossier City, Louisiana. I need to take this time to acknowledge La Tasha Washington, former Representative Roy Burrell, Senator Gregory Tarver, Linda Johnson, Mayor Ollie Tyler, former Mayor Keith Hightower, Mary Rounds, Sherricka Fields, Councilwoman Stephanie Lynch, Mayor Lorenz Walker, Commissioner Stormy Gage-Watts, Pastor Tommy Nard, Sr. and First Lady Kimberly Nard, Dr. Curley White, Deacon Rickey Lee, Karla McCulloch, former Representative Ernest Baylor, Jr. and a heartfelt gratitude to Pastor Bertnard Bailey and First Lady Victoria Bailey, for being faithful servants in this assignment, in your lives.

For the final acknowledgements, I am grateful for the support of Lee Boyd, Tammy Smith, Elder Christopher Martin, Sr., Alfred and Emily Heath, Kerys Walker, Brandon and Tiffany Davis, Mother Hattie Strong, Lisa Strong-Dobson, Lakita Strong, Theresa Hindsman, Doris Matthews and her children, Pierre Ruff, Celena and Tinika Bostic, Doris Royal, Sharon Dean, Janell Leaks, Latressa Wilson-Alford, Adrienne Ursino, Neku Pogue, Sheena McCrary, Amy Maginnis-Honey, Michelle Pillow, Dr. Anthony Gantt, Dorinda Lawrence, Cora Jackson-Fossett, Dr. Jeremiah Enoch, the Southern Poverty Law Center in Montgomery, Alabama, the administration, facility and students at Regent University in Virginia Beach, Virginia, the Gospel Music Workshop of America, Pastor Gloria Perkins, and Dr. Christopher Bowen, for writing the forward to this book.

There will a special place in my heart for my Facebook and Twitter followers. Your comments and tweets are a blessing. Lastly, to our children around the world, you are loved and appreciated. I will always have you in my thoughts and prayers. Just know that the best is yet to come for you, and the future

THE BEST IS YET TO COME

God has in store

JAMES C. BIRDSONG, JR.

THE BEST IS YET TO COME

AWARDS AND RECOGNITION

Proclamations and Resolutions

City of Richmond – Richmond, California
Presented by Mayor Irma L. Anderson on March 18, 2003.

Contra Costa County - Contra Costa County, California
Presented by Supervisor John Gioia in May 2003.

Texas State Senate - State of Texas
Introduced by Senator Rodney Ellis at the legislative session in Austin on July 26, 2003.

Parish of Caddo - Caddo Parish, Louisiana
Presented by Commissioner Clifford Collins on March 26, 2004.

Louisiana House of Representatives - State of Louisiana (March 18, 2004)
Introduced by Representative Ernest Baylor at the legislative session in Baton Rouge.

City of Richmond - Richmond, California
Presented by Mayor Irma L. Anderson on June 4, 2004.

California State Senate - Sacramento, California
Presented by Senator Don Perata on June 4, 2004.

City of Shreveport - Shreveport, Louisiana

Presented by Mayor Keith Hightower on March 18, 2005.

Parish of Caddo - Caddo Parish, Louisiana
Presented by Commissioner Clifford Collins on March 18, 2005.

Louisiana House of Representatives - State of Louisiana
Presented by Representative Ernest Baylor, Jr. on March 18, 2005.

City of Pinole - Pinole, California
Presented by Mayor David Cole on July 19, 2005.

City of Vallejo - Vallejo, California
Presented by Mayor Anthony J. Intintoli, Jr. on June 25, 2005.

California State Assembly - State of California
Introduced by Assemblywoman Noreen Evans and Senator Wesley Chesbro on July 31, 2005.

Texas State Senate - State of Texas
Introduced by Senator Rodney Ellis during the legislative session in Austin on July 18, 2005.

Louisiana House of Representatives - State of Louisiana
Presented by Representative Roy Burrell on July 18, 2005.

City of Richmond - Richmond, California
Presented by Mayor Gayle McLaughlin on November 5, 2009.

City of Pinole - Pinole, California
Presented by Mayor Peter J. Murray on September 1, 2015

THE BEST IS YET TO COME

City of Shreveport - Shreveport, Louisiana
Presented by Mayor Ollie Tyler September 26, 2015.

City of Shreveport City Council - Shreveport, Louisiana (November 24, 2015)
Introduced by Councilwoman Stephanie Lynch, at the city council meeting in Shreveport.

City of Bossier City - Bossier City, Louisiana
Presented by Mayor Lorenz Walker on September 26, 2015.

Parish of Caddo - Caddo Parish, Louisiana
Presented by Commissioners Lyndon B. Johnson and Stormy Gage-Watts on September 26, 2015.

Louisiana House of Representatives - State of Louisiana
Presented by Representative Roy Burrell on September 26, 2015.

Louisiana State Senate - State of Louisiana
Presented by Senator Gregory Tarver on September 26, 2015.

City of Marietta - Marietta, Georgia
Presented by Mayor R. Steve "Thunder" Tumlin, Jr. on April 1, 2016.

Louisiana State Senate - State of Louisiana
Presented by Senator Gregory Tarver on April 1, 2016.

City of Shreveport - Shreveport, Louisiana

Presented by Mayor Ollie Tyler on May 16, 2017.

Louisiana State Legislative
House of Representatives and Senate – State of Louisiana (May 1, 2017)
Introduced by Senator Gregory Tarver at the legislative session in Baton Rouge.

Certificates
Booker T. Washington Revisited Student Conference
Solano County Office of Education - Fairfield, California
Presented by Seretha Jefferson and Wendall Kuykendall on March 27, 1998.

Alpha Kappa Alpha Sorothy
Tau Upsilon Omega Chapter - Fairfield, California
Presented by Muzetta Thrower on June 7, 1998.

Award of Honor
Fairfield High School- Fairfield, California
Presented by Fairfield High School on June 8, 1998.

Booker T. Washington Revisited Student Conference
Solano County Office of Education - Fairfield, California
Presented by Seretha Jefferson and Wendall Kuykendall on March 27, 1999.

California State Senate - Sacramento, California
Presented by Senator Don Perata on June 6, 2003.

Contra Costa County - Contra Costa County, California

THE BEST IS YET TO COME

Presented by Supervisor John Gioia on June 4, 2004.

United States House of Representatives - Washington, D.C.
Presented by Congresswoman Ellen O. Tauscher (D-California) on August 23, 2004.

United States House of Representatives - Washington, D.C.
Presented by Congressman George Miller (D-California) on May 27, 2005.

United States House of Representatives - Washington, D.C.
Presented by Congressman George Miller (D-California) on July 30, 2005.

City of Los Angeles - Los Angeles, California
Presented by Mayor Antonio Villaraigosa on July 31, 2005.

Solano County - Solano County, California
Presented by Supervisor Barbara R. Kondylis on July 31, 2005.

United Negro College Fund – Fairfax, Virginia
Presented by Michael Lomax in 2008.

Albert T. Mills Enrichment Center - Atlanta, Georgia
Presented by Rosa Mills-Arnold on May 27, 2010.

Black Essence Awards - South Bend, Indiana
Presented by Prophetess Gwendolyn Spinks on October 20, 2010.

Wall of Tolerance (Civil Rights Memorial Center)

Southern Poverty Law Center - Montgomery, Alabama
Presented by Morris Dees, Joseph J. Levin, Jr., and J. Richard Cohen.

Gospel Music Association (Individual Member) - Nashville, Tennessee
Presented by Jackie Patillo in February 2015.

Gospel Music Association (Professional Member) - Nashville, Tennessee
Presented by Jackie Patillo in February 2016.

Gospel Music Association (Professional Member) - Nashville, Tennessee
Presented by Jackie Patillo in February 2017.

Citations

State of California - Sacramento, California
Presented by Governor Gray Davis on June 6, 2003.

State of Louisiana - Baton Rouge, Louisiana
Presented by Governor Kathleen Blanco on April 2, 2004.

Letters

Booker T. Washington Revisited Student Conference
Solano County Office of Education - Fairfield, California
Written by Seretha Jefferson and Wendall Kuykendall on May 26, 1998.

Booker T. Washington Revisited Student Conference
Solano County Office of Education - Fairfield, California

Written by Seretha Jefferson and Wendall Kuykendall on May 18, 1999.

Marquis Who's Who in America - New Providence, New Jersey
Written by Robert Docherty in March 2002.

Marquis Who's Who in America – New Providence, New Jersey
Written by Karen Chassie in July and August 2003.

The King Center - Atlanta, Georgia
Written by Kelvin L. Cothern on behalf of Coretta Scott King on September 6, 2002.

The Carter Center - Atlanta, Georgia
Written by Nancy Konigsmark on behalf of President Jimmy Carter on September 11, 2002.

United States Senate - Washington, D.C.
Written by Senator Mary L. Landrieu (D-Louisiana) on February 19, 2004.

United States Senate - Washington, D.C.
Written by Senator Barbara Boxer (D-California) on June 4, 2004.

United States House of Representatives - Washington, D.C.
Written by Congresswoman Ellen O. Tauscher (D-California) on August 23, 2004.

City of Fairfield - Fairfield, California
Written by Mayor Karin MacMillian on July 30, 2005.

United States Senate - Washington, D.C.
Written by Senator Barbara Boxer (D-California) on July 30, 2005.

United States Senate - Washington, D.C.
Written by Senator Dianne Feinstein (D-California) on August 9, 2005.

Plaques
Blue Ribbon Honorees Award
Nystrom Elementary School – Richmond, California
Presented by Nystrom Elementary School on June 6, 2003.

ENDNOTES

Chapter One
John Gray, *Mars and Venus on a Date: A Guide for Navigating the 5 Stages of Dating to Create a Loving Lasting Relationship* (New York: HarperCollins, 1997), 109.

Chapter Two
The 1980s, <http://www.history.com/topics/1980s> (December 7, 2016).

Olympics Games, International Encyclopedia of the Social Sciences <https://www.encyclopedia.com> (February 25, 2017).

The Olympic Boycott, 1980, *United States Department of State Archive,* http://www.2001-2009.state.gov/r/pa/ho/time/qfp/104481.htm> (December 7, 2016).

Jackie Nash, "John Lennon's Death, 33 Years Later: A Timeline of Events," 6 December 2013, *History.com* http://www.history.com> (February 26, 2017).

William F. Harley, Jr., *His Needs Her Needs Building an Affair-Proof Marriage* (Grand Rapids, MI: Baker Publishing Group, 2011), 25.

Joan and Richard Hunt, *Preparing for Christian Marriage*

(Nashville, TN: Abingdon Press, 1982), 11.

Chapter Three
Kent Branch, *A Kingdom Calling: How to Identify Your Divine Assignment* (Apopka, FL: Higher Level Solutions, 2010), 50.

John Gray, *Children are from Heaven: Positive Parenting Skills for Raising Cooperative, Confident, and Compassionate Children* (New York: HarperCollins, 1999), 1.

T.D. Jakes, *Destiny: Step into Your Purpose* (New York: Faith Words, 2015), 35.

Ibid, 35.

Karl Pillemer, *30 Lessons of Loving: Advice from the Wisest Americans on Love, Relationships and Marriage* (New York: Penguin Publishing Group, 2015),

William and Martha Sears, *The Successful Child: What Parents Can Do to Help Kids Turn out Well* (New York: Little, Brown and Company, 2002), 1.

Chapter Four
Rick Warren, *The Purpose Driven Life: What on Earth I am Here For?* (Nashville, TN: Zondervan, 2002), 22.

Chapter Five
John C. Maxwell, *The 360 Leader: Developing Your Influence from Anywhere in the Organization* (New York: Little, Brown

and Company, 2005).

Chapter Six
The 1930s, <http://www.history.com/topics/1930s> (December 7, 2016).

Franklin D. Roosevelt, https://www.whitehouse.gov/1600/presidents/franklindroosevelt> (December 7, 2016).

Chapter Seven
The 1930s, <http://www.history.com/topics/1930s> (December 7, 2016).

Stokesbury, James L., "World War II." *The World Book Encyclopedia.* 2015 ed. Print.

Chapter Eight
Mengesha Francis, "The Jacksons Victory Tour 1984 on DVD and Blu-Ray," *Ipetitions.* < http://www.ipetitions.com/petition/jacksons_victory_tour_dvd/> (December 7, 2016).

What Is HIV/AIDS? 13 July 2016 <https://www.aids.gov/hiv-aids- basics/hiv-aids-101/what-is-hiv-aids/> (December 7, 2016).

Space Shuttle Overview: Challenger (OV-099), *NASA Orbiter Fleet,* 12 April 2013 https://www.nasa.gov/centers/kennedy/shuttleoperations/orbiters/challenger-info.html > (December 7, 2016).

Chapter Ten
Earthquake Loma Prieta California 1989," 11 June 2011" <https://www.nist.gov/el/earthquake-loma-prieta-california-1989> (December 7, 2016).

Loma Prieta Strikes, <http://baybridgeinfo.org/1989> (December 7, 2016).

1989 San Francisco Earthquake, http://www.history.com/topics/1989-san-francisco-earthquake> (December 7, 2016).

Chapter Eleven
Triumph [Def. 1]. (n.d.). *Merriam-Webster Online*. Retrieved February 15, 2017, from http://www.merriam-webster.com/dictionary/triumph.

Kyle Anderson, "Janet Jackson's 'Rhythm Nation 1814:' Still Dancing and Dreaming 25 Years Later," *Entertainment Weekly*, 19 September 2014, <http://www.ew.com/article/2014/19/19/janet-jackson-rhythm-nation-1814-25th-anniversary> (December 4, 2016).

Ranker, "The Dopest Rappers of the '90s," <http: //www.m.ranker.com/crowdranked-list/best_-90s-rappers> (December 4, 2016).

D.L. Chandler, "Nelson Mandela Freed from Prison on This Day in 1990," *Newsone*, <http://newsone.com/2199801/nelson-mandela-prison-release-1990/> (December 7, 2016).

Chickenpox (Varicella) - Topic Overview, *WebMD* <http://www.webmd.com/
/vaccines/tc/chickenpox-varicella-topic-overview#1> (December 7, 2016)

Chapter Thirteen
Dave Johns, "The Crimes of Saddam Hussein," *Frontline World* <http://www.pbs.org/frontlineworld/stories/iraq501/events_kuwait.html> (December 8, 2016)

The Human Dog, *Dog Breed Info Center* <http://www.dogbreedinfo.com/articles/humandog.htm> (December 7, 2016)

Chapter Sixteen

Eric Speir, "One Thing Sons Need from their Fathers," *Charisma* <http://www.charismamag.com/life/men/23077-one-thing-sons-need-from-their-fathers> (February 19, 2017).

Chapter Twenty-Two
9/11 Attacks, *History.com* <http://www.history.com/topics/9-11-attacks> (December 8, 2016).

George W. Bush, "Text of Bush's Address," September 11, 2001, *CNN.com* <http://edition.cnn.com/2001/US/09/11/bush.speech.text/> (May 13, 2017).

Chapter Twenty-Four
D.A.R.E. <http://www.dare.org> (February 20, 2017).

Reproductive Health: Teen Pregnancy, "Teen Pregnancy in the United States", *CDC.gov* <https://www.cdc.gov/teenpregnancy/about/index.htm?mobile=nocontent> (February 20, 2017).

Ken Sande, *The Peacemaker: A Biblical Guide to Resolving Personal Conflict* (Grand Rapids, MI: Baker Books, 2004), 43.

Chapter Twenty-Five
James C. Birdsong, Jr., *One Marriage, Many Tales, and a Separation: A Message of Hope*
(Bloomington, IN: 1st Books Library, 2000), 72.

John Borek, Danny Lovett and Elmer Towns, *The Good Book: Case Studies from the Bible* (Nashville, TN: B&H Publishing Group, 2005), 22.

JAMES C. BIRDSONG, JR.

THE BEST IS YET TO COME

JAMES C. BIRDSONG, JR.

ABOUT THE AUTHOR

James C. Birdsong, Jr. is a respected leader in the 21st century. He has established himself as one of the latest voices and editions today under the age of forty. Consider by his peers as "the pastor," he is a gifted aspiring gospel artist, songwriter, author, pastor, motivational speaker, entrepreneur, and humanitarian. He is also an advocate and supporter of our children.

His list of numerous awards, proclamations, and accolades nationally reads like an encyclopedia. A nominee for inclusion in the 2003 57th Edition of the renowned autobiographical reference publication, Marquis Who's who in America and his name added to the Wall of Tolerance at the Civil Rights Memorial Center in Montgomery, Alabama, he holds a Bachelor of Arts in Biblical Education from Beulah Heights University in Atlanta, Georgia and a Standard Teacher's Diploma by the Evangelical Training Association in Wheaton, Illinois.

He serves as the founder and senior pastor of Gospel Outreach Tabernacle Church, a non-denominational and multicultural church in the plans of being re-established in Marietta Georgia. His memberships among national and global organizations include the Global United Fellowship, the NAACP, the Southern Poverty Law Center, the Gospel Music Workshop of America, the Gospel Music Association (GMA Dove Awards) and SAGMA (Stellar Awards). As of now, he resides in Austell, Georgia.

JAMES C. BIRDSONG, JR.

www.ingramcontent.com/pod-product-compliance
Lightning Source LLC
Chambersburg PA
CBHW021116300426
44113CB00006B/170